LYONS PR

MW00984465

GREAT

AMERICAN

EXPLORER

STORIES

EDITED BY

CHENEY GARDNER

GUILFORD,
CONNECTICUT

An imprint of The Rowman & Littlefield Publishing Group, Inc.
4501 Forbes Blvd., Ste. 200
Lanham, MD 20706
www.rowman.com

Distributed by NATIONAL BOOK NETWORK

Copyright © 2018 The Rowman & Littlefield Publishing Group, Inc.

British Library Cataloguing in Publication Information available

Library of Congress Cataloging-in-Publication Data available

ISBN 978-1-4930-3553-3 (paperback)
ISBN 978-1-4930-3554-0 (e-book)

♾ ™ The paper used in this publication meets the minimum requirements
of American National Standard for Information Sciences—Permanence of
Paper for Printed Library Materials, ANSI/NISO Z39.48-1992.

Printed in the United States of America

CONTENTS

INTRODUCTION

CHENEY GARDNER

The need to explore is among our most primal. It's taken us out of Africa, across all corners of the globe, deep under the ocean, high in the Himalayas, and into orbit among the stars. We're not the only species driven to seek out new resources and habitat, but we're unique, even from our Neanderthal cousins, in our obsessive desire to know what's out there.

There are many motivators that guide exploration—gold, glory, competition—but it's the knowledge gleaned that endures. Whether huddling around a fire with Yeti hunters in Siberia or swinging machetes to reach ruins buried deep in the jungle, we're adding to the database of human understanding that has been building for millennia.

As Americans, the need to explore pumps through our veins. When Christopher Columbus first laid eyes upon what is now the Bahamas, he, as Spanish American poet George Santayana wrote, "gave the world a new world." Some 500 years later, we've continued to find new waters to cross. "We set sail on this new sea because there is new knowledge to be gained, and new rights to be won, and they must be won and used for the progress of all people," said President John F. Kennedy in a 1962 speech at Rice

University as he turned the country's attention skyward. Seven years later, Apollo11 landed on the moon's Sea of Tranquility.

The modern history of exploration comes heavily footnoted, among the asides that European (and American) explorers "discovered" places that were already populated by native people. (Another, that misguided exploration into new territories was often scarred by racism and exploitation, cannot be ignored.) But the definition of explore—"to travel in or through (an unfamiliar country or area) in order to learn about or familiarize oneself with it"—allows that exploration is not so much about the finality of a discovery as the exchange that comes when hitherto separated worlds meet.

Native people had already seen the Pacific, bathed in its water, and eaten its fish before Lewis and Clark reached the shore. But their meeting opened up new worlds—physical and psychological—for our young nation. Lewis and Clark brought home knowledge of the topography, ecology, and ethnic groups of the areas that made up the Louisiana Purchase, lands that were until then totally unknown but now represented a new frontier.

In this book, you'll be taken along mile-high canyon walls, across Andean glaciers, around a bustling Baghdad market, deep into the silent Siberian tundra, and through thick Mexican jungle teeming with ancient life. We may not all want to bike across the Algerian desert or sail through turbulent Polynesian gales, but, to some degree, we are all intoxicated by the draw of unfamiliar places, people, and lands—and the stories of those who chase them.

1

TWO BEAUTIFUL BLACK EYES AND ADEN TO COLOMBO

NELLIE BLY

Elizabeth Cochran Seaman launched her career with a ferocious rebuke to an article published in the Pittsburgh Dispatch *condemning women who pursued an education or vocation. The* Dispatch *put out a call for the writer of the scathing response, and Seaman (under the pen name Nellie Bly) joined the staff. After moving to New York, Bly wrote of the pitiable conditions in a box-making factory and went undercover to expose abuse in the Women's Lunatic Asylum on Blackwell's Island, along the way pioneering a new form of investigative journalism. When she suggested to her editors at* New York World *a trip around the world to beat Jules Verne's fictional character Phileas Fogg's 80-day record, she was again breaking new ground. In this excerpt from her race around the world, her steamer has docked in Aden, Yemen, and issued a warning for women to stay aboard to avoid the assault of the Arabian sun. Nellie makes a beeline for the shore.*

CHAPTER VII: TWO BEAUTIFUL BLACK EYES

The nights were so warm while on the Red Sea that the men left their cabins and spent their nights on deck. It is usually customary for the women to sleep on deck, one side of which, at such times, is reserved exclusively for them. During this trip none of the women had the courage to set the example, so the men had the decks to themselves.

Sleeping down below was all the more reason why women arising early would go on the decks before the sun began to boil in search of a refreshing spot where they could get a breath of cool air. At this hour the men were usually to be seen promenading about in their pajamas, but I heard no objections raised until much to the dismay of the women the Captain announced that the decks belonged to the men until after eight o'clock in the morning, and that the women were expected to remain below until after that hour.

Just before we came to Aden we passed in the sea a number of high brown mountains. They are known as the Twelve Apostles. Shortly after this we came in sight of Aden. It looked to us like a large, bare mountain of wonderful height, but even by the aid of glasses we were unable to tell that it was inhabited. Shortly after eleven o'clock in the morning we anchored in the bay. Our boat was soon surrounded by a number of small boats, which brought to us men who had things to sell, and the wonderful divers of the East.

The passengers had been warned by the officers on board not to go ashore at Aden because of the intense heat. So the women spent their time bargaining with the Jews who came to the ship to sell ostrich feathers and feather boas. The men helped them to close with the sellers always to the sellers' advantage, much as they might congratulate themselves to the contrary.

I, in company with a few of the more reckless ones, decided to brave the heat and go ashore and see what Aden had to offer.

CHAPTER VIII: ADEN TO COLOMBO

HIRING a large boat, I went ashore with a half dozen acquaintances who felt they could risk the sun. The four oarsmen were black fellows, thin of limb, but possessed of much strength and tireless good humor. They have, as have all the inhabitants of Aden, the finest white teeth of any mortals. This may be due to the care they take of them and the manner of that care. From some place, I am unable to state where, as I failed to see one living thing growing at Aden, they get tree branches of a soft, fibrous wood which they cut into pieces three and four inches in length. With one end of this stick, scraped free of the bark, they rub and polish their teeth until they are perfect in their whiteness. The wood wears into a soft pulp, but as one can buy a dozen sticks for a penny one can well afford to throw the stick away after once using; although, if necessary, a stick can be used many times. I bought several sticks and found them the most efficient as well as pleasant tooth brush I had ever tried. I felt a regret that some enterprising firm had not thought of importing this useful bit of timber to replace the tooth-destroying brush used in America.

The man in charge of the boat that carried us to land was a small black fellow with the thinnest legs I ever saw. Somehow they reminded me of smoked herrings, they were so black, flat and dried looking. He was very gay notwithstanding his lack of weight. Around his neck and over his bare breast were twined strings of beads, black and gold and silver. Around his waist was a highly colored sash, and on his arms and ankles were heavy bracelets, while his fingers and toes seemed to be trying to outdo one another in the way of rings. He spoke English quite well, and to my rather impertinent question as to what number constituted his family told me that he had three wives and eleven children, which number, he added piously, by the grace of the power of his faith, he hoped to increase.

His hair was yellow which, added to his very light dress of jewelry and sash, gave him rather a strange look. The bright yellow hair and the black skin forming a contrast which was more startling than the black eyes and yellow hair that flashed upon the astonished vision of the American public some years ago, but has become since an old and tiresome sight. Some of the boatmen had their black wool pasted down and hidden under a coating of lime. I was very curious about it until the first man explained that they were merely bleaching their hair; that it was always done by covering the head with lime, which, being allowed to remain on for several days, exposed to the hot sun and the water, bleached the hair yellow or red at the expiration of that time. This bleaching craze, he also informed me, was confined to the men of Aden. So far, none of the women had tried to enhance their black beauty in that way, but it was considered very smart among the men.

While we were talking our men were vigorously pulling to the time of a rousing song, one line of which was sung by one man, the others joining in the refrain at the end. Their voices were not unpleasant, and the air had a monotonous rhythm that was very fascinating.

We landed at a well-built pier and walked up the finely-cut, white-stone steps from the boat to the land. Instantly we were surrounded by half-clad black people, all of whom, after the manner of hack-drivers at railway stations, were clamoring for our favor. They were not all drivers, however. Mingling with the drivers were merchants with jewelry, ostrich plumes and boas to sell, runners for hotels, beggars, cripples and guides. This conglomeration besought us to listen to every individual one of them until a native policeman, in the Queen's uniform, came forward and pushed the black fellows back with his hands, sometimes hastening their retreat with his boot.

A large board occupied a prominent position on the pier. On it was marked the prices that should be paid drivers, boatmen, and like people. It was, indeed, a praiseworthy thoughtfulness that caused the erection of that board, for it prevented tourists being robbed. I looked at it, and thought that even in that land there was more precaution taken to protect helpless and ignorant strangers than in New York city, where the usual custom of night hack-men is to demand exorbitant prices, and if they are not forthcoming, to pull off their coats and fight for it.

Perched on the side of this bleak, bare mountain is a majestic white building, reached by a fine road cut in the stone that forms the mountain. It is a club house, erected for the benefit of the English soldiers who are stationed on this barren spot. In the harbor lay an English man-of-war, and near a point where the land was most level, numbers of white tents were pitched for soldiers.

From the highest peak of the black, rocky mountain, probably 1700 feet above sea level, floated the English flag. As I traveled on and realized more than ever before how the English have stolen almost all, if not all, desirable sea-ports, I felt an increased respect for the level-headedness of the English government, and I cease to marvel at the pride with which Englishmen view their flag floating in so many different climes and over so many different nationalities.

Near the pier were shops run by Parsees. A hotel, post-office and telegraph office are located in the same place. The town of Aden is five miles distant. We hired a carriage and started at a good pace, on a wide, smooth road that took us along the beach for a way, passing low rows of houses, where we saw many miserable, dirty-looking natives; passed a large graveyard, liberally filled, which looked like the rest of that stony point, bleak, black and bare, the graves often being shaped by cobblestones.

The roads at Aden are a marvel of beauty. They are wide and as smooth as hardwood, and as they twist and wind in pleasing curves up the mountain, they are made secure by a high, smooth wall against mishap. Otherwise their steepness might result in giving tourists a serious roll down a rough mountain-side.

Just before we began to ascend we saw a black man at his devotions. He was kneeling in the centre of a little square formed by rocks. His face was turned heavenward, and he was oblivious to all else except the power before which he was laying bare his inmost soul, with a fervor and devotion that commanded respect, even from those who thought of him as a heathen. I inferred that he was a sun worshipper from the way in which he constantly had his face turned upward, except when he bent forward to kiss the ground on which he knelt.

On the road we saw black people of many different tribes. A number of women I noticed, who walked proudly along, their brown, bare feet stepping lightly on the smooth road. They had long purple-black hair, which was always adorned with a long, stiff feather, dyed of brilliant red, green, purple, and like striking shades. They wore no other ornament than the colored feather, which lent them an air of pride, when seen beside the much-bejeweled people of that quaint town. Many of the women, who seemed very poor indeed, were lavishly dressed in jewelry. They did not wear much else, it is true, but in a place as hot as Aden, jewelry must be as much as anyone would care to wear.

To me the sight of these perfect, bronze-like women, with a graceful drapery of thin silk wound about the waist, falling to the knees, and a corner taken up the back and brought across the bust, was most bewitching. On their bare, perfectly modeled arms were heavy bracelets, around the wrist and muscle, most times joined by chains. Bracelets were also worn about the ankles, and their fingers and toes were laden with rings. Sometimes large rings were suspended from the nose, and the ears were almost always outlined with hoop rings, that reached from the inmost edge of the lobe to the top of the ear joining the head. So closely were these rings placed that, at a distance, the ear had the appearance of being rimmed in gold. A more pleasing style of nose ornament was a large gold ornament set in the nostril and fastened there as screw rings fasten in the ear. Still, if that nose ornamentation was more pleasing than the other, the ear adornment that accompanied it was disgusting. The lobe of the ear was split from the ear, and pulled down to such length that it usually rested on the shoulder. The enormous loop of flesh was partially filled with large gold knobs.

At the top of the hill we came to a beautiful, majestic, stone double gate, the entrance to the English fort and also spanning the road that leads to the town. Sentinels were pacing to and fro but we drove past them without stopping or being stopped, through a strange, narrow cut in the mountain, that towered at the sides a hundred feet above the road bed. Both these narrow, perpendicular sides are strongly fortified. It needs but one glance at Aden, which is in itself a natural fort, to strengthen the assertion that Aden is the strongest gate to India.

The moment we emerged from the cut, which, besides being so narrow that two carriages pass with great difficulty, is made on a dangerous steep grade, we got a view of the white town of Aden, nestling in the very heart of what seems to be an extinct volcano. We were driven rapidly down the road, catching glimpses of gaudily attired mounted policemen, water-carriers from the bay, with their well-filled goat-skins flung across their backs, camels loaded with cut stone, and black people of every description.

When we drove into the town, which is composed of low adobe houses, our carriage was surrounded with beggars. We got out and walked through an unpaved street, looking at the dirty, uninviting shops and the dirty, uninviting people in and about them. Very often we were urged to buy, but more frequently the natives stared at us with quiet curiosity. In the heart of the town we found the camel market, but beyond a number of camels standing, lying, and kneeling about, the sight was nothing extraordinary. Near by was a goat market, but business seemed dull in both places.

Without buying anything we started to return to the ship. Little naked children ran after us for miles, touching their foreheads humbly and crying for money. They all knew enough English to be able to ask us for charity.

When we reached the pier, we found our driver had forgotten all the English he knew when we started out. He wanted one price for the carriage and we wanted to pay another. It resulted in our appealing to a native policeman, who took the right change from us, handed it to the driver, and gave him, in addition, a lusty kick for his dishonesty.

Our limited time prevented our going to see the water tanks, which are some miles distant from Aden. When we returned to the ship we found Jews there, selling ostrich eggs and plumes, shells, fruit, spears of sword-fish, and such things. In the water, on one side of the boat, were numbers of men, Somali boys, they called them, who were giving an exhibition of wonderful diving and swimming.

They would actually sit in the water looking like bronze statues, as the sun rested on their wet, black skins. They sat in a row, and turning their faces up towards the deck, would yell methodically, one after the other, down the entire line:

"Oh! Yo! Ho!"

It sounded very like a chorus of bull-frogs and was very amusing. After finishing this strange music they would give us a duet, half crying, persuasively, in a sing-song style:

"Have a dive! Have a dive! Have a dive!"

The other half, meanwhile, would put their hands before their widely opened mouths, yelling through their rapidly moving fingers with such energy that we gladly threw over silver to see them dive and stop the din.

The moment the silver flashed over the water all the bronze figures would disappear like flying fish, and looking down we would see a few ripples on the surface of the blue water—nothing more. After a time that seemed dangerously long to us, they would bob up through the water again. We could see them coming before they finally appeared on the surface, and one among the number would have the silver between his teeth, which would be most liberally displayed in a broad smile of satisfaction. Some of these divers were children not more than eight years old, and they ranged from that up to any age. Many of them had their hair bleached. As they were completely naked, excepting a small cloth twisted about the loins, they found it necessary to make a purse out of their cheeks, which they did with as much ease as a cow stows away grass to chew at her leisure.

I have often envied a cow this splendid gift. One wastes so much time eating, especially when traveling, and I could not help picturing the comfort it would be sometimes to dispose of our food wholesale and consume it at our leisure afterwards. I am certain there would be fewer dyspeptics then.

No animal, waterborn and bred, could frisk, more gracefully in the water than do these Somali boys. They swim about, using the legs alone, or the arms alone, on their backs, or sides, and, in most cases, with their faces under water. They never get out of the way of a boat. They merely sink and come up in the same spot when the boat passes. The bay at Aden is filled with sharks, but they never touch these black men, so they tell me, and the safety with which they spend their lives in the water proves the truth of the assertion. They claim that a shark will not attack a black man, and after I had caught the odor of the grease with which these men annoint their bodies, I did not blame the sharks.

After a seven hours stay at Aden we left for Colombo, being followed a long ways out from land by the divers. One little boy went out with us on the ship, and when he left us he merely took a plunge from the upper deck into the sea and went happily back towards Aden, on his side, waving a farewell to us with his free hand.

2

A DAY IN THE AFRICAN ALPS—THE COL DE TIROURDA

FANNY BULLOCK WORKMAN

Fanny Bullock Workman is best known for her role in breaking down gender barriers in alpinism through her pioneering expeditions in the Himalayas. Due to the notoriety of her ascents in the Karakoram and Western Himalayas, she was invited to be the first woman to lecture at the Sorbonne and the second at the Royal Geographical Society. (Bullock, remembered for a biting determination, was also fiercely competitive. After Annie Smith Peck claimed to have broken her altitude record by summiting Huascarán in Peru, Workman sent a team of surveyors to determine the peak's true elevation, proving that her own Himalayan summit was a thousand feet higher.) But before she established herself as a climber, Fanny and her husband, William Hunter Workman, explored India, Switzerland, and, in this chapter, Algeria by bike.

CHAPTER XVIII: A DAY IN THE AFRICAN ALPS – THE COL DE TIROURDA

THE town of Fort National stands on the crest of a long narrow *crête* running parallel with the Djurjura, with a commanding view of the country on both sides. The town is mostly French, and presents nothing of especial interest except the Wednesday market. The fort, on a hill overhanging the town, is quite an imposing structure, suitable to the importance of the place as a military post. It was enlarged after the insurrection of 1871. At that time it was termed by the natives, 'A thorn in the eye of the Kabylie,' and such they probably still consider it, as it is kept well garrisoned, and, in case of insurrection, the houses of sixty thousand Kabyles could be destroyed in a few hours by its guns.

While looking about on the afternoon after our arrival, we chanced to go into the shop of the only *bijoutier* in the town, and while examining Kabyle ornaments we remarked, in the course of conversation, we should like to visit the place where they were made. The jeweller, a very friendly Kabyle, who spoke French, said it would give him much pleasure to entertain us as his guests at his house at Beni Yenni, if we would come there. He added, – 'To-morrow is the beginning of the feast of the Ramadan. I am going home early in the morning to remain with my people four days. Will you not go with me?'

'No,' we said, 'we cannot go to-morrow, for, fair, we have arranged a trip to the Col de Tirourda. Perhaps the day after to-morrow.'

'As you please. I will be there.'

'But how far is Beni Yenni from here?'

'Four hours on a good mule.'

As we looked at the fine form before us, wrapped in the soft folds of his burnous, which fell to his sandled feet, his face bright, his eye eager with apparently real desire to have us visit him, a strong wish to see the land of the Beni Yenni seized us, and we promised to go on the second day after.

That night it rained, as it can in the mountains, in torrents, and we feared our attempt on the Col de Tirourda from this side would prove as unsuccessful as the one proposed from Tasmalt. But at five o'clock in the morning, when a small Arab boy knocked at the door to awaken us, the brilliant African stars were palpitating in the heavens – for stars do not twinkle in Algeria – and the dark blue sky was full of mysterious premonition of a cloudless dawn.

We decided to use our cycles as far as the road would permit, and then climb the Col on foot. No one at Fort National could tell us anything about the route beyond Michelet, twenty-five kilometres distant. As we rode out of the sleeping town, past the house of the *bijoutier*, a cloaked figure appeared at the door, and the words 'Je vous attendrais' greeted us. We answered, 'A demain a Beni Yenni.'

The road, though well made, was muddy after the rainy night, and we had to ride with care, but we would not have hurried if we could on this magnificent ride from Fort National to Michelet. The road runs along a high horizontal *crête*, and as it circles in and out of the curling contour of the mountain, brings into sight peak after peak of the Djurjura, and ridge after ridge of the village-covered Kabylie. We could not help recalling the road from Sorrento to Positano and Amalfi, and that from Taormina toward Messina, not on account of any similarity in the landscape, but because each in its way is so superlatively lovely.

We passed a number of villages, and many Kabyles on the highway returning home from the market of the previous day. Most of them carried pieces of meat strung on strings, for the long fast was over and the people were about to celebrate the feast which was to follow by free indulgence in meat and *couscous*. Some of the men were without the usual cloak, being dressed only in large yellowish white shirts confined at the waist by a belt, their legs and arms bare. The only addition to this costume is the cloak ordinarily worn in cold weather, or sometimes two or three when the cold is extreme.

Michelet is a small official station consisting of a few houses and a sort of fort or strong house to which the inhabitants may fly for protection in case of necessity. Its situation, facing the highest peaks of the Djurjura, is even more beautiful than that of Fort National. Fifty villages are seen from here. On one long spur running out from the mountain we counted fifteen, the first nestling on the limit of the green, overhung by the high crags above, the last perched on the end, where it fell off sharply to the valley below.

The knowledge of the inhabitants of Michelet as to the road did not extend beyond the next station, the 'Maison Cantonniere,' nine kilometres farther, to which point they thought we could ride. They did not tell us that the road was unfinished, and converted by the rain of the preceding night into a sea of mud, as we found to be the case after going on a short distance. Returning to Michelet, we left the cycles at the inn and started on foot for the 'Maison Cantonniere,' which, by picking our way along the sides of the road, we reached in two hours.

Here we found only two tattooed, bejewelled Kabyle women, who spoke no French, and could tell us nothing about the route to the pass. We were now well up on the mountain side. The road, or the attempt at one, ceased, and we struck into a mule path, which led directly upward around the edge of the mountain. The scenery had become Alpine in character, the fertile lands were left behind, and the region grew milder and more desolate with every step. The path was obstructed in places with *débris* and rocks, which had been loosened by the frost and rains and had rolled down from above, so that progress was oftentimes slow. In one place we had to climb over a chaos of good-sized boulders, which covered the path for two hundred feet, the result of a landslide. This was the route across the mountains which we had been told in Algiers was available to bicyclists. We found it difficult enough to follow on foot and were thankful our machines were safely housed.

A turn of the path now brought into view the village of Tirourda far below, on the top of a desolate *crête*, the last village of the Kabylie in this direction, and the last to fall into the hands of the French in 1857, noted for having been the home of the Berber prophetess, Lalla Fathma.

Built almost upon the snow-beds of the mountain, amid nature's sternest aspects, it looked more like a deserted eagle's nest than the home of man. In 1857 it and Takleh, an adjoining village belonging to the marabouts of the tribe of Illilten, were governed by Sidi Thaieb, who, with his sister Lalla Fathma, lived like a petty monarch, surrounded by every luxury. Lalla had a wide reputation as a prophetess, and was consulted by the people of the whole Kabylie.

At the approach of the French, Sidi Thaieb, whose family had for centuries governed these two villages, went to MacMahon and succeeded in making an arrangement by which, in return for certain services on his part, these villages should remain unmolested. This compact would have been carried out by the French had not an unfortunate mistake occurred. Several zouaves in pursuit of some fugitives from another town came, without realising the fact, into Tirourda. The people, supposing them to come with hostile intent, fixed upon them, killing and wounding them all. A detachment of the army, which was in the neighbourhood, hearing the firing came up, and before either side was aware of it, a general engagement took place.

Lalla Fathma and her brother were taken prisoners, and their arms, clothing, furniture and jewels were confiscated. As we sit on a boulder, looking down upon lifeless Tirourda, fancy pictures the procession of three hundred men and women, with torn garments and dishevelled hair, starting down the narrow steep path on their way to the marshal's camp, following their idol seated on her mule, who, in the midst of the tumult of battle, had found time to braid carefully her jet black tresses, paint her cheeks with carmine, blacken her eyelids and stain her finger-nails with henna.

A light rustling breaks the silence. Is it the voices of the sobbing women and children driven from their homes by the relentless conqueror, or is it the spring wind playing about the jutting crags of the Pic de Tirourda?

The path became narrower and ran along dangerous precipices. Evidences of the action of frost appeared in cracks on its outer side, where the loosened edge threatened to slide off in places should any extra weight be placed upon it.

All this part of the mountain is composed of a loose, crumbling material, which at this season affords an uncertain and precarious foothold. Patches of snow lay across the path, and were seen to cover it ahead in great slanting sheets running to the edge of the cliffs. These must be crossed if we would go on.

We had now arrived within two kilometres of the goal in regard to which, we had so long sought for information in vain – the Col de Tirourda – from which an extended view over the Kabylie of the country south of Djurjura of the sea, and of Algiers was to be obtained. Should we go on, or give up farther attempt? It was hard to give up now, after so much effort and being so near to success, but common prudence dictated that we go no further. We knew nothing of the character of the ground under the slanting masses of snow ahead, or what foothold they had upon the mountain. We had no Alpine-stocks, and no hobnails in our boots. Reluctantly we turned our backs upon the Col, feeling that we could at least give somewhat more information about the route than we had ever succeeded in gathering from others. The grandeur of the region, however, amply repaid all exertion, and we consoled ourselves for the failure to accomplish all we had desired, by the reflection that we were not the only tourists who had had mountain luck.

We were now thankful that the mules had failed to put in an appearance that morning at Tasmalt, for had it been otherwise, we might have been deposited with our bicycles on the top of the Col, there to wait perhaps until the snow melted.

By the time we reached Michelet again we had walked eighteen miles up and down, and were glad enough to mount and ride back over the splendid road to Fort National. Over the green setting of dozens of villages hovered in the evening light a thin blue film of smoke, a sign that the labours of the day were over and the people had gathered around their hearthstones to enjoy their evening meal. The clouds behind the mountains grew pink in sunset hues, and faded into the cold greys of crepuscule before the day's trip ended.

3

SACRED CITY OF THE LIVING BUDDHA

ROY CHAPMAN ANDREWS

It's been said that Roy Chapman Andrews provided the inspiration for George Lucas's Indiana Jones. True or not, he lived a fittingly thrilling life and is credited with, among other things, exploring the outer reaches of Mongolia, unearthing one of the first known nests of dinosaur eggs, and later serving as the director of the American Museum of Natural History. On the subject of close calls during his first 15 years of fieldwork, he wrote, "Two were from drowning in typhoons, one was when our boat was charged by a wounded whale, once my wife and I were nearly eaten by wild dogs, once we were in great danger from fanatical lama priests, two were close calls when I fell over cliffs, once was nearly caught by a huge python, and twice I might have been killed by bandits." This excerpt, taken from Chapman's account of a year-long hunting expedition across North China and Mongolia, provides a glimpse into why he continued to succumb to the intoxicating pull of the world's hidden corners.

CHAPTER VI: SACRED CITY OF THE LIVING BUDDHA

Far up in northern Mongolia, where the forests stretch in an unbroken line to the Siberian frontier, lies Urga, the Sacred City of the Living Buddha. The world has other sacred cities, but none like this. It is a relic of medieval times overlaid with a veneer of twentieth-century civilization; a city of violent contrasts and glaring anachronisms. Motor cars pass camel caravans fresh from the vast, lone spaces of the Gobi Desert; holy lamas, in robes of flaming red or brilliant yellow, walk side by side with black-gowned priests; and swarthy Mongol women, in the fantastic headdress of their race, stare wonderingly at the latest fashions of their Russian sisters.

We came to Urga from the south. All day we had been riding over rolling, treeless uplands, and late in the afternoon we had halted on the summit of a hill overlooking the Tola River valley. Fifteen miles away lay Urga, asleep in the darkening shadow of the Bogdo-ol (God's Mountain). An hour later the road led us to our first surprise in Mai-ma-cheng, the Chinese quarter of the city. Years of wandering in the strange corners of the world had left us totally unprepared for what we saw. It seemed that here in Mongolia we had discovered an American frontier outpost of the Indian fighting days. Every house and shop was protected by high stockades of unpeeled timbers, and there was hardly a trace of Oriental architecture save where a temple roof gleamed above the palisades.

Before we were able to adjust our mental perspective we had passed from colonial America into a hamlet of modern Russia. Gayly painted cottages lined the road, and, unconsciously,

I looked for a white church with gilded cupolas. The church was not in sight, but its place was taken by a huge red building of surpassing ugliness, the Russian Consulate. It stands alone on the summit of a knoll, the open plains stretching away behind it to the somber masses of the northern forests. In its imposing proportions it is tangible evidence of the Russian Colossus which not many years ago dominated Urga and all that is left of the ancient empire of the Khans.

For two miles the road is bordered by Russian cottages; then it debouches into a wide square which loses its distinctive character and becomes an indescribable mixture of Russia, Mongolia, and China. Palisaded compounds, gay with fluttering prayer flags, ornate houses, felt-covered *yurts*, and Chinese shops mingle in a dizzying chaos of conflicting personalities. Three great races have met in Urga and each carries on, in this far corner of Mongolia, its own customs and way of life. The Mongol *yurt* has remained unchanged; the Chinese shop, with its wooden counter and blue-gowned inmates, is pure Chinese; and the ornate cottages proclaim themselves to be only Russian.

But on the street my wife and I could never forget that we were in Mongolia. We never tired of wandering through the narrow alleys, with their tiny native shops, or of watching the ever-changing crowds. Mongols in half a dozen different tribal dresses, Tibetan pilgrims, Manchu Tartars, or camel drivers from far Turkestan drank and ate and gambled with Chinese from civilized Peking.

The barbaric splendor of the native dress fairly makes one gasp for breath. Besides gowns and sashes of dazzling brilliance, the men wear on their heads all the types of covering one learned to know in the pictures of ancient Cathay, from the high-peaked

hat of yellow and black—through the whole, strange gamut—
to the helmet with streaming peacock plumes. But were I to
tell about them all I would leave none of my poor descriptive
phrases for the women.

It is hopeless to draw a word-picture of a Mongol woman.
A photograph will help, but to be appreciated she must be seen
in all her colors. To begin with the dressing of her hair. If all
the women of the Orient competed to produce a strange and
fantastic type, I do not believe that they could excel what the
Mongol matrons have developed by themselves.

Their hair is plaited over a frame into two enormous flat
bands, curved like the horns of a mountain sheep and reënforced
with bars of wood or silver. Each horn ends in a silver plaque,
studded with bits of colored glass or stone, and supports a pendent braid like a riding quirt. On her head, between the horns,
she wears a silver cap elaborately chased and flashing with
"jewels." Surmounting this is a "saucer" hat of black and yellow.
Her skirt is of gorgeous brocade or cloth, and the jacket is of like
material with prominent "puffs" upon the shoulders. She wears
huge leather boots with upturned, pointed toes, similar to those
of the men, and when in full array she has a whole portiere of
beadwork suspended from the region of her ears.

She is altogether satisfying to the lover of fantastic Oriental
costumes, except in the matter of footgear, and this slight exception might be allowed, for she has so amply decorated every
other available part of her anatomy.

Moreover, the boots form a very necessary adjunct to her personal equipment, besides providing a covering for her feet. They
are many sizes too large, of course, but they furnish ample space
during the bitter cold of winter for the addition of several pairs

of socks, varying in number according to the thermometer. During the summer she often wears no socks at all, but their place is taken by an assortment of small articles which cannot be carried conveniently on her person. Her pipe and tobacco, a package of tea, or a wooden bowl can easily be stuffed into the wide top boots, for pockets are an unknown luxury even to the men.

In its kaleidoscopic mass of life and color the city is like a great pageant on the stage of a theater, with the added fascination of reality. But, somehow, I could never quite make myself believe that it *was* real when a brilliant group of horsemen in pointed, yellow hats and streaming, peacock feathers dashed down the street. It seemed too impossible that I, a wandering naturalist of the drab, prosaic twentieth century, and my American wife were really a living, breathing part of this strange drama of the Orient.

4

THE CONVICT TRAIL

WILLIAM BEEBE

The career of naturalist William Beebe crossed land, sea, and sky.
From the canopy of the British Guinea jungle, through the interior of
Borneo and a half-mile under the ocean off the coast of Bermuda, Beebe
established himself as one of the country's foremost ornithologists,
entomologists, and explorers. (He also struck up a friendship with
another distinguished American conservationist, President Theodore
Roosevelt, who reviewed a number of Beebe's books, including this
one.) Though it was his ocean descent—made in a groundbreaking
cast-iron "Bathysphere" and providing the first opportunity to study
deep-sea animals—that brought him fame, Beebe also made a name as
a writer capable of communicating scientific discovery to the masses.
Here, from a field research station he established in British Guinea, he
describes the lure of a quiet jungle.

VIII: THE CONVICT TRAIL

I am thinking of a very wonderful thing and words come laggardly. For it is a thing which more easily rests quietly in the deep pool of memory than stirred up and crystalized into words and phrases. It is of the making of a new trail, of the need and the planning and the achievement, of the immediate effects and the possible consequences. For the effects became manifest at once, myriad, unexpected, some sinister, others altogether thrilling and wholly delightful to the soul of a naturalist. And now, many months after, they are still spreading, like a forest fire which has passed beyond control. Only in this case the land was no worse and untold numbers of creatures were better off because of our new trail.

Of the still more distant consequences I cannot write, for the book of the future is tightly sealed. But we may recall that a trail once was cut through coarse, high grass and belts of cedar, which in time became the Appian Way. And a herd of aurochs breasting in single file dense shrubby oaks and heather toward a salt lick may well have foreshadowed Regent Street; the Place d'Etoile was perhaps first adumbrated by wild boars concentrating on a root-filled marsh. And why should not the Indian trail which became a Dutch road and our Fifth Avenue, have had its first hint in a moose track down the heart of a wooded island, leading to some hidden spring!

We left our boats stranded on the Mazaruni River bank and climbed the steep ascent to our new home in the heart of British Guiana. Our outfit was unpacked, and the laboratory and kitchen and bedrooms in the big Kalacoon house were at last more than names.

And now we surveyed our little kingdom. One path led down to our boats, another meandered eastwards through the hills. But like the feathered end of the magnetic arrow, we drifted as with one will to the south. Here at the edge of our cleared compound we were confronted by a tangle. It was not very high—twenty feet or so—but dense and unbroken. Like newly trapped creatures we paced back and forth along it looking for an opening. It was without a break. We examined it more closely and saw a multitude of slender, graceful cane stems hung with festoons and grass-like drapery. One of us seized a wisp of this climbing grass and pulled downward. When he dropped it his hand dripped blood. He might as well have run a scroll saw over his fingers. The jungle had shown its teeth.

We laughed and retreated to the upper floor for consultation. The sight we saw there decided us. In the distance "not too far," to use the hopelessly indefinite Guiana vernacular, high over the tumbled lower growths towered the real jungle—the high bush. This was the edge of that mighty tropical ocean of foliage, that sea of life with its surface one hundred, two hundred feet above the earth, stretching unbroken to the Andes: leagues of unknown wonderland. And here we were, after thousands of miles of voyaging to study the life of this great jungle, to find our last few yards blocked by a mass of vegetation. There was no dissenting voice. We must cut a trail, and at once, straight to the jungle.

Before we begin our trail, it will be wise to try to understand this twenty-foot tangle, stretching almost a mile back from Kalacoon. Three years before it was pure jungle. Then man came with ax and saw and fire and one by one the great giants were felled—mora, greenheart, crabwood—each crashing its way to earth after centuries of upward growth. The underbrush in the dark, high jungle is comparatively scanty. Light-starved and fungus-plagued, the shrubs and saplings are stunted and weak. So when only the great stumps were left standing, the erstwhile jungle showed as a mere shambles of raw wood and shriveled foliage. After a time fire was applied, and quickly, as in the case of resinous trees, or with long, slow smolderings of half-rotted, hollow giants, the huge boles were consumed.

For a period, utter desolation reigned. Charcoal and gray ash covered everything. No life stirred. Birds had flown, reptiles and insects made their escape or succumbed. Only the saffron-faced vultures swung past, on the watch for some half-charred creature. Almost at once, however, the marvelous vitality of the tropical vegetation asserted itself. Phoenix-like, from the very heart of the ashes, appeared leaves of strange shape and color. Stumps whose tissues seemed wholly turned to charcoal sent forth adventitious shoots, and splintered boughs blossomed from their wounds. Now was the lowest ebb of the jungle's life, when man for the success of his commercial aims, should take instant advantage. But plans miscarried and the ruin wrought was left to nature.

The destruction of the jungle had been complete and the searing flames had destroyed all forest seeds. In their place, by some magic, there sprang up at once a maze of weeds, vines and woody shrubs, reeds, ferns and grasses, all foreign to the dark jungle and whose nearest congeners were miles away. Yet here were their seeds and spores, baffling all attempts at tracing their migration or the time they had laid dormant.

When we had begun to penetrate this newborn tangle we found it possible, by comparing various spots, to follow its growth in past time. The first things to appear in the burned jungle area were grasses or grass-like plants and prostrate vines. These latter climbed over the fallen tree-trunks and covered the charred stumps with a glory of blossoms—white convolvulus gleaming everywhere, then pale yellow allamandas, and later, orchid-like, violet, butterfly peas which at first flowered among the ashes on the ground, but climbed as soon as they found support. Little by little, a five-finger vine flung whole chains of bloom over stumps, logs and bushes, a beautiful, blood-red passion flower, whose buds looked like strings of tiny Chinese lanterns.

Soon another type of plant appeared, with hollow and jointed stems, pushing out fans of fingered leaves, swiftly, wasting no time in branching, but content with a single spike piercing up through strata of grass and reeds, through shrubs and bushes until it won to the open sky. This was the cecropia or trumpet tree, falsely appearing firm and solid stemmed, but quite dominant in the neglected tangle.

We started early one morning with small axes and sharp machetes, and single file, began to cut and hew and tear a narrow trail southward. For some distance we found almost a pure culture of the cecropia trees, through which we made rapid progress which aroused entirely false hopes. It was a joy to crash obliquely through the crisp hollow stems at one blow from our great knives. The second man cut again at the base and the rest took the severed stems and threw or pushed them to one side, cutting away any smaller growths. We soon learned to be careful in handling the stems for they were sanctuary for scores of a small stinging ant, whose race had practiced preparedness for many generations and who rushed out when the stem was split by cutlass or ax.

As we went on we learned that differences in soil which were not apparent when the great jungle covered everything, had now become of much importance. On high sandy spots the cecropias did not get that flying start which they needed for their vertical straightaway dash. Here a community of hollow reeds or bamboo grass appeared from no one knows where. They had grown and multiplied until their stems fairly touched one another, forming a dense, impenetrable thicket of green, silicious tubes eight to twelve feet in length. These were smooth and hard as glass and tapered beautifully, making wonderfully light and strong arrows with which our Akawai Indians shot fish. Slow indeed was our progress through this. The silica dulled and chipped our blades and the sharp points of the cut stems lamed us at a touch.

But whatever the character of the vegetation, whether a tangle of various thorny nightshades, a grove of cecropias, or a serried phalanx of reeds, the terrible razor-grass overran all. Gracefully it hung in emerald loops from branch to branch, festooning living foliage and dead stump alike, with masses of slender fronds. It appeared soft and loose-hung as if one could brush it away with a sweep of the hand. But it was the most punishing of all living things, insidiously cutting to the bone as we grasped it, and binding all this new growth together with bands more efficient than steel.

An age-old jungle is kind to the intruder, its floor is smooth and open, one's footsteps fall upon soft moss, the air is cooled and shadowed by the foliage high overhead. Here, in this mushroom growth of only three years, our progress became slower and ever more difficult. Our hands bled and were cut until we could barely keep them gripped about the cutlass handles; our trail opened up a lane down which poured the seething heat of the sun's direct rays; thorns penetrated our moccasins and ants dropped down our necks and bit and stung simultaneously with opposite ends of their anatomy. Five minutes' chopping and hacking was all that the leader could stand, who would then give way to another. Fifty yards of a narrow lane represented our combined efforts the first day.

Direction was a constant source of trouble. Every three or four feet we had to consult a compass, so confusing was the tangle. Sudden gullies blocked us, a barren, half-open, sandy slope cheered us for a few yards. It was nature's defense and excelled any barbed-wire entanglement I have ever seen at the battle-front.

Once I came to a steep concealed gully. The razor-grass had been particularly bad, giving like elastic to blows of the cutlass and then flying back across my face. I was adrip with perspiration, panting in the heat when I slid part way down the bank, and chopping away a solid mass of huge elephant's ears, uncovered a tree-trunk bridging the swamp. It brought to mind the bridge from Bad to Worse in the terrible Dubious Land. Strange insects fled from the great leaves, lizards whisked past me, hummingbirds whirred close to my face—the very sound seeming to increase the heat. I slipped and fell off the log, splashing into the hot water and warm mud, and sat in it for a while, too fagged to move. Then the rest of the party came up and we clambered slowly to the top of the next rise, and there caught sight of the jungle's edge, and it seemed a trifle nearer and we went on with renewed courage. Shortly afterwards two of us were resting in a patch of reeds while the third worked some distance ahead, when there came a sudden low growl and rush. Instinctively we rose on the instant, just in time to see a jaguar swerve off on one side and disappear in a swish of swaying reed stems. I have never known one of these animals to attack a man, and in this case the jaguar had undoubtedly heard but not scented us, and the attack ceased the moment we proved to be other than deer or similar prey. The incident had come and passed too swiftly for thought, but now when we realized that this was a bit of the real wild life of the jungle, our enthusiasm never flagged, and we kept steadily at the heart-breaking work, resting only now and then for our cuts to heal.

Then a government official who was our guest, took pity on us, and for science' sake, obtained special dispensation. One morning we went out and found in our compound several huge, blue-uniformed policemen, who saluted and with real black magic, produced twenty convicts—negroes and coolies—armed with cutlasses. So began the second phase of what we now named the Convict Trail. We had already fought our painful way through a half-mile of the terrible maze, and now we heartily welcomed this new aid, whether good-natured murderers, and burglars, or like Sippy, Slorg and Slith, mere thieves. We watched them strip to their black skins and begin a real assault. On a front of ten to fifteen feet, the tangle fairly dissolved before our eyes, and their great tough palms and soles made little moment of the razor-grass and thorns. In one of the slight-bodied coolies, whose task was to clear away the cut débris, I recognized Ram Narine, whose trial had been the cause of my traveling another trail.

With my friend, Hope, an honest forger, I went on far ahead and laid the course for the jungle. In especially dense parts we climbed to the summit of great jungle stumps and stretched a white sheet to guide the oncoming trail cutters.

Day after day the score of convicts returned with their guards and at last we saw the path unite with an old game and Indian trail in the cool shade of the jungle, and Kalacoon was in direct contact with the great tropical forest itself. I have passed lightly over the really frightful pain and exhaustion which we experienced in the initial part of this work, and which emphasized the tremendous difference between the age-old jungle untouched by man, and the terrible tangle which springs after he has destroyed the primeval vegetation.

After this came our reward, and never a day passed but the trail yielded many wonderful facts. The creatures of the wilderness soon found this wide swath, and used it by day and night, making it an exciting thing for us to peer around a corner, to see what strange beings were sitting or feeding in our little street.

Before the trail was quite completed, it yielded one of the most exciting hunts of our trip—the noosing of a giant bushmaster—the most deadly serpent of the tropics. Nupee—my Akawai Indian hunter, two nestling trogons and Easter eve—these things led to the capture of the Master of the Bush: For nothing in the tropics is direct, premeditated.

My thoughts were far from poisonous serpents when Nupee came into our Kalacoon laboratory late on a Saturday afternoon. Outdoors he had deposited the coarser game intended for the mess, consisting, today, of a small deer, a tinamou or maam and two agoutis. But now with his quiet smile, he held out his lesser booty, which he always brought in to me, offering in his slender, effeminate hands his contribution to science. Usually this was a bird of brilliant plumage, or a nestful of maam's eggs with shells like great spheres of burnished emeralds. These he would carry in a basket so cunningly woven from a single palm frond that it shared our interest in its contents. Today, he presented two nestling trogons, and this was against rules. For we desired only to know where such nests were, there to go and study and photograph.

"Nupee,—listen! You sabe we no want bird here. Must go and show nest, eh?"

"Me sabe."

Accompanied by one of us, off he started again, without a murmur. In the slanting rays of the sun he walked lightly down the trail from Kalacoon as if he had not been hunting since early dawn. An hour passed and the sun swung still lower when a panting voice gasped out:

"Huge labaria, yards long! Big as leg!"

The flight of queen bees and their swarms, the call to arms in a sleeping camp creates somewhat the commotion that the news of the bushmaster aroused with us. For he is really what his name implies. What the elephant is to the African jungles and the buffalo to Malaysia, this serpent is to the Guiana wilderness. He fears nothing—save one thing, hunting ants, before which all the world flees. And this was the first bushmaster of the rainy season.

Nupee had been left to mount guard over the serpent which had been found near the trogon tree. Already the light was failing; so we walked rapidly with gun, snake-pole and canvas bag. Parrakeets hurtled bamboowards to roost; doves scurried off and small rails flew from our path and flopped into the reeds. Our route led from the open compound of Kalacoon, through the freshly cut Convict Trail, toward the edge of the high bush, and we did not slacken speed until we were in the dim light which filtered through the western branches.

At the top of the slope we heard a yell—a veritable Red Indian yell—and there our Akawai hunter was dancing excitedly about, shouting to us to come on. "Snake, he move! Snake, he move!" We arrived panting, and he tremblingly led me along a fallen tree and pointed to the dead leaves. I well knew the color and pattern of the bushmaster. I had had them brought to me dead and had killed them myself, and I had seen them in their cage behind glass. But now, though I was thinking bushmaster and looking bushmaster, my eyes insisted on registering dead leaves. Eager as I was to begin operations before darkness closed down, it was a full three minutes before I could honestly say, "This is leaf; that is snake."

The pattern and pigment of the cunningly arranged coils were that of the jungle floor, anywhere; a design of dead leaves, reddish-yellow, pinkish, dark-brown, etched with mold, fungus and decay, and with all the shadows and high lights which the heaped-up plant tissues throw upon one another. In the center of this dread plaque, this reptilian mirage, silent and motionless, rested the head. I knew it was triangular and flattened, because I had dissected such heads in times past, but now my senses revealed to me only an irregularity in the contour, a central focus in this jungle mat, the unraveling of which spelt death.

It was a big snake, seven or eight feet long, and heavy bodied—by no means a one-man job. Again we carefully examined the screw-eyes on the pole, and each looked behind for a possible line of escape.

I quickly formed my method of attack. Nupee was sent to cut forked sticks, but his enthusiasm at having work to do away from the scene of immediate conflict was so sincere that he vanished altogether and returned with the sticks only when our shouts announced the end of the struggle. An Indian will smilingly undergo any physical hardship, and he will face any creature in the jungle, except the bushmaster.

We approached from three sides, bringing snake-pole, free noose and gun to bear. Slowly the noose on the pole pushed nearer and nearer. I had no idea how he would react at the attack, whether he would receive it quietly, or, as I have seen the king cobra in Burma, become enraged and attack in turn.

The cord touched his nose, and he drew back close to some bushy stems. Again it dangled against his head, and his tongue played like lightning. And now he sent forth the warning of his mastership—a sharp *whirrrrr!* and the tip of his tail became a blur, the rough scales rasping and vibrating against the dead leaves, and giving out a sound not less sharp and sinister than the instrumental rattling of his near relatives.

For a moment the head hung motionless, then the noose-man made a lunge and pulled his cord. The great serpent drew back like a flash, and turning, undulated slowly away toward the darker depths of the forest. There was no panic, no fear of pursuit in his movements. He had encountered something quite new to his experience, and the knowledge of his own power made it easy for him to gauge that of an opponent. He feared neither deer nor tapir, yet at their approach he would sound his warning as a reciprocal precaution, poison against hoofs. And now, when his warning had no effect on this new disturbing thing, he chose dignifiedly to withdraw.

I crept quickly along on one side and with the gun-barrel slightly deflected his course so that he was headed toward an open space, free from brush and bush-ropes. Here the pole-man awaited him, the noose spread and swaying a few inches from the leaves. Steadily the snake held to his course, and without sensing any danger pushed his head cleanly into the circle of cord. A sudden snap of the taut line and pandemonium began. The snake lashed and curled and whipped up a whirlpool of débris, while one of us held grimly on to the noose and the rest tried to disentangle the whirling coils and make certain of a tight grip close behind the head, praying for the screw-eyes to hold fast. Even with the scant inch of neck ahead of the noose, the head had such play that I had to pin it down with the gun-barrel before we dared seize it. When our fingers gained their safe hold and pressed, the great mouth opened wide, a gaping expanse of snowy white tissue, and the inch-long fangs appeared erect, each draped under the folds of its sheath like a rapier outlined beneath a courtier's cloak.

When once the serpent felt himself conquered, he ceased to struggle; and this was fortunate, for in the dim light we stumbled more than once as we sidled and backed through the maze of lianas and over fallen logs.

Nupee now appeared, unashamed and wide-eyed with excitement. He followed and picked up the wreck of battle—gun, hats and bags which had been thrown aside or knocked off in the struggle. With locked step, so as not to wrench the long body, we marched back to Kalacoon. Now and then a great shudder would pass through the hanging loops and a spasm of muscular stress that tested our strength. It was no easy matter to hold the snake, for the scales on its back were as rough and hard as a file, and a sudden twist fairly took the skin off one's hand.

I cleaned his mouth of all dirt and débris, and then we laid him upon the ground and, without stretching, found that he measured a good eight feet and a half. With no relaxing of care we slid him into the wired box which would be his home until he was liberated in his roomier quarters in the Zoölogical Park in New York.

Close to the very entrance of the Convict Trail behind Kalacoon stood four sentinel trees. Every day we passed and repassed them on the way to and from the jungle. For many days we paid very little attention to them, except to be grateful for the shade cast by their dense foliage of glossy leaves. Their trunks were their most striking feature, the bark almost concealed by a maze of beautifully colored lichens, different forms overlapping one another in many places, forming a palimpsest of gray, white, pink, mauve and lilac. One day a streaked flycatcher chose the top of a branch for her nest, and this we watched and photographed and robbed for science' sake, and again we thought no more of the four trees.

Late in April, however, a change came over the trees. The leaves had been shed some time in January and the fallen foliage formed a dry mass on the ground which crackled under foot. Now each branch and twig began to send out clusters of small buds, and one day,—a week after Easter,—these burst into indescribable glory. Every lichened bough and branch and twig was lined with a soft mass of bloom, clear, bright cerise, which reflected its brilliance on the foliage itself. After two days a rain of stamens began and soon the ground beneath the trees was solid cerise, a carpet of tens of thousands of fallen stamens, and within the length of a foot on one small branch were often a score of blooms. This feast of color was wonderful enough, and it made us want to know more of these trees. But all the information we could glean was that they were called French cashew. Yet they had not nearly finished with the surprises they had in store. A hummingbird or two was not an uncommon sight along the trail at any time, but now we began to notice an increase in numbers. Then it was observed that the tiny birds seemed to focus their flight upon one part of the clearing, and this proved to be the four cashew trees.

The next few days made the trees ever memorable: they were the Mecca of all the hummingbirds in the jungle. In early morning the air for many yards resounded with a dull droning, as of a swarming of giant bees. Standing or sitting under the tree we could detect the units of this host and then the individuals forced themselves on our notice. Back and forth the hummers swooped and swung, now poising in front of a mass of blossom and probing deeply among the stamens, now dashing off at a tangent, squeaking or chattering their loudest. The magnitude of the total sound made by these feathered atoms was astounding; piercing squeaks, shrill insect-like tones, and now and then a real song, diminutive trills and warbles as if from a flock of song birds a long distance away. Combats and encounters were frequent, some mere sparring bouts, while, when two would go at it in earnest, their humming and squeaks and throb of wings were audible above the general noise.

This being an effect, I looked for the cause. The massed cerise bloom gave forth comparatively little perfume, but at the base of each flower, hidden and protected by the twenty score densely ranked stamens, was a cup of honey; not a nectary with one or two delicately distilled drops, but a good thimbleful, a veritable stein of liquor. No creature without a long proboscis or bill could penetrate the chevaux-de-frise of stamens, and to reach the honey the hummingbirds had to probe to their eyes. They came out with forehead well dusted with pollen and carried it to the next blossom. The destiny of the flower was now fulfilled, the pot of honey might dry up, the stamens rain to the earth and the glory of Tyrian rose pass into the dull hues of decay.

Day after day as we watched this kaleidoscope of vegetable and avian hues, we came to know more intimately the units which formed the mass. There were at least fifteen species and all had peculiarities of flight and plumage so marked that they soon became recognizable at sight.

After our eyes had become accustomed to specific differences in these atoms of birds we began to notice the eccentricities of individuals. This was made easy by the persistence with which certain birds usurped and clung to favorite perches. One glowing hermit clad in resplendent emerald armor selected a bare twig on a nearby shrub and from there challenged every hummer that came in sight; whether larger, smaller or of his own kind made no difference. He considered the cashew trees as his own special property and as far as his side of them went he made good his claim. I have never seen such a concentration of virile combative force in so condensed a form.

In some such way as vultures concentrate upon carrion, so news of the cashew sweets had passed through the jungle. Not by any altruistic agency we may be certain, as we watch the selfish, irritable little beings, but by subtile scent, or as with the vultures, by the jealous watching of each other's actions. I observed closely for one hour and counted one hundred and forty-six hummingbirds coming to the tree. During the day at least one thousand must visit it.

They did not have a monopoly of the cashew manna, for now and then a honey-creeper or flower-pecker flew into the tree and took toll of the sweets. But they were scarcely noticeable. We had almost a pure culture of hummingbirds to watch and vainly to attempt to study, for more elusive creatures do not exist. Convict Trail revealed no more beautiful a sight than this concentration of the smallest, most active and the most gorgeous birds in the world.

Such treats—floral and avian—were all that might be expected of any tree, but the cashews had still more treasures in store. The weeks passed and we had almost forgotten the flowers and hummingbirds, when a new odor greeted us, the sweet, intense smell of overripe fruit. We noticed a scattering of soft yellow cashews fallen here and there, and simultaneously there arrived the hosts of fruit-eating birds. From the most delicate turquoise honey-creepers to great red and black grosbeaks, they thronged the trees. All day a perfect stream of tanagers—green, azure and wine-colored—flew in and about the manna, callistes and silver-beaks, dacnis and palm tanagers. And for a whole week we gloried in this new feast of color, before the last riddled cashew dropped, to be henceforth the prize of great wasps and gauze-winged flies, who guzzled its fermented juice and helped in the general redistribution of its flesh—back to the elements of the tropic mold, to await the swarms of fingering rootlets, a renewed synthesis—to rise again for a time high in air, again to become part of blossom and bird and insect.

It was along this Convict Trail that I sank the series of pits which trapped unwary walkers of the night, and halfway out at pit number five, the army ants waged their wonderful warfare.

In fact it was while watching operations in another sector of this same battle-front that I found myself all unintentionally in the sleeping chamber of the heliconias.

Tired from a long day's work in the laboratory, I wandered slowly along the Convict Trail, aimlessly, in that wholly relaxed state which always seems to invite small adventures. It is a mental condition wholly desirable, but not to be achieved consciously. One cannot say, "Lo, I will now be relaxed, receptive." It must come subconsciously, unnoticed, induced by a certain wearied content of body or mind—and then—many secret doors stand ajar, any one of which may be opened and passed if the gods approve. My stroll was marked at first, however, by only one quaint happening. For several weeks the jolly little trail-lizards had been carrying on most enthusiastic courtships, marked with much bowing and posing, and a terrific amount of scrambling about. The previous day—that of the first rains—numbers of lizardlets appeared, and at the same time the brown tree-lizards initiated their season of love-making. I had often watched them battle with one another—combats wholly futile as far as any damage was concerned. But the vanquished invariably gave up to his conqueror the last thing he had swallowed, the victor receiving it in a gluttonly rather than a gracious spirit, but allowing his captive to escape. I surprised one of these dark-brown chaps in the trail and seized him well up toward the head, to preserve his tail intact. Hardly had I lifted him from the ground, when he turned his head, considered me calmly with his bright little eyes, and forthwith solemnly spat out a still living ant in my direction. The inquiring look he then gave me, was exceedingly embarrassing. Who was I not to be bound in chivalry by the accredited customs of his race?

With dignity and certainty of acceptance he had surrendered, calmly and without doubt he had proffered his little substitute of sword. It was, I felt, infinitely preferable to any guttural and cowardly "kamerad!" Feeling rather shamefaced I accepted the weakly struggling ant, gently lowered the small saurian to the ground and opened my fingers. He went as he had surrendered, with steadiness and without terror. From the summit of a fallen log he turned and watched me walk slowly out of sight, and I at least felt the better for the encounter.

Of all tropical butterflies, heliconias seem the most casual and irresponsible. The background of the wings of many is jet-black, and on this sable canvas are splashed the boldest of yellow streaks and the most conspicuous of scarlet spots. Unquestionably protected by nauseous body fluids, they flaunt their glaring colors in measured, impudent flight, weaving their way slowly through the jungle, in the face of lizard and bird. Warningly colored they assuredly are. One cannot think of them except as flitting aimlessly on their way, usually threading the densest part of the undergrowth. No butterflies are more conspicuous or easier to capture. They must feed, they must pay court and mate, and they must stop long enough in their aimless wanderings to deposit their eggs on particular plants by an instinct which we have never fathomed. But these are consummations hidden from the casual observer.

Now, however, I am prepared for any unexpected meaningful trait, for I have surprised them in a habit, which presupposes memory, sociability and caution, manifested at least subconsciously.

The afternoon had worn on, and after leaving my lizard, I had squatted at the edge of a small glade. This glade was my private property, and the way by which one reached it from the nearby Convict Trail was a pressure trail, not a cut one. One pushed one's way through the reeds, which flew back into place and revealed nothing. Lifting my eyes from the tragedies of a hastening column of army ants, I saw that an unusual number of heliconias were flitting about the glade, both species, the Reds and the Yellows. All were fluttering slowly about and as I watched, one by one they alighted on the very tips of bare twigs, upside down with closed wings. In this position they were almost invisible, even a side view showing only the subdued under-wing pigments which blended with the pastel colors of twilight in the glade, reflected from variegated leaves and from the opening blossoms of the scarlet passion vine. Perhaps the most significant fact of this sleeping posture, was the very evident protection it afforded to butterflies which in motion during their waking hours are undoubtedly warningly colored and advertised to the world as inedible. Hanging perpendicularly beneath the twig, although they were almost in the open with little or no foliage overhead, yet they presented no surface to the rain of the night, and all faced northeast—the certain direction of both rain and wind.

The first one or two roosting butterflies I thought must be due to accidental association, but I soon saw my error. I counted twelve of the Red-spots and eight Yellows on two small bushes and a few minutes' search revealed forty-three more. All were swung invariably from the tips of bare twigs, and there was very evident segregation of the two kinds, one on each side of the glade.

When I disturbed them, they flew up in a colorful flurry, flapped about for a minute or less and returned, each to its particular perch. After two or three gentle waves of the wings and a momentary shifting of feet they settled again to perfect rest. This persistent choice of position was invariably the case, as

I observed in a number of butterflies which had recognizable tears in their wings. No matter how often they were disturbed they never made a mistake in the number of their cabin. A certain section of a particular twig on a definite branch was the resting place of some one heliconia, and he always claimed it.

Several were bright and fresh, newly emerged, but the remainder were somewhat faded and chipped at the edges. The delicate little beings slept soundly. I waited until dusk began finally to settle down and crept gently toward a Red-spot. I brought my face close and aroused no sign of life. Then I reached up and slowly detached the butterfly from its resting place. It moved its feet slightly, but soon became quiet. Then I gently replaced it, and at the touch of the twig, its feet took new hold. When I released its wings it did not fly but sank back into the same position as before. I wondered if I was the first scientist to pluck a sleepy butterfly from a jungle tree and replace it unawakened. At the time I was more impressed by the romantic beauty of it all than by its psychological significance. I wondered if heliconias ever dreamed, I compared the peacefulness of this little company with the fierce ants which even now were just disappearing from view. These were my thoughts rather than later meditations on whether this might not be a sort of atavistic social instinct, faintly reminiscent of the gregariousness of their caterpillar youth.

From any point of view I shall think better of all butterflies for this discovery; their desire for company, the instinctive wisdom of place and posture, the gentleness and silence of the little foregathering in the jungle. As I walked back along the trail several late comers passed me, vibrating softly through the twilight, headed for their glade of dreams.

Subsequent visits to this glade emphasized the strength of association of this little fraternity, by realization of its temporal brevity. Three weeks after I first discovered the glade, I returned in late afternoon and waited silently. For a time I feared that the mariposal friendship was a thing of the past. But a few minutes before five the first Red-spot fluttered by, in and out among the twigs and leaves, as one slips an aeroplane through openings in drifting clouds. One by one, from all directions, the rest followed, until I counted twelve, twenty, thirty-four. Many of the twigs were now vacant, and most of the heliconias were tattered and forlorn, just able to keep at their fluttering level. There was something infinitely pathetic in this little company, which in less than a month had become so out at elbow, so aged, with death close ahead, yet with all their remaining strength making their way from north and from south, from dense and from open jungle, to keep tryst for this silent, somnolent communion. I rose quietly and passed carefully from the glade, disturbing none of the paper-thin silhouettes, so like the foliage in outward seeming, yet so individual, each perhaps with dim dreams of flowers and little meetings and wind tossings; certainly with small adventures awaiting their awakening on the morrow, and a very certain kismet such a short way ahead.

Two weeks after this, only three butterflies came to the glade, one newly painted, freshly emerged, the other two old and tattered and very weary.

I loitered on my homeward way and before I reached Kalacoon found myself in the Convict Trail in full moonlight. At one turn of the path a peculiar tinkling reached my ear. It was a veritable silver wire of sound—so high, so tenuous that one had to think as well as listen to keep it in audible focus. I pushed through a growth of cecropias and at once lost the sound never to hear it again, but in its place there appeared a very wonderful thing—a good-sized tree standing alone and exposed, bathed in full moonlight, and yet gleaming, as brightly as if silhouetted against complete darkness, by the greenish light of numberless fireflies. After the first marvel of the sudden sight, I approached and pulled down a branch and counted twenty-six glowing insects, as close together as the blossoms on a Japanese cherry branch. There were hundreds upon hundreds, all clustered together in candelabred glory, hidden from the view of all, at the farther side of this dense thicket. As I left I remembered with gratitude the silver wire of sound which had guided me, and in a far corner of my mind I stored a new memory—one which I could draw upon at need in distant times of pain, or of intolerance or perhaps in some lull of battle—the thought of a tree all aglow with living flames, in the moonlight of the Convict Trail.

5

MACHU PICCHU

HIRAM BINGHAM

While directing a 1911 Yale archaeological expedition in search of Vilcabamba, the "Lost City of the Incas," Hiram Bingham was led by local farmers to the long-ignored and overgrown site of Machu Picchu. Although it's now thought that Machu Picchu served as a royal retreat, not the last Inca stronghold as Bingham believed, the excavation of the site ignited a fiery interest in the study of the pre-Columbian empire. (Incidentally, Bingham was actually guided to and wrote about the similarly overlooked site of Espíritu Pampa that experts now believe to be the "Lost City" he sought.) Bingham later pursued a career in politics but is best remembered for the indelible impression he left on the region, whose millions of visitors still travel up the "Hiram Bingham Highway" to reach this wonder of the world.

CHAPTER XVII: MACHU PICCHU

It was in July, 1911, that we first entered that marvelous canyon of the Urubamba, where the river escapes from the cold regions near

Cuzco by tearing its way through gigantic mountains of granite. From Torontoy to Colpani the road runs through a land of matchless charm. It has the majestic grandeur of the Canadian Rockies, as well as the startling beauty of the Nuuanu Pali near Honolulu, and the enchanting vistas of the Koolau Ditch Trail on Maul. In the variety of its charms and the power of its spell, I know of no place in the world which can compare with it. Not only has it great snow peaks looming above the clouds more than two miles overhead; gigantic precipices of many-colored granite rising sheer for thousands of feet above the foaming, glistening, roaring rapids; it has also, in striking contrast, orchids and tree ferns, the delectable beauty of luxurious vegetation, and the mysterious witchery of the jungle. One is drawn irresistibly onward by ever-recurring surprises through a deep, winding gorge, turning and twisting past overhanging cliffs of incredible height. Above all, there is the fascination of finding here and there under the swaying vines, or perched on top of a beetling crag, the rugged masonry of a bygone race; and of trying to understand the bewildering romance of the ancient builders who ages ago sought refuge in a region which appears to have been expressly designed by Nature as a sanctuary for the oppressed, a place where they might fearlessly and patiently give expression to their passion for walls of enduring beauty. Space forbids any attempt to describe in detail the constantly changing panorama, the rank tropical foliage, the countless terraces, the towering cliffs, the glaciers peeping out between the clouds.

We had camped at a place near the river, called Mandor Pampa. Melchor Arteaga, proprietor of the neighboring farm, had told us of ruins at Machu Picchu.

The morning of July 24th dawned in a cold drizzle. Arteaga shivered and seemed inclined to stay in his hut. I offered to pay him well if he would show me the ruins. He demurred and said it was too hard a climb for such a wet day. When he found that we were willing to pay him a sol, three or four times the ordinary daily wage in this vicinity, he finally agreed to guide us to the ruins. No one supposed that they would be particularly interesting. Accompanied by Sergeant Carrasco I left camp at ten o'clock and went some distance upstream. On the road we passed a venomous snake which recently had been killed. This region has an unpleasant notoriety for being the favorite haunt of "vipers." The lance-headed or yellow viper, commonly known as the fer-de-lance, a very venomous serpent capable of making considerable springs when in pursuit of its prey, is common hereabouts. Later two of our mules died from snake-bite.

After a walk of three quarters of an hour the guide left the main road and plunged down through the jungle to the bank of the river. Here there was a primitive "bridge" which crossed the roaring rapids at its narrowest part, where the stream was forced to flow between two great boulders. The bridge was made of half a dozen very slender logs, some of which were not long enough to span the distance between the boulders. They had been spliced and lashed together with vines. Arteaga and Carrasco took off their shoes and crept gingerly across, using their somewhat prehensile toes to keep from slipping. It was obvious that no one could have lived for an instant in the rapids, but would immediately have been dashed to pieces against granite boulders. I am frank to confess that I got down on hands and knees and crawled across, six inches at a time. Even after we reached the other side I could not help wondering what would happen to the "bridge" if a particularly heavy shower should fall in the valley above. A light rain had fallen during the night. The river had risen so that the bridge was already threatened by the foaming rapids. It would not take much more rain to wash away the bridge entirely. If this should happen during the day it might be very awkward. As a matter of fact, it did happen a few days later and the next explorers to attempt to cross the river at this point found only one slender log remaining.

Leaving the stream, we struggled up the bank through a dense jungle, and in a few minutes reached the bottom of a precipitous slope. For an hour and twenty minutes we had a hard climb. A good part of the distance we went on all fours, sometimes hanging on by the tips of our fingers. Here and there, a primitive ladder made from the roughly hewn trunk of a small tree was placed in such a way as to help one over what might otherwise have proved to be an impassable cliff. In another place the slope was covered with slippery grass where it was hard to find either handholds or footholds. The guide said that there were lots of snakes here. The humidity was great, the heat was excessive, and we were not in training.

Shortly after noon we reached a little grass-covered hut where several good-natured Indians, pleasantly surprised at our unexpected arrival, welcomed us with dripping gourds full of cool, delicious water. Then they set before us a few cooked sweet potatoes, called here *cumara*, a Quichua word identical with the Polynesian *kumala*, as has been pointed out by Mr. Cook.

Apart from the wonderful view of the canyon, all we could see from our cool shelter was a couple of small grass huts and a few ancient stone-faced terraces. Two pleasant Indian farmers, Richarte and Alvarez, had chosen this eagle's nest for their home. They said they had found plenty of terraces here on which to grow their crops and they were usually free from undesirable visitors. They did not speak Spanish, but through Sergeant Carrasco I learned that there were more ruins "a little farther along." In this country one never can tell whether such a report is worthy of credence. "He may have been lying" is a good footnote to affix to all hearsay evidence. Accordingly, I was not unduly excited, nor in a great hurry to move. The heat was still great, the water from the Indian's spring was cool and delicious, and the rustic wooden bench, hospitably covered immediately after my arrival with a soft, woolen poncho, seemed most comfortable. Furthermore, the view was simply enchanting. Tremendous green precipices fell away to the white rapids of the Urubamba below. Immediately in front, on the north side of the valley, was a great granite cliff rising 2000 feet sheer. To the left was the solitary peak of Huayna Picchu, surrounded by seemingly inaccessible precipices. On all sides were rocky cliffs. Beyond them cloud-capped mountains rose thousands of feet above us.

The Indians said there were two paths to the outside world. Of one we had already had a taste; the other, they said, was more difficult—a perilous path down the face of a rocky precipice on the other side of the ridge. It was their only means of egress in the wet season, when the bridge over which we had come could not be maintained. I was not surprised to learn that they went away from home only "about once a month."

Richarte told us that they had been living here four years. It seems probable that, owing to its inaccessibility, the canyon had been unoccupied for several centuries, but with the completion of the new government road settlers began once more to occupy this region. In time somebody clambered up the precipices and found on the slopes of Machu Picchu, at an elevation of

9000 feet above the sea, an abundance of rich soil conveniently situated on artificial terraces, in a fine climate. Here the Indians had finally cleared off some ruins, burned over a few terraces, and planted crops of maize, sweet and white potatoes, sugar cane, beans, peppers, tree tomatoes, and gooseberries. At first they appropriated some of the ancient houses and replaced the roofs of wood and thatch. They found, however, that there were neither springs nor wells near the ancient buildings. An ancient aqueduct which had once brought a tiny stream to the citadel had long since disappeared beneath the forest, filled with earth washed from the upper terraces. So, abandoning the shelter of the ruins, the Indians were now enjoying the convenience of living near some springs in roughly built thatched huts of their own design.

Without the slightest expectation of finding anything more interesting than the stone-faced terraces of which I already had a glimpse, and the ruins of two or three stone houses such as we had encountered at various places on the road between Ollantaytambo and Torontoy, I finally left the cool shade of the pleasant little hut and climbed farther up the ridge and around a slight promontory. Arteaga had "been here once before," and decided to rest and gossip with Richarte and Alvarez in the hut. They sent a small boy with me as a guide.

Hardly had we rounded the promontory when the character of the stonework began to improve. A flight of beautifully constructed terraces, each two hundred yards long and ten feet high, had then recently rescued from the jungle by the Indians. A forest of large trees had been chopped down and burned over to make a clearing for agricultural purposes. Crossing these terraces, I entered the untouched forest beyond, and suddenly found myself in a maze of beautiful granite houses! They were covered with trees and moss and the growth of centuries, but in the dense shadow, hiding in bamboo thickets and tangled vines, could be seen, here and there, walls of white granite ashlars most carefully cut and exquisitely fitted together. Buildings with windows were frequent. Here at least was a "place far from town and conspicuous for its windows."

Under a carved rock the little boy showed me a cave beautifully lined with the finest cut stone. It was evidently intended to be a Royal Mausoleum. On top of this particular boulder a semicircular building had been constructed. The wall followed the natural curvature of the rock and was keyed to it by one of the finest examples of masonry I have ever seen. This beautiful wall, made of carefully matched ashlars of pure white granite, especially selected for its fine grain, was the work of a master artist. The interior surface of the wall was broken by niches and square stone-pegs. The exterior surface was perfectly simple and unadorned. The lower courses, of particularly large ashlars, gave it a look of solidity. The upper courses, diminishing in size toward the top, lent grace and delicacy to the structure. The flowing lines, the symmetrical arrangement of the ashlars, and the gradual gradation of the courses, combined to produce a wonderful effect, softer and more pleasing than that of the marble temples of the Old World. Owing to the absence of mortar, there are no ugly spaces between the rocks. They might have grown together.

The elusive beauty of this chaste, undecorated surface seems to me to be due to the fact that the wall was built under the eye of a master mason who knew not the straight edge, the plumb rule, or the square. He had no instruments of precision, so he had to depend on his eye. He had a good eye, an artistic eye, an eye for symmetry and beauty of form. His product received none of the harshness of mechanical and mathematical accuracy. The apparently rectangular blocks are not really rectangular. The apparently straight lines of the courses are not actually straight in the exact sense of that term.

To my astonishment I saw that this wall and its adjoining semicircular temple over the cave were as fine as the finest stonework in the far-famed Temple of the Sun in Cuzco. Surprise followed surprise in bewildering succession. I climbed a marvelous great stairway of large granite blocks, walked along a *pampa* where the Indians had a small vegetable garden, and came into a little clearing. Here were the ruins of two of the finest structures I have ever seen in Peru. Not only were they made of selected blocks of beautifully grained white granite; their walls contained ashlars of Cyclopean size, ten feet in length, and higher than a man. The sight held me spellbound.

Each building had only three walls and was entirely open on the side toward the clearing. The principal temple was lined with exquisitely made niches, five high up at each end, and seven on the back wall. There were seven courses of ashlars in the end walls. Under the seven rear niches was a rectangular block fourteen feet long, probably a sacrificial altar. The building did not look as though it had ever had a roof. The top course of beautifully smooth ashlars was not intended to be covered.

The other temple is on the east side of the *pampa*. I called it the Temple of the Three Windows. Like its neighbor, it is unique among Inca ruins. Its eastern wall, overlooking the citadel, is a massive stone framework for three conspicuously large windows, obviously too large to serve any useful purpose, yet most beautifully made with the greatest care and solidity. This was clearly a ceremonial edifice of peculiar significance. Nowhere else in Peru, so far as I know, is there a similar structure conspicuous as "a masonry wall with three windows."

These ruins have no other name than that of the mountain on the slopes of which they are located. Had this place been occupied uninterruptedly, like Cuzco and Ollantaytambo, Machu Picchu would have retained its ancient name, but during the centuries when it was abandoned, its name was lost. Examination showed that it was essentially a fortified place, a remote fastness protected by natural bulwarks, of which man took advantage to create the most impregnable stronghold in the Andes. Our subsequent excavations and the clearing made in 1912, to be described in a subsequent volume, has shown that this was the chief place in Uilcapampa.

It did not take an expert to realize, from the glimpse of Machu Picchu on that rainy day in July, 1911, when Sergeant Carrasco and I first saw it, that here were most extraordinary and interesting ruins. Although the ridge had been partly cleared by the Indians for their fields of maize, so much of it was still underneath a thick jungle growth—some walls were actually supporting trees ten and twelve inches in diameter—that it was impossible to determine just what would be found here. As soon as I could get hold of Mr. Tucker, who was assisting Mr. Hendriksen, and Mr. Lanius, who had gone down the Urubamba with Dr. Bowman, I asked them to make a map of the ruins. I knew it would be a difficult undertaking and that it was essential for Mr. Tucker to join me in Arequipa not later than the first of October for the ascent of Coropuna. With the hearty aid of Richarte and Alvarez, the surveyors did better than I expected. In the ten days while they were at the ruins they were able to secure data from which Mr. Tucker afterwards prepared a map which told better than could any words of mine the importance of this site and the necessity for further investigation.

With the possible exception of one mining prospector, no one in Cuzco had seen the ruins of Machu Picchu or appreciated their importance. No one had any realization of what an extraordinary place lay on top of the ridge. It had never been visited by any of the planters of the lower Urubamba Valley who annually passed over the road which winds through the canyon two thousand feet below.

It seems incredible that this citadel, less than three days' journey from Cuzco, should have remained so long undescribed by travelers and comparatively unknown even to the Peruvians themselves. If the *conquistadores* ever saw this wonderful place, some reference to it surely would have been made; yet nothing can be found which clearly refers to the ruins of Machu Picchu. Just when it was first seen by a Spanish-speaking person is uncertain. When the Count de Sartiges was at Huadquiña in 1834 he was looking for ruins; yet, although so near, he heard of none here. From a crude scrawl on the walls of one of the finest buildings, we learned that the ruins were visited in 1902 by Lizarraga, lessee of the lands immediately below the bridge of San Miguel. This is the earliest local record. Yet some one must have visited Machu Picchu long before that; because in 1875, as has been said, the French explorer Charles Wiener heard in Ollantaytambo of there being ruins at "Huaina-Picchu or Matcho-Picchu." He tried to find them. That he failed was due to there being no road through the canyon of Torontoy and the necessity of making a wide detour through the pass of Panticalla and the Lucumayo Valley, a route which brought him to the Urubamba River at the bridge of Chuquichaca, twenty-five miles below Machu Picchu.

It was not until 1890 that the Peruvian Government, recognizing the needs of the enterprising planters who were opening up the lower valley of the Urubamba, decided to construct a mule trail along the banks of the river through the grand canyon to enable the much-desired *coca* and *aguardiente* to be shipped from Huadquiña, Maranura, and Santa Ann to Cuzco more quickly and cheaply than formerly. This road avoids the necessity of carrying the precious cargoes over the dangerous snowy passes of Mt. Veronica and Mt. Salcantay, so vividly described by Raimondi, de Sartiges, and others. The road, however, was very expensive, took years to build, and still requires frequent repair. In fact, even to-day travel over it is often suspended for several days or weeks at a time, following some tremendous avalanche. Yet it was this new road which had led Melchor Arteaga to build his hut near the arable land at Mandor Pampa, where he could raise food for his family and offer rough shelter to passing travelers. It was this new road which brought Richarte, Alvarez, and their enterprising friends into this little-known region, gave them the opportunity of occupying the ancient terraces of Machu Picchu, which had lain fallow for centuries, encouraged them to keep open a passable trail over the precipices, and made it feasible for us to reach the ruins. It was this new road which offered us in 1911 a virgin field between Ollantaytambo and Huadquiña and enabled us to learn that the Incas, or their predecessors, had once lived here in the remote fastnesses of the Andes, and had left stone witnesses of the magnificence and beauty of their ancient civilization, more interesting and extensive than any which have been found since the days of the Spanish Conquest of Peru.

6

FROM THE LITTLE COLORADO TO THE FOOT OF THE GRAND CANYON

JOHN WESLEY POWELL

When John Wesley Powell—a one-armed veteran of the Civil War and amateur geologist—and his party of nine clambered aboard their heavy wooden boats in 1869, they were pushing off into the unknown. Three months later, they were spit out of the mouth of the Grand Canyon, the first white men to travel the length of the Colorado River. But in the shadow of those towering canyon walls, they faced bloodthirsty rapids, starvation, leaking boats (plugged daily with tree sap), and wavering morale. At this juncture, in a place now known as Separation Canyon, Powell was approached by O. G. Howland, who, along with two others, believed the journey was too dangerous to continue.

CHAPTER XI: FROM THE LITTLE COLORADO TO THE FOOT OF THE GRAND CANYON

August 27—This morning the river takes a more southerly direction. The dip of the rocks is to the north and we are running rapidly into lower formations. Unless our course changes we shall very soon run again into the granite. This gives some anxiety. Now and then the river turns to the west and excites hopes that are soon destroyed by another turn to the south. About nine o'clock we come to the dreaded rock. It is with no little misgiving that we see the river enter these black, hard walls. At its very entrance we have to make a portage; then let down with lines past some ugly rocks. We run a mile or two farther, and then the rapids below can be seen.

About eleven o'clock we come to a place in the river which seems much worse than any we have yet met in all its course. A little creek comes down from the left. We land first on the right and clamber up over the granite pinnacles for a mile or two, but can see no way by which to let down, and to run it would be sure destruction. After dinner we cross to examine on the left. High above the river we can walk along on the top of the granite, which is broken off at the edge and set with crags and pinnacles, so that it is very difficult to get a view of the river at all. In my eagerness to reach a point where I can see the roaring fall below, I go too far on the wall, and can neither advance nor retreat. I stand with one foot on a little projecting rock and cling with my hand fixed in a little crevice. Finding I am caught here, suspended 400 feet above the river, into which I must fall if my footing fails, I call for help. The men come and pass me a line, but I cannot let go of the rock long enough to take hold of it. Then they bring two or three of the largest oars. All this takes time which seems very precious to me; but at last they arrive. The blade of one of the oars is pushed into a little crevice in the rock beyond me in such a manner that they can hold me pressed against the wall. Then another is fixed in such a way that I can step on it; and thus I am extricated.

Still another hour is spent in examining the river from this side, but no good view of it is obtained; so now we return to the side that was first examined, and the afternoon is spent in clambering among the crags and pinnacles and carefully scanning the river again. We find that the lateral streams have washed boulders into the river, so as to form a dam, over which the water makes a broken fall of 18 or 20 feet; then there is a rapid, beset with rocks, for 200 or 300 yards, while on the other side, points of the wall project into the river. Below, there is a second fall; how great, we cannot tell. Then there is a rapid, filled with huge rocks, for 100 or 200 yards. At the bottom of it, from the right wall, a great rock projects quite halfway across the river. It has a sloping surface extending up stream, and the water, coming down with all the momentum gained in the falls and rapids above, rolls up this inclined plane many feet, and tumbles over to the left. I decide that it is possible to let down over the first fall, then run near the right cliff to a point just above the second, where we can pull out into a little chute, and, having run over that in safety, if we pull with all our power across the stream, we may avoid the great rock below. On my return to the boat I announce to the men that we are to run it in the morning. Then we cross the river and go into camp for the night on some rocks in the mouth of the little side canyon.

After supper Captain Howland asks to have a talk with me. We walk up the little creek a short distance, and I soon find that his object is to remonstrate against my determination to proceed. He thinks that we had better abandon the river here. Talking with him, I learn that he, his brother, and William Dunn have determined to go no farther in the boats. So we return to camp. Nothing is said to the other men.

For the last two days our course has not been plotted. I sit down and do this now, for the purpose of finding where we are by dead reckoning. It is a clear night, and I take out the sextant to make observation for latitude, and I find that the astronomic determination agrees very nearly with that of the plot—quite as closely as might be expected from a meridian observation on a planet. In a direct line, we must be about 45 miles from the mouth of the Rio Virgen. If we can reach that point, we know that there are settlements up that river about 20 miles. This 45 miles in a direct line will probably be 80 or 90 by the meandering line of the river. But then we know that there is comparatively open country for many miles above the mouth of the Virgen, which is our point of destination.

As soon as I determine all this, I spread my plot on the sand and wake Howland, who is sleeping down by the river, and show him where I suppose we are, and where several Mormon settlements are situated.

We have another short talk about the morrow, and he lies down again; but for me there is no sleep. All night long I pace up and down a little path, on a few yards of sand beach, along by the river. Is it wise to go on? I go to the boats again to look at our rations. I feel satisfied that we can get over the danger immediately before us; what there may be below I know not. From our outlook yesterday on the cliffs, the canyon seemed to make another great bend to the south, and this, from our experience heretofore, means more and higher granite walls. I am not sure that we can climb out of the canyon here, and, if at the top of the wall, I know enough of the country to be certain that it is a desert of rock and sand between this and the nearest Mormon town, which, on the most direct line, must be 75 miles away. True, the late rains have been favorable to us, should we go out, for the probabilities are that we shall find water still standing in holes; and at one time I almost conclude to leave the river. But for years I have been contemplating this trip. To leave the exploration unfinished, to say that there is a part of the canyon which I cannot explore, having already nearly accomplished it, is more than I am willing to acknowledge, and I determine to go on.

I wake my brother and tell him of Howland's determination, and he promises to stay with me; then I call up Hawkins, the cook, and he makes a like promise; then Sumner and Bradley and Hall, and they all agree to go on.

August 28—At last daylight comes and we have breakfast without a word being said about the future. The meal is as solemn as a funeral. After breakfast I ask the three men if they still think it best to leave us. The elder Howland thinks it is, and Dunn agrees with him. The younger Howland tries to persuade them to go on with the party; failing in which, he decides to go with his brother.

Then we cross the river. The small boat is very much disabled and unseaworthy. With the loss of hands, consequent on the departure of the three men, we shall not be able to run all of the boats; so I decide to leave my "Emma Dean."

Two rifles and a shotgun are given to the men who are going out. I ask them to help themselves to the rations and take what they think to be a fair share. This they refuse to do, saying they have no fear but that they can get something to eat; but Billy, the cook, has a pan of biscuits prepared for dinner, and these he leaves on a rock.

Before starting, we take from the boat our barometers, fossils, the minerals, and some ammunition and leave them on the rocks. We are going over this place as light as possible. The three men help us lift our boats over a rock 25 or 30 feet high and let them down again over the first fall, and now we are all ready to start. The last thing before leaving, I write a letter to my wife and give it to Howland. Sumner gives him his watch, directing that it be sent to his sister should he not be heard from again. The records of the expedition have been kept in duplicate. One set of these is given to Howland; and now we are ready. For the last time they entreat us not to go on, and tell us that it is madness to set out in this place; that we can never get safely through it; and, further, that the river turns again to the south into the granite, and a few miles of such rapids and falls will exhaust our entire stock of rations, and then it will be too late to climb out. Some tears are shed; it is rather a solemn parting; each party thinks the other is taking the dangerous course.

My old boat left, I go on board of the "Maid of the Canyon." The three men climb a crag that overhangs the river to watch us off. The "Maid of the Canyon" pushes out. We glide rapidly along the foot of the wall, just grazing one great rock, then pull out a little into the chute of the second fall and plunge over it. The open compartment is filled when we strike the first wave below, but we cut through it, and then the men pull with all their power toward the left wall and swing clear of the dangerous rock below all right. We are scarcely a minute in running it, and find that, although it looked bad from above, we have passed many places that were worse. The other boat follows without more difficulty. We land at the first practicable point below, and fire our guns, as a signal to the men above that we have come over in safety. Here we remain a couple of hours, hoping that they will take the smaller boat and follow us. We are behind a curve in the canyon and cannot see up to where we left them, and so we wait until their coming seems hopeless, and then push on.

And now we have a succession of rapids and falls until noon, all of which we run in safety. Just after dinner we come to another bad place. A little stream comes in from the left, and below there is a fall, and still below another fall. Above, the river tumbles down, over and among the rocks, in whirlpools and great waves, and the waters are lashed into mad, white foam. We run along the left, above this, and soon see that we cannot get down on this side, but it seems possible to let down on the other. We pull up stream again for 200 or 300 yards and cross. Now there is a bed of basalt on this northern side of the canyon, with a bold escarp- . ment that seems to be a hundred feet high. We can climb it and walk along its summit to a point where we are just at the head of the fall. Here the basalt is broken down again, so it seems to us, and I direct the men to take a line to the top of the cliff and let the boats down along the wall. One man remains in the boat to keep her clear of the rocks and prevent her line from being caught on the projecting angles. I climb the cliff and pass along to a point just over the fall and descend by broken rocks, and find that the break of the fall is above the break of the wall, so that we cannot land, and that still below the river is very bad, and that there is no possibility of a portage. Without waiting further to examine and determine what shall be done, I hasten back to the top of the cliff to stop the boats from coming down. When I arrive I find the men have let one of them down to the head of the fall. She is in swift water and they are not able to pull her back; nor are they able to go on with the line, as it is not long enough to reach the higher part of the cliff which is just before them; so they take a bight around a crag. I send two men back for the other line. The boat is in very swift water, and Bradley is standing in the open compartment, holding out his oar to prevent her from striking against the foot of the cliff. Now she shoots out into the stream and up as far as the line will permit, and then, wheeling, drives headlong against the rock, and then out and back again, now straining on the line, now striking against the rock. As soon as the second line is brought, we pass it down to him; but his attention is all taken up with his own situation, and he does not see that we are passing him the line. I stand on a projecting rock, waving my hat to gain his attention, for my voice is drowned by the roaring of the falls. Just at this moment I see him take his knife from its sheath and step forward to cut the line. He has evidently decided that it is better to go over with the boat as it is than to wait for her to be broken to pieces. As he leans over, the boat sheers again into the stream, the stem-post breaks away and she is loose. With perfect composure Bradley seizes the great scull oar, places it in the stern rowlock, and pulls with all his power (and he is an athlete) to turn the bow of the boat down stream, for he wishes to go bow down, rather than to drift broadside on. One, two strokes he makes, and a third just as she goes over, and the boat is fairly turned, and she goes down almost beyond our sight, though we are more than a hundred feet above the river. Then she comes up again on a great wave, and down and up, then around behind some great rocks, and is lost in the mad, white foam below. We stand frozen with fear, for we see no boat. Bradley is gone! so it seems. But now, away below, we see something coming out of the waves. It is evidently a boat. A moment more, and we see Bradley standing on deck, swinging his hat to show that he is all right. But he is in a whirlpool. We have the stem-post of his boat attached to the line. How badly she may be disabled we know not. I direct Sumner and Powell to pass along the cliff and see if they can reach him from below. Hawkins, Hall, and myself run to the other boat, jump aboard, push out, and away we go over the falls. A wave rolls over us and our boat is unmanageable. Another great wave strikes us, and the boat rolls over, and tumbles and tosses, I know not how. All I know is that Bradley is picking us up. We soon have all right again, and row to the cliff and wait until Sumner and Powell can come. After a difficult climb they reach us. We run two or three miles farther and turn again to the northwest, continuing until night, when we have run out of the granite once more.

7

LEWIS AND
CLARK: THURSDAY 13

JOURNALS OF MERIWETHER LEWIS AND
WILLIAM CLARK, EDITED BY PAUL ALLEN

In 1804, while the ink was still wet on the Louisiana Purchase, Meriwether Lewis and William Clark undertook the nation's first expedition to cross the western half of the country and explore the newly acquired territory. Commissioned by Thomas Jefferson, the expedition served to suss out whether the French and English trappers threatened American control and offered an opportunity to study the area's geography, ecology, and native people. In mid-June 1805, as the party was moving along the Missouri River in central Montana, they heard the sound of rushing water. Cue a very Wild West chain of events involving the discovery of a national landmark, a first look at native westslope cutthroat trout (scientific name: Oncorhynchus clarki lewisi), and a grizzly bear.

Thursday 13. They left their encampment at sunrise, and ascending the river hills went for six miles in a course generally southwest, over a country which though more waving than that of yesterday may still be considered level. At the extremity of this course they overlooked a most beautiful plain, where were infinitely more buffaloe than we had ever before seen at a single view. To the southwest arose from the plain two mountains of a singular appearance and more like ramparts of high fortifications than works of nature. They are square figures with sides rising perpendicularly to the height of two hundred and fifty feet, formed of yellow clay, and the tops seemed to be level plains. Finding that the river here bore considerably to the south, and fearful of passing the falls before reaching the Rocky mountains, they now changed their course to the south, and leaving those insulated hills to the right proceeded across the plain. In this direction captain Lewis had gone about two miles when his ears were saluted with the agreeable sound of a fall of water, and as he advanced a spray which seemed driven by the high southwest wind arose above the plain like a column of smoke and vanished in an instant. Towards this point he directed his steps, and the noise increasing as he approached soon became too tremendous to be mistaken for any thing but the great falls of the Missouri. Having travelled seven miles after first hearing the sound he reached the falls about twelve o'clock, the hills as he approached were difficult of access and two hundred feet high: down these he hurried with impatience and seating himself on some rocks under the centre of the falls, enjoyed the sublime spectacle of this stupendous object which has since the creation had been lavishing its magnificence upon the desert, unknown to civilization.

The river immediately at its cascade is three hundred yards wide, and is pressed in by a perpendicular cliff on the left, which rises to about one hundred feet and extends up the stream for a mile; on the right the bluff is also perpendicular for three hundred yards above the falls. For ninety or a hundred yards from the left cliff, the water falls in one smooth even sheet, over a precipice of at least eighty feet. The remaining part of the river precipitates itself with a more rapid current, but being received as it falls by the irregular and somewhat projecting rocks below, forms a splendid prospect of perfectly white foam two hundred yards in length, and eighty in perpendicular elevation. This spray is dissipated into a thousand shapes, sometimes flying up in columns of fifteen or twenty feet, which are then oppressed by larger masses of the white foam, on all which the sun impresses the brightest colours of the rainbow. As it rises from the fall it beats with fury against a ledge of rocks which extend across the river at one hundred and fifty yards from the precipice. From the perpendicular cliff on the north, to the distance of one hundred and twenty yards, the rocks rise only a few feet above the water, and when the river is high the stream finds a channel across them forty yards wide, and near the higher parts of the ledge which then rise about twenty feet, and terminate abruptly within eighty or ninety yards of the southern side. Between them and the perpendicular cliff on the south, the whole body of water runs with great swiftness. A few small cedars grow near this ridge of rocks which serves as a barrier to defend a small plain of about three acres shaded with cottonwood, at the lower extremity of which is a grove of the same tree, where are several Indian cabins of sticks; below the point of them the river is divided by a large rock, several feet above the surface of the water, and extending down the stream for twenty yards. At the distance of three hundred yards from the same ridge is a second abutment of solid perpendicular rock about sixty feet high, projecting at right angles from the small plain on the north for one hundred and thirty-four yards into the river. After leaving this, the Missouri again spreads itself to its usual distance of three hundred yards, though with more than its ordinary rapidity.

The hunters who had been sent out now returned loaded with buffaloe meat, and captain Lewis encamped for the night under a tree near the falls. The men were again despatched to hunt for food against the arrival of the party, and captain Lewis walked down the river to discover if possible some place where the canoes might be safely drawn on shore, in order to be transported beyond the falls. He returned however without discovering any such spot, the river for three miles below being one continued succession of rapids and cascades, overhung with perpendicular bluffs from one hundred and fifty to two hundred feet high; in short, it seems to have worn itself a channel through the solid rock. In the afternoon they caught in the falls some of both kinds of the white fish, and half a dozen trout from sixteen to twenty-three inches long, precisely resembling in form and the position of its fins the mountain or speckled trout of the United States, except that the specks of the former are of a deep black, while those of the latter are of a red or gold colour: they have long sharp teeth on the palate and tongue, and generally a small speck of red on each side behind the front ventral fins; the flesh is of a pale yellowish red, or when in good order of a rose-coloured red.

Friday 14. This morning one of the men was sent to captain Clarke with an account of the discovery of the falls, and after employing the rest in preserving the meat which had been killed yesterday, captain Lewis proceeded to examine the rapids above. From the falls he directed his course southwest up the river: after passing one continued rapid, and three small cascades, each three or four feet high, he reached at the distance of five miles a second fall. The river is about four hundred yards wide, and for the distance of three hundred throws itself over to the depth of nineteen feet, and so irregularly that he gave it the name of the Crooked falls. From the southern shore it extends obliquely upwards about one hundred and fifty yards, and then forms an acute angle downwards nearly to the commencement of four small islands close to the northern side. From the perpendicular pitch to these islands, a distance of more than one hundred yards, the water glides down a sloping rock with a velocity almost equal to that of its fall. Above this fall the river bends suddenly to the northward: while viewing this place captain Lewis heard a loud roar above him, and crossing the point of a hill for a few hundred yards, he saw one of the most beautiful objects in nature: the whole Missouri is suddenly stopped by one shelving rock, which without a single niche and with an edge as straight and regular as if formed by art, stretches itself from one side of the river to the other for at least a quarter of a mile. Over this it precipitates itself in an even uninterrupted sheet to the perpendicular depth of fifty feet, whence dashing against the rocky bottom it rushes rapidly down, leaving behind it a spray of the purest foam across the river. The scene which it presented was indeed singularly beautiful, since without any of the wild irregular sublimity of the lower falls, it combined all the regular elegances which the fancy of a painter would select to form a beautiful waterfall. The eye had scarcely been regaled with this charming prospect, when at the distance of half a mile captain Lewis observed another of a similar kind: to this he immediately hastened, and found a cascade stretching across the whole river for a quarter of a mile with a descent of fourteen feet, though the perpendicular pitch was only six feet. This too in any other neighborhood would have been an object of great magnificence, but after what he had just seen it became of secondary interest; his curiosity being however awakencd, he determined to go on even should night overtake him to the head of the falls. He therefore pursued the southwest course of the river, which was one constant succession of rapids and small cascades, at every one of which the bluffs grew lower, or the bed of the river became more on a level with the plains. At the distance of two and a half miles he arrived at another cataract of twenty-six feet. The river is here six hundred yards wide, but the descent is not immediately perpendicular, though the river falls generally with a regular and smooth sheet; for about one third of the descent a rock protrudes to a small distance, receives the water in its passage and gives it a curve. On the south side is a beautiful plain a few feet above the level of the falls; on the north the country is more broken, and there is a hill not far from the river. Just below the falls is a little island in the middle of the river well covered with timber. Here on a cottonwood tree an eagle had fixed its nest, and seemed the undisputed mistress of a spot, to contest whose dominion neither man nor beast would venture across the gulfs that surround it, and which is further secured by the mist rising from the falls. This solitary bird could not escape the observation of the Indians who made the eagle's nest a part of their description of the falls, which now proves to be correct in almost every particular, except that they did not do justice to their height. Just above this is a cascade of about five feet, beyond which, as far as could be discerned, the velocity of the water seemed to abate. Captain Lewis now ascended the hill which was behind him, and saw from its top a delightful plain extending from the river to the base of the Snow mountains to the south and southwest. Along this wide level country the Missouri pursued its winding course, filled with water to its even and grassy banks, while about four miles above it was joined by a large river flowing from the northwest through a valley three miles in width, and distinguished by the timber which adorned its shores; the Missouri itself stretches to the south in one unruffled stream of water as if unconscious of the roughness it must soon encounter, and bearing on its bosom vast flocks of geese, while numerous herds of buffaloe are feeding on the plains which surround it.

Captain Lewis then descended the hill, and directed his course towards the river falling in from the west. He soon met a herd of at least a thousand buffaloe, and being desirous of providing for supper shot one of them; the animal began to bleed, and captain Lewis who had forgotten to reload his rifle, was intently watching to see him fall, when he beheld a large brown bear who was stealing on him unperceived, and was already within twenty steps. In the first moment of surprise he lifted his rifle, but remembering instantly that it was not charged, and that he had not time to reload, he felt that there was no safety but in flight. It was in the open level plain, not a bush nor a tree within three hundred yards, the bank of the river sloping and not more than three feet high, so that there was no possible mode of concealment: captain Lewis therefore thought of retreating in a quick walk as fast as the bear advanced towards the nearest tree; but as soon as he turned the bear ran open mouth and at full speed upon him. Captain Lewis ran about eighty yards, but finding that the animal gained on him fast, it flashed on his mind that by getting into the water to such a depth that the bear would be obliged to attack him swimming, there was still some chance of his life, he therefore turned short, plunged into the river about waist deep, and facing about presented the point of his espontoon. The bear arrived at the water's edge within twenty feet of him, but as soon as he put himself in this position of defence, he seemed frightened, and wheeling about, retreated with as much precipitation as he had pursued. Very glad to be released from this danger, captain Lewis returned to the shore, and observed him run with great speed, sometimes looking back as if he expected to be pursued, till he reached the woods. He could not conceive the cause of the sudden alarm of the bear, but congratulated himself on his escape when he saw his own track torn to pieces by the furious animal, and learnt from the whole adventure never to suffer his rifle to be a moment unloaded. He now resumed his progress in the direction which the bear had taken towards the western river, and found it a handsome stream about two hundred yards wide, apparently deep, with a gentle current; its waters clear, and its banks, which were formed principally of dark brown and blue clay, are about the same height as those of the Missouri, that is from three to five feet. What was singular was that the river does not seem to overflow its banks at any season, while it might be presumed from its vicinity to the mountains, that the torrents arising from the melting of the snows, would sometimes cause it to swell beyond its limits. The contrary fact would induce a belief that the Rocky mountains yield their snows very reluctantly and equably to the sun, and are not often drenched by very heavy rains.

This river is no doubt that which the Indians call Medicine river, which they mentioned as emptying into the Missouri, just above the falls. After examining Medicine river, captain Lewis set out at half after six o'clock in the evening on his return towards the camp, which he estimated at the distance of twelve miles. In going through the low grounds on Medicine river he met an animal which at a distance he thought was a wolf, but on coming within sixty paces, it proved to be some brownish yellow animal standing near its burrow, which, when he came nigh, crouched and seemed as if about to spring on him. Captain Lewis fired and the beast disappeared in its burrow. From the track and the general appearance of the animal he supposed it to be of the tiger kind. He then went on, but as if the beasts of the forests had conspired against him, three buffaloe bulls which were feeding with a large herd at the distance of half a mile, left their companions and ran at full speed towards him. He turned round, and unwilling to give up the field advanced towards them: when they came within a hundred yards, they stopped, looked at him for some time, and then retreated as they came. He now pursued his route in the dark, reflecting on the strange adventures and sights of the day which crowded on his mind so rapidly that he should have been inclined to believe it all enchantment if the thorns of the prickly pear piercing his feet did not dispel at every moment the illusion. He at last reached the party, who had been very anxious for his safety, and who had already decided on the route which each should take in the morning to look for him. Being much fatigued he supped and slept well during the night.

8

SEVENTY-TWO DAYS
WITHOUT A PORT

JOSHUA SLOCUM

Joshua Slocum—a Nova Scotian–born naturalized American—made his first escape for the ocean at 13, running away for a job as a cook on a schooner; until the crew tasted his pudding and sent him packing. Nearly 40 years later, the 51-year-old left Boston on a self-repaired 36-foot sailboat in 1895 with plans to sail around the world. Aboard the Spray he encountered pirates, swells, coral reefs, and "savages," and more than 3 years and 46,000 miles later, he docked in Newport, Rhode Island, having completed history's first solo circumnavigation. The account of the journey catapulted to a surprise best seller, with English author Arthur Ransome concluding that those "who do not like this book ought to be drowned at once." And though Slocum and his wife purchased land in Martha's Vineyard upon his return, he was drawn to the ocean until the end, when he disappeared while aboard the Spray somewhere en route to the West Indies.

CHAPTER XII: SEVENTY-TWO DAYS WITHOUT A PORT

To be alone forty-three days would seem a long time, but in reality, even here, winged moments flew lightly by, and instead of my hauling in for Nukahiva, which I could have made as well as not, I kept on for Samoa, where I wished to make my next landing. This occupied twenty-nine days more, making seventy-two days in all. I was not distressed in any way during that time. There was no end of companionship; the very coral reefs kept me company, or gave me no time to feel lonely, which is the same thing, and there were many of them now in my course to Samoa.

First among the incidents of the voyage from Juan Fernandez to Samoa (which were not many) was a narrow escape from collision with a great whale that was absent-mindedly plowing the ocean at night while I was below. The noise from his startled snort and the commotion he made in the sea, as he turned to clear my vessel, brought me on deck in time to catch a wetting from the water he threw up with his flukes. The monster was apparently frightened. He headed quickly for the east; I kept on going west. Soon another whale passed, evidently a companion, following in its wake. I saw no more on this part of the voyage, nor did I wish to.

Hungry sharks came about the vessel often when she neared islands or coral reefs. I own to a satisfaction in shooting them as one would a tiger. Sharks, after all, are the tigers of the sea. Nothing is more dreadful to the mind of a sailor, I think, than a possible encounter with a hungry shark.

A number of birds were always about; occasionally one poised on the mast to look the *Spray* over, wondering, perhaps, at her odd wings, for she now wore her Fuego mainsail, which, like Joseph's coat, was made of many pieces. Ships are less common on the Southern seas than formerly. I saw not one in the many days crossing the Pacific.

My diet on these long passages usually consisted of potatoes and salt cod and biscuits, which I made two or three times a week. I had always plenty of coffee, tea, sugar, and flour. I carried usually a good supply of potatoes, but before reaching Samoa I had a mishap which left me destitute of this highly prized sailors' luxury. Through meeting at Juan Fernandez the Yankee Portuguese named Manuel Carroza, who nearly traded me out of my boots, I ran out of potatoes in mid-ocean, and was wretched thereafter. I prided myself on being something of a trader; but this Portuguese from the Azores by way of New Bedford, who gave me new potatoes for the older ones I had got from the *Colombia*, a bushel or more of the best, left me no ground for boasting. He wanted mine, he said, "for changee the seed." When I got to sea I found that his tubers were rank and unedible, and full of fine yellow streaks of repulsive appearance. I tied the sack up and returned to the few left of my old stock, thinking that maybe when I got right hungry the island potatoes would improve in flavor. Three weeks later I opened the bag again, and out flew millions of winged insects! Manuel's potatoes had all turned to moths. I tied them up quickly and threw all into the sea.

Manuel had a large crop of potatoes on hand, and as a hint to whalemen, who are always eager to buy vegetables, he wished me to report whales off the island of Juan Fernandez, which I have already done, and big ones at that, but they were a long way off.

Taking things by and large, as sailors say, I got on fairly well in the matter of provisions even on the long voyage across the Pacific. I found always some small stores to help the fare of luxuries; what I lacked of fresh meat was made up in fresh fish, at least while in the trade-winds, where flying-fish crossing on the wing at night would hit the sails and fall on deck, sometimes two or three of them, sometimes a dozen. Every morning except when the moon was large I got a bountiful supply by merely picking them up from the lee scuppers. All tinned meats went begging.

On the 16th of July, after considerable care and some skill and hard work, the *Spray* cast anchor at Apia, in the kingdom of Samoa, about noon. My vessel being moored, I spread an awning, and instead of going at once on shore I sat under it till late in the evening, listening with delight to the musical voices of the Samoan men and women.

A canoe coming down the harbor, with three young women in it, rested her paddles abreast the sloop. One of the fair crew, hailing with the naive salutation, "Talofa lee" ("Love to you, chief"), asked:

"Schoon come Melike?"

"Love to you," I answered, and said, "Yes."

"You man come 'lone?"

Again I answered, "Yes."

"I don't believe that. You had other mans, and you eat 'em."

At this sally the others laughed. "What for you come long way?" they asked.

"To hear you ladies sing," I replied.

"Oh, talofa lee!" they all cried, and sang on. Their voices filled the air with music that rolled across to the grove of tall palms on the other side of the harbor and back. Soon after this six young men came down in the United States consul-general's boat, singing in parts and beating time with their oars. In my interview with them I came off better than with the damsels in the canoe. They bore an invitation from General Churchill for me to come and dine at the consulate. There was a lady's hand in things about the consulate at Samoa. Mrs. Churchill picked the crew for the general's boat, and saw to it that they wore a smart uniform and that they could sing the Samoan boatsong, which in the first week Mrs. Churchill herself could sing like a native girl.

Next morning bright and early Mrs. Robert Louis Stevenson came to the *Spray* and invited me to Vailima the following day. I was of course thrilled when I found myself, after so many days of adventure, face to face with this bright woman, so lately the companion of the author who had delighted me on the voyage. The kindly eyes, that looked me through and through, sparkled when we compared notes of adventure. I marveled at some of her experiences and escapes. She told me that, along with her husband, she had voyaged in all manner of rickety craft among the islands of the Pacific, reflectively adding, "Our tastes were similar."

Following the subject of voyages, she gave me the four beautiful volumes of sailing directories for the Mediterranean, writing on the fly-leaf of the first:

To CAPTAIN SLOCUM. These volumes have been read and re-read many times by my husband, and I am very sure that he would be pleased that they should be passed on to the sort of seafaring man that he liked above all others. FANNY V. DE G. STEVENSON.

Mrs. Stevenson also gave me a great directory of the Indian Ocean. It was not without a feeling of reverential awe that I received the books so nearly direct from the hand of Tusitala, "who sleeps in the forest." Aolele, the *Spray* will cherish your gift.

The novelist's stepson, Mr. Lloyd Osbourne, walked through the Vailima mansion with me and bade me write my letters at the old desk. I thought it would be presumptuous to do that; it was sufficient for me to enter the hall on the floor of which the "Writer of Tales," according to the Samoan custom, was wont to sit.

Coming through the main street of Apia one day, with my hosts, all bound for the *Spray*, Mrs. Stevenson on horseback, I walking by her side, and Mr. and Mrs. Osbourne close in our wake on bicycles, at a sudden turn in the road we found ourselves mixed with a remarkable native procession, with a somewhat primitive band of music, in front of us, while behind was a festival or a funeral, we could not tell which. Several of the stoutest men carried bales and bundles on poles. Some were evidently bales of tapa-cloth. The burden of one set of poles, heavier than the rest, however, was not so easily made out. My curiosity was whetted to know whether it was a roast pig or something of a gruesome nature, and I inquired about it. "I don't know," said Mrs. Stevenson, "whether this is a wedding or a funeral. Whatever it is, though, captain, our place seems to be at the head of it."

The *Spray* being in the stream, we boarded her from the beach abreast, in the little razeed Gloucester dory, which had been painted a smart green. Our combined weight loaded it gunwale to the water, and I was obliged to steer with great care to avoid swamping. The adventure pleased Mrs. Stevenson greatly, and as we paddled along she sang, "They went to sea in a pea-green boat." I could understand her saying of her husband and herself, "Our tastes were similar."

As I sailed farther from the center of civilization I heard less and less of what would and what would not pay. Mrs. Stevenson, in speaking of my voyage, did not once ask me what I would make out of it. When I came to a Samoan village, the chief did not ask the price of gin, or say, "How much will you pay for roast pig?" but, "Dollar, dollar," said he; "white man know only dollar."

"Never mind dollar. The *tapo* has prepared ava; let us drink and rejoice." The tapo is the virgin hostess of the village; in this instance it was Taloa, daughter of the chief. "Our taro is good; let us eat. On the tree there is fruit. Let the day go by; why should we mourn over that? There are millions of days coming. The breadfruit is yellow in the sun, and from the cloth-tree is Taloa's gown. Our house, which is good, cost but the labor of building it, and there is no lock on the door."

While the days go thus in these Southern islands we at the North are struggling for the bare necessities of life.

For food the islanders have only to put out their hand and take what nature has provided for them; if they plant a banana-tree, their only care afterward is to see that too many trees do not grow. They have great reason to love their country and to fear the white man's yoke, for once harnessed to the plow, their life would no longer be a poem.

The chief of the village of Caini, who was a tall and dignified Tonga man, could be approached only through an interpreter and talking man. It was perfectly natural for him to inquire the object of my visit, and I was sincere when I told him that my reason for casting anchor in Samoa was to see their fine men, and fine women, too. After a considerable pause the chief said: "The captain has come a long way to see so little; but," he added, "the tapo must sit nearer the captain." "Yack," said Taloa, who had so nearly learned to say yes in English, and suiting the action to the word, she hitched a peg nearer, all hands sitting in a circle upon mats. I was no less taken with the chiefs eloquence than delighted with the simplicity of all he said. About him there was nothing pompous; he might have been taken for a great scholar or statesman, the least assuming of the men I met on the voyage. As for Taloa, a sort of Queen of the May, and the other tapo girls, well, it is wise to learn as soon as possible the manners and customs of these hospitable people, and meanwhile not to mistake for over-familiarity that which is intended as honor to a guest. I was fortunate in my travels in the islands, and saw nothing to shake one's faith in native virtue.

To the unconventional mind the punctilious etiquette of Samoa is perhaps a little painful. For instance, I found that in partaking of ava, the social bowl, I was supposed to toss a little of the beverage over my shoulder, or pretend to do so, and say, "Let the gods drink," and then drink it all myself; and the dish, invariably a cocoanut-shell, being empty, I might not pass it politely as we would do, but politely throw it twirling across the mats at the tapo.

My most grievous mistake while at the islands was made on a nag, which, inspired by a bit of good road, must needs break into a smart trot through a village. I was instantly hailed by the chief's deputy, who in an angry voice brought me to a halt. Perceiving that I was in trouble, I made signs for pardon, the safest thing to do, though I did not know what offense I had committed. My interpreter coming up, however, put me right, but not until a long palaver had ensued. The deputy's hail, liberally translated, was: "Ahoy, there, on the frantic steed! Know you not that it is against the law to ride thus through the village of our fathers?" I made what apologies I could, and offered to dismount and, like my servant, lead my nag by the bridle. This, the interpreter told me, would also be a grievous wrong, and so I again begged for pardon. I was summoned to appear before a chief; but my interpreter, being a wit as well as a bit of a rogue, explained that I was myself something of a chief, and should not be detained, being on a most important mission. In my own behalf I could only say that I was a stranger, but, pleading all this, I knew I still deserved to be roasted, at which the chief showed a fine row of teeth and seemed pleased, but allowed me to pass on.

The chief of the Tongas and his family at Caini, returning my visit, brought presents of tapa-cloth and fruits. Taloa, the princess, brought a bottle of cocoa-nut oil for my hair, which another man might have regarded as coming late.

It was impossible to entertain on the *Spray* after the royal manner in which I had been received by the chief. His fare had included all that the land could afford, fruits, fowl, fishes, and flesh, a hog having been roasted whole. I set before them boiled salt pork and salt beef, with which I was well supplied, and in the evening took them all to a new amusement in the town, a rocking-horse merry-go-round, which they called a "kee-kee," meaning theater; and in a spirit of justice they pulled off the horses' tails, for the proprietors of the show, two hard-fisted countrymen of mine, I grieve to say, unceremoniously hustled them off for a new set, almost at the first spin. I was not a little proud of my Tonga friends; the chief, finest of them all, carried a portentous club. As for the theater, through the greed of the proprietors it was becoming unpopular, and the representatives of the three great powers, in want of laws which they could enforce, adopted a vigorous foreign policy, taxing it twenty-five per cent, on the gate-money. This was considered a great stroke of legislative reform!

It was the fashion of the native visitors to the *Spray* to come over the bows, where they could reach the head-gear and climb aboard with ease, and on going ashore to jump off the stern and swim away; nothing could have been more delightfully simple. The modest natives wore *lava-lava* bathing-dresses, a native cloth from the bark of the mulberry-tree, and they did no harm to the *Spray*. In summer-land Samoa their coming and going was only a merry every-day scene. One day the head teachers of Papauta College, Miss Schultze and Miss Moore, came on board with their ninety-seven young women students. They were all dressed in white, and each wore a red rose, and of course came in boats or canoes in the cold-climate style. A merrier bevy of girls it would be difficult to find. As soon as they got on deck, by request of one of the teachers, they sang "The Watch on the Rhine," which I had never heard before. "And now," said they all, "let's up anchor and away." But I had no inclination to sail from Samoa so soon. On leaving the *Spray* these accomplished young women each seized a palm-branch or paddle, or whatever else would serve the purpose, and literally paddled her own canoe. Each could have swum as readily, and would have done so, I dare say, had it not been for the holiday muslin.

It was not uncommon at Apia to see a young woman swimming alongside a small canoe with a passenger for the *Spray*. Mr. Trood, an old Eton boy, came in this manner to see me, and he exclaimed, "Was ever king ferried in such state?" Then, suiting his action to the sentiment, he gave the damsel pieces of silver till the natives watching on shore yelled with envy. My own canoe, a small dugout, one day when it had rolled over with me, was seized by a party of fair bathers, and before I could get my breath, almost, was towed around and around the *Spray*, while I sat in the bottom of it, wondering what they would do next. But in this case there were six of them, three on a side, and I could not help myself. One of the sprites, I remember, was a young English lady, who made more sport of it than any of the others.

9

THE POLE! AND THE FAST TREK BACK TO LAND

MATTHEW HENSON

Matthew Henson was an African American Arctic explorer, the in-trepid "first man" of Robert Peary, and part of the small party recognized as the first to reach the North Pole. Together, Peary and Henson made half a dozen voyages to the Arctic before finally finding success in 1909. On the last of those, when the rest of the crew had turned back, Peary reportedly mandated that "Henson must go all the way. I can't make it there without him." But while Peary was smothered in glory upon their return, Henson was quietly honored by the black community and then spent most of the next 30 years working in the US Customs House in New York. It wasn't until 1937 that Henson was invited to join the Explorers Club, the first African American to be accepted, and then, in 1954, received personal commendation by President Dwight Eisenhower at the White House. The lives of Henson and Peary were intertwined until the end when, three decades after his death, by presidential order in 1988, the remains of Henson and his wife were reinterred at Arlington National Cemetery to lie near those of Peary and his wife.

CHAPTER XV: THE POLE!

Captain Bartlett and his two boys had commenced their return journey, and the main column, depleted to its final strength, started northward. We were six: Peary, the commander, the Esquimos, Ootah, Egingwah, Seegloo and Ooqueah, and myself.

Day and night were the same. My thoughts were on the going and getting forward, and on nothing else. The wind was from the southeast, and seemed to push us on, and the sun was at our backs, a ball of livid fire, rolling his way above the horizon in never-ending day.

The Captain had gone, Commander Peary and I were alone (save for the four Esquimos), the same as we had been so often in the past years, and as we looked at each other we realized our position and we knew without speaking that the time had come for us to demonstrate that we were the men who, it had been ordained, should unlock the door which held the mystery of the Arctic. Without an instant's hesitation, the order to push on was given, and we started off in the trail made by the Captain to cover the Farthest North he had made and to push on over one hundred and thirty miles to our final destination.

The Captain had had rough going, but, owing to the fact that his trail was our track for a short time, and that we came to good going shortly after leaving his turning point, we made excellent distance without any trouble, and only stopped when we came to a lead barely frozen over, a full twenty-five miles beyond. We camped and waited for the strong southeast wind to force the sides of the lead together. The Esquimos had eaten a meal of stewed dog, cooked over a fire of wood from a discarded sledge, and, owing to their wonderful powers of recuperation, were in good condition; Commander Peary and myself, rested and invigorated by our thirty hours in the last camp, waiting for the return and departure of Captain Bartlett, were also in fine fettle, and accordingly the accomplishment of twenty-five miles of northward progress was not exceptional. With my proven ability in gauging distances, Commander Peary was ready to take the reckoning as I made it and he did not resort to solar observations until we were within a hand's grasp of the Pole.

The memory of those last five marches, from the Farthest North of Captain Bartlett to the arrival of our party at the Pole, is a memory of toil, fatigue, and exhaustion, but we were urged on and encouraged by our relentless commander, who was himself being scourged by the final lashings of the dominating influence that had controlled his life. From the land to 87° 48′ north, Commander Peary had had the best of the going, for he had brought up the rear and had utilized the trail made by the preceding parties, and thus he had kept himself in the best of condition for the time when he made the spurt that brought him to the end of the race. From 87° 48′ north, he kept in the lead and did his work in such a way as to convince me that he was still as good a man as he had ever been. We marched and marched, falling down in our tracks repeatedly, until it was impossible to go on. We were forced to camp, in spite of the impatience of the Commander, who found himself unable to rest, and who only waited long enough for us to relax into sound sleep, when he would wake us up and start us off again. I do not believe that he slept for one hour from April 2 until after he had loaded us up and ordered us to go back over our old trail, and I often think that from the instant when the order to return was given until the land was again sighted, he was in a continual daze.

Onward we forced our weary way. Commander Peary took his sights from the time our chronometer-watches gave, and I, knowing that we had kept on going in practically a straight line, was sure that we had more than covered the necessary distance to insure our arrival at the top of the earth.

It was during the march of the 3d of April that I endured an instant of hideous horror. We were crossing a lane of moving ice. Commander Peary was in the lead setting the pace, and a half hour later the four boys and myself followed in single file. They had all gone before, and I was standing and pushing at the upstanders of my sledge, when the block of ice I was using as a support slipped from underneath my feet, and before I knew it the sledge was out of my grasp, and I was floundering in the water of the lead. I did the best I could. I tore my hood from off my head and struggled frantically. My hands were gloved and I could not take hold of the ice, but before I could give the "Grand Hailing Sigh of Distress," faithful old Ootah had grabbed me by the nape of the neck, the same as he would have grabbed a dog, and with one hand he pulled me out of the water, and with the other hurried the team across.

He had saved my life, but I did not tell him so, for such occurrences are taken as part of the day's work, and the sledge he safeguarded was of much more importance, for it held, as part of its load, the Commander's sextant, the mercury, and the coils of piano-wire that were the essential portion of the scientific part of the expedition. My kamiks (boots of sealskin) were stripped off, and the congealed water was beaten out of my bearskin trousers, and with a dry pair of kamiks, we hurried on to overtake the column. When we caught up, we found the boys gathered around the Commander, doing their best to relieve him of his discomfort, for he had fallen into the water also, and while he was not complaining, I was sure that his bath had not been any more voluntary than mine had been.

When we halted on April 6, 1909, and started to build the igloos, the dogs and sledges having been secured, I noticed Commander Peary at work unloading his sledge and unpacking several bundles of equipment. He pulled out from under his kooletah (thick, fur outer-garment) a small folded package and unfolded it. I recognized his old silk flag, and realized that this was to be a camp of importance. Our different camps had been known as Camp Number One, Number Two, etc., but after the turning back of Captain Bartlett, the camps had been given names such as Camp Nansen, Camp Cagni, etc., and I asked what the name of this camp was to be—"Camp Peary"? "This, my boy, is to be Camp Morris K. Jesup, the last and most northerly camp on the earth." He fastened the flag to a staff and planted it firmly on the top of his igloo. For a few minutes it hung limp and lifeless in the dead calm of the haze, and then a slight breeze, increasing in strength, caused the folds to straighten out, and soon it was rippling out in sparkling color. The stars and stripes were "nailed to the Pole."

A thrill of patriotism ran through me and I raised my voice to cheer the starry emblem of my native land. The Esquimos gathered around and, taking the time from Commander Peary, three hearty cheers rang out on the still, frosty air, our dumb dogs looking on in puzzled surprise. As prospects for getting a sight of the sun were not good, we turned in and slept, leaving the flag proudly floating above us.

This was a thin silk flag that Commander Peary had carried on all of his Arctic journeys, and he had always flown it at his last camps. It was as glorious and as inspiring a banner as any battle-scarred, blood-stained standard of the world—and this badge of honor and courage was also blood-stained and battle-scarred, for at several places there were blank squares marking the spots where pieces had been cut out at each of the "Farthests" of its brave bearer, and left with the records in the cairns, as mute but eloquent witnesses of his achievements. At the North Pole a diagonal strip running from the upper left to the lower right corner was cut and this precious strip, together with a brief record, was placed in an empty tin, sealed up and buried in the ice, as a record for all time.

Commander Peary also had another American flag, sewn on a white ground, and it was the emblem of the "Daughters of the Revolution Peace Society"; he also had and flew the emblem of the Navy League, and the emblems of a couple of college fraternities of which he was a member.

It was about ten or ten-thirty a. m., on the 7th of April, 1909, that the Commander gave the order to build a snow-shield to protect him from the flying drift of the surface-snow. I knew that he was about to take an observation, and while we worked I was nervously apprehensive, for I felt that the end of our journey had come. When we handed him the pan of mercury the hour was within a very few minutes of noon. Laying flat on his stomach, he took the elevation and made the notes on a piece of tissue-paper at his head. With sun-blinded eyes, he snapped shut the vernier (a graduated scale that subdivides the smallest divisions on the sector of the circular scale of the sextant) and with the resolute squaring of his jaws, I was sure that he was satisfied, and I was confident that the journey had ended. Feeling that the time had come, I ungloved my right hand and went forward to congratulate him on the success of our eighteen years of effort, but a gust of wind blew something into his eye, or else the burning pain caused by his prolonged look at the reflection of the limb of the sun forced him to turn aside; and with both hands covering his eyes, he gave us orders to not let him sleep for more than four hours, for six hours later he purposed to take another sight about four miles beyond, and that he wanted at least two hours to make the trip and get everything in readiness.

I unloaded a sledge, and reloaded it with a couple of skins, the instruments, and a cooker with enough alcohol and food for one meal for three, and then I turned in to the igloo where my boys were already sound asleep. The thermometer registered 29° below zero. I fell into a dreamless sleep and slept for about a minute, so I thought, when I was awakened by the clatter and noise made by the return of Peary and his boys.

The Commander gave the word, "We will plant the stars and stripes—*at the North Pole!*" and it was done; on the peak of a huge paleocrystic floeberg the glorious banner was unfurled to the breeze, and as it snapped and crackled with the wind, I felt a savage joy and exultation. Another world's accomplishment was done and finished, and as in the past, from the beginning of history, wherever the world's work was done by a white man, he had been accompanied by a colored man. From the building of the pyramids and the journey to the Cross, to the discovery of the new world and the discovery of the North Pole, the Negro had been the faithful and constant companion of the Caucasian, and I felt all that it was possible for me to feel, that it was I, a lowly member of my race, who had been chosen by fate to represent it, at this, almost the last of the world's great work.

The four Esquimos who stood with Commander Peary at the North Pole, were the brothers, Ootah and Egingwah, the old campaigner, Seegloo, and the sturdy, boyish Ooqueah. Four devoted companions, blindly confident in the leader, they worked only that he might succeed and for the promise of reward that had been made before they had left the ship, which promise they were sure would be kept. Together with the faithful dogs, these men had insured the success of the master. They had all of the characteristics of the dogs, including the dogs' fidelity. Within their breasts lingered the same infatuations that Commander Peary seemed to inspire in all who were with him, and though frequently complaining and constantly requiring to be urged to do their utmost, they worked faithfully and willingly. Ootah, of my party, was the oldest, a married man, of about thirty-four years, and regarded as the best all around member of the tribe, a great hunter, a kind father, and a good provider. Owing to his strong character and the fact that he was more easily managed by me than by any of the others, he had been a member of my party from the time we left the ship. Without exaggeration, I can say that we had both saved each other's lives more than once, but it had all gone in as part of the day's work, and neither of us dwelt on our obligations to the other.

My other boy, Ooqueah, was a young man of about nineteen or twenty, very sturdy and stocky of build, and with an open, honest countenance, a smile that was "child-like and bland,"

and a character that was child-like and bland. It was alleged that the efforts of young Ooqueah were spurred on by the shafts of love, and that it was in the hopes of winning the hand of the demure Miss Anadore, the charming daughter of Ikwah, the first Esquimo of Commander Peary's acquaintance, that he worked so valiantly. His efforts were of an ardent character, but it was not due to the ardor of love, as far as I could see, but to his desire to please and his anxiety to win the promised rewards that would raise him to the grade of a millionaire, according to Esquimo standards.

Commander Peary's boy, Egingwah, was the brother of my boy Ootah, also married and of good report in his community, and it was he who drove the Morris K. Jesup sledge.

If there was any sentiment among the Esquimos in regard to the success of the venture, Ootah and Seegloo by their unswerving loyalty and fidelity expressed it. They had been members of the "Farthest North party" in 1906, the party that was almost lost beyond and in the "Big Lead," and only reached the land again in a state of almost complete collapse. They were the ones who, on bidding Commander Peary farewell in 1906, when he was returning, a saddened and discouraged man, told him to be of good cheer and that when he came back again Ootah and Seegloo would go along, and stay until Commander Peary had succeeded, and they did. The cowardice of their fellow Esquimos at the "Big Lead" on this journey did not in the least demoralize them, and when they were absolutely alone on the trail, with every chance to turn back and return to comfort, wife, and family, they remained steadfast and true, and ever northward guided their sledges.

CHAPTER XVI: THE FAST TREK BACK TO LAND

The long trail was finished, the work was done, and there was only left for us to return and tell the tale of the doing. Reaction had set in, and it was with quavering voice that Commander Peary gave the order to break camp. Already the strain of the hard upward-journey was beginning to tell, and after the first two marches back, he was practically a dead weight, but do not think that we could have gotten back without him, for it was due to the fact that he was with us, and that we could depend upon him to direct and order us, that we were able to keep up the break-neck pace that enabled us to cover three of our upward marches on one of our return marches, and we never forgot that he was still the heart and head of the party.

It was broad daylight and getting brighter, and accordingly I knew little fear, though I did think of the ghosts of other parties, flitting in spectral form over the ice-clad wastes, especially of that small detachment of the Italian expedition of the Duke D'Abruzzi, of which to this day neither track, trace, nor remembrance has ever been found. We crossed lead after lead, sometimes like a bare-back rider in the circus, balancing on cake after cake of ice, but good fortune was with us all of the way, and it was not until the land of recognizable character had been lifted that we lost the trail, and with the land in sight as an incentive, it was no trouble for us to gain the talus of the shore ice and find the trail again.

When we "hit the beach for fair" it was early in the morning of April 23, 1909, nearly seventeen days since we had left the Pole, but such a seventeen days of haste, toil, and misery as cannot be comprehended by the mind. We who experienced it, Commander Peary, the Esquimos, and myself, look back to it as to a horrid nightmare, and to describe it is impossible for me.

Commander Peary had taken the North Pole by conquest, in the face of almost insuperable natural difficulties, by the tremendous fighting-power of himself. The winning of the North Pole was a fight with nature; the way to the Pole that had been covered and retraced by Commander Peary lay across the ever moving and drifting ice of the Arctic Ocean. For more than a hundred miles from Cape Columbia it was piled in heavy pressure ridges, ridge after ridge, some more than a hundred feet in height. In addition, open lanes of water held the parties back until the leads froze up again, and continually the steady drift of the ice carried us back on the course we had come, but due to his deathless ambition to know and to do, he had conquered. He had added to the sum of Earth's knowledge, and proven that the mind of man is boundless in its desire.

The long quest for the North Pole is over and the awful space that separated man from the *Ultima Thule* has been bridged. There is no more beyond; from Cape Columbia to Cape Chelyuskin, the route northward to the Pole, and southward again to the plains of Asia, is an open book and the geographical mind is at rest.

We found the abandoned igloos of Crane City and realized that Captain Bartlett had reached the land safely. The damage due to the action of the storms was not material. We made the necessary repairs, and in a few minutes tea was boiled and rations eaten, and we turned in for sleep. For practically all of the two days following, that was what we did: sleep and eat; men and dogs thoroughly exhausted; and we slept the sleep of the just, without apprehensions or misgivings. Our toboggan from the Pole was ended.

Different from all other trips, we had not on this one been maddened by the pangs of hunger, but instead we felt the effects of lack of sleep, and brain- and body-fatigue. After reaching the land again, I gave a keen searching look at each member of the party, and I realized the strain they had been under. Instead of the plump, round countenances I knew so well, I saw lean, gaunt faces, seamed and wrinkled, the faces of old men, not those of boys, but in their eyes still shone the spark of resolute determination.

Commander Peary's face was lined and seamed, his beard was fully an inch in length, and his mustaches, which had been closely cropped before he left the ship, had again attained their full flowing length. His features expressed fatigue, but the heart-breaking look of sadness, that had clung to him since the failure of the 1906 expedition, had vanished. From his steel-gray eyes flashed forth the light of glorious victory, and though he always carried himself proudly, there had come about him an air of erect assurance that was exhilarating.

When I reached the ship again and gazed into my little mirror, it was the pinched and wrinkled visage of an old man that peered out at me, but the eyes still twinkled and life was still entrancing. This wizening of our features was due to the strain of travel and lack of sleep; we had enough to eat, and I have only mentioned it to help impress the fact that the journey to the Pole and back is not to be regarded as a pleasure outing, and our so-called jaunt was by no means a cake-walk.

10

HOW TO TRAVEL IN TROPICAL AFRICA

WILLIAM EDGAR GEIL

Though most famous for being likely the first person—Chinese included—to travel the length of the Great Wall of China, William Edgar Geil's travels also took him down the Malay Peninsula, through Africa's "pigmy forest" and into village life among headhunters in Borneo. A furious chronicler, he kept boxes of diaries, field notes, and photographs, which he turned into the backbone for ten published books. (Remarkably, Geil has since been called "America's Forgotten Explorer," although the recent unearthing of some of his personal effects has stirred renewed interest in his achievements.) In this excerpt from his account of travels through "Pigmy Land," he provides a how-to list for traveling in tropical Africa, injecting it with dark humor, pervasive racial prejudice, and both asking and answering why anyone would want to keep going.

CHAPTER XIX: HOW TO TRAVEL IN TROPICAL AFRICA

Tropical Africa differs from all other tropical countries through which I have travelled, and this setting down in writing the result of personal observations and experience is a duty which the traveller owes to literature and those who may follow after him. I hold this ancient Avakubi at the end of the fourth stage of the journey and the finish-point to the caravan travelling a suitable if not convenient spot for marking down in order some meditations on HOW TO TRAVEL IN TROPICAL AFRICA.

Travellers who anticipate as extensive and novel a journey as myself and secretary are making across East Africa, past Sultan Hamud, around the Ruwenzori range, through the vast Treeland of the Pigmies, to Banana-on-the-Sea, should take considerable forethought and certain articles with them. I shall presently name in categorical fashion some things to be taken along. But before starting to cross this Dark Continent from sea to sea it is advisable to make decisions and abide by them. An important decision which I strongly recommend is this,— decide not to start! If you do not start across Tropical Africa, your funeral will probably be delayed some years. But if you *will* go, meditate upon the following:

FIRST. Take advice from any and everybody — fools, idiots, semi, quarter and fully insane people and persons of long and short residence in the country. Take this advice smilingly and with an expression of thanks, take it genteelly, take it politely; and then go into a room and close the door and lock it and push a pair of bedsteads up against it. Look in every closet and under the bed, close the windows and fasten them, then gather up all the advice and hermetically seal it. The man who has been long in the country may not best understand its present conditions. No one doubts that early impressions are the deepest and most lasting; therefore old men's advice is not to be implicitly trusted concerning recently existing conditions.

Of course it is to be listened to with the highest respect, but should be balanced by the vision of the young man who has had but a year's experience in the country, but having a well-balanced mind, gets a correct up-to-date view of the present actual conditions. Take advice from consumptive people, dyspeptics, and especially follow the instructions of the man who always has fever and has never learned to cure himself. He is the individual to tell you how to treat fever. Let the baldheaded man tell you how to make your hair grow. Take advice of the man who has been sufficiently long in the country without a vacation to have the wheels of his mind rusted by the atmosphere of Negro thought. He has got his bearings, but they are worn by perpetual repetition; his intellect no longer works freely or clearly. A gentleman long resident in the tropics, one of the shrewdest and most active officials of the Congo Government, acknowledged that after a year or eighteen months' residence in Congo his mind slackens its pace and gradually but certainly fails in prompt, clear decisions and vigorous projects; but that a change into the temperate zone, even though brief, rejuvenates the mind as it does the body. Other men, of strong individuality, and rising rapidly in political positions, tell me that three years is the utmost limit to safely remain in these fever-stricken regions, and that to tarry four years without a vacation is unwise. The Congo Government, appreciating the situation, and clearly seeing the advantage of having officers with minds and bodies in the best condition, insists that employees return to Europe at the end of thirty-six months. Major Woodruff thinks the extreme limit of safety as a period of duty in parts of the Philippines is twelve months, and I certainly think the same applies to many parts of the Congo basin. This leads me to gravely question the advisability of mission boards permitting missionaries from Tropical Africa to address audiences or conduct any sort of meetings until after at least three months of rest and recuperation in the best home-land climate. Here is a new idea hatched out in the heat made by the circumstances of this overland tour.

Take advice from delicate people. If you are not unusually strong and robust, do not be fool enough to attempt the most exacting of all trans-continental journeys of modern times. Take advice of cranks and wise men, and make use of as little of it as possible. No one should attempt a journey along the equator in this country until after he has travelled at least two years in other parts of the world.

To dose this department of the subject: take my advice.

SECOND. Take a square yard of good oiled baize, and attach it to the bag which the *traveller* always has with him. Also fasten on the under side of the flap on one of the pockets of your hunting coat six large size safety pins. This piece of oiled baize will be useful to sit on, to wrap a camera in during a sudden tropical storm, and when tramping through tall wet grass in the early morning, to wear as an apron. Remember how English bishops do not die of fever in Africa; they have aprons and gaiters. With the safety pins I fastened it securely to my coat, and let it hang down in front of my shoe-tops. This turned off more than ninety percent of the water from the grass and prevented me from getting wet feet, which otherwise must have resulted from the moisture running into my high shoes. The piece of oiled baize proved one of my most useful articles. Two good rubber blankets, light in weight, will be of great service. The traveller should always have these things with him.

THIRD. You will require a hypodermic instrument for snake bites, some people will tell you. That may be; I have heard of huge monsters that wiggle and hiss and do dreadful things snake-like, poisonous and vicious. I make no objection, although in crossing Africa thus far I have seen but two snakes, one a thin, green water snake, which was killed by my cannibal paddlers in the Ituri river, and the other a bronze snake coiled up on the limb of a tree. A revolver shot pulverized a part of its backbone and it permanently went out of business. So far as my personal observation goes, there are now no live snakes in Africa. However, take some snake bite medicine with you. On similar cautious principles, it is advisable of course to be vaccinated for everything before you start on the trip- smallpox, cholera, corns, bubonic plague, consumption, indigestion and all fevers known and unknown. In fact, get vaccinated until it will be understood by the savage races among whom you pass that you have been tattooed according to the most modern fashion.

The medicine chest should contain, in real earnest: first a good cathartic, second a better cathartic, and third a first-class cathartic. The best-known physician in Tropical Africa and probably the best-informed of the diseases thereof, quaintly says: "Purgation is salvation." I would recommend Epsom-salts. I have tried Epsom-salts. I tried them here at Avakubi. If you want to see wonders and feel wonders and wonder take two quarts of Epsom-salts; and when you take a dose of it, do as I did, take ten times too much. You will then feel a series of electric chills go up your spinal column and you will conclude that you have taken poison and that your life insurance policies will presently become due; but you will learn what Epsom-salts can do for you.

If you leave everything else at home in the line of medicine and medical equipment, do not fail to take with you an enema. A constipated person is ten times more likely to be attacked by a tropical sun than a person who is not. It is the door through which fever enters. An enema will prove of inestimable value and will keep you from becoming disgusted with everything and everybody. There are few things more to be desired in Tropical Africa than an internal bath. A gallon of water boiled and cooled to blood heat, with a teaspoonful of table salt added will be satisfactory.

The medicine case should contain something to make you perspire, say three pounds of Griffith Bros.' tea, a teakettle and a box of matches. Some red pepper should also be taken along. If you have a mighty strong heart get a bottle of phenacetin. Some people will tell you to take quinine. I think that is advisable. I am no friend of quinine, but I believe in it as I believe in rough-on-rats. It is useful to make you deaf; give you a headache, and will probably act as a tonic to assist the system in resisting a new attack of fever. About that I am not certain, but it is advisable to take quinine along with you to be distributed to the natives. In fact, as a general rule use your medicines in that way. I have taken quinine on this journey.

Your physician will give you a little strong ammonia, and will tell you to take ten drops in a tablespoonful of water as a stimulant should a stimulant be necessary. Under no circumstances carry intoxicating liquors. The missionary who has been longest in Congo says: "When I came to Congo in January, 1878, there were five houses at Boma and one this side. Gin and rum were the currency. The first house I lived in was paid for with a case of gin. I would not pay for it, but a friend bought it for me. I was not an abstainer for years, but now I am and I am better without it. Fevers hit me with less force now; that is my experience. There is no doubt that alcohol is inimical to the health." The Government, recognizing the detrimental effect of intoxicants upon the black and white races, prohibits the sale to the blacks except within a very limited area, and limits the allowance of whiskey to its agents. I know of a Government station which has been occupied not above twelve years, and nine of the foreigners who have held positions there are now dead. They all used alcoholic stimulants and insisted that in the tropics they are necessary. In the meantime the missionaries in that region have lived comfortably and are still living.

Have ipecac in your chest, so that should you change your mind after having swallowed something and desire to have it out of you, you can transfer from chest to stomach. A small bottle of pure carbolic acid will be useful to put where the jigger came out. A drop of this will end the career of any little jiggers that may be just beginning to jig. Corrosive sublimate is not a bad thing if not taken inwardly. Take red or yellow cough syrup. Your friends who have never passed through the vast Tree-land will insist on your taking it, for they will be emphatic that you will be troubled with coughs and colds. I passed through the Forest in the rainy season. Neither the secretary nor myself experimented with coughs or colds. But the cough syrup will be useful, for if it be red, yellow, or any other bright colour, the natives will appreciate it. Take along an anti-diarrhea tablet, a pound of red pepper, and of course wear a heavy belt night and day.

FOURTH. Take strong shoes and always travel on your feet. This will furnish exercise and will be a great protection to your wig if you wear one. The use of a horse or donkey in the Great Forest becomes an exceedingly difficult and inconvenient undertaking. In the first place it is necessary to have a large number of extra men accompany you to be ready to carry the animal. If you take a horse, rope and tackle should be taken along to lift the quadruped over fallen trees and to drag it through vines and overhanging briars. This will somewhat disturb the horse's coat and necessitate the presence of a veterinary surgeon and likely of another surgeon. For ten days in the Forest a cow accompanied me. With the greatest difficulty was she gotten over fallen trees. Plump and round at the beginning, she showed her ribs and looked crestfallen at the finish. There is nothing like two good feet shod with perfectly fitting shoes made of heavy leather, double-soled and at least ten inches high. Put a layer of wool between the foot and the shoe and let it come up and meet a strong pair of knickerbockers. It is advisable to have several pairs of long hose very heavy and reserved for night wear, as a precaution against cold and bites of various kinds. Heavy woolen undergarments should be worn at all times. Always wear a hunting coat with a layer of wool between it and the skin.

FIFTH. Take care of the sun; not that it is out of repair and requires special attention. It is like an emperor who never requests anybody but commands everybody. When I landed in Africa, Bishop Peel said to me a half-dozen different times, "If you don't look out for the sun, the sun will look out for you." "Mistakes may cost as ldcar as crimes." I bring my clenched right fist heavily down on this rough native-made table and strike it such a frightful blow that it trembles even in its legs as I say. Mind the African Sun. Do not disobey it; take the slightest hint from it; do not wait for a hint. It is a smiling but most insidious enemy. For headgear take a pith hat, an enormous one. Take also three felt hats, one fitting over the other, each having a broad brim and ventilator. Keep a good heavy shade on your spinal column. Now there is no objection to the traveller having a hammock convenient, but be careful not to fall asleep in it. The sun caught me napping in the wrong place when I was travelling in one of the Mountains-of-the-Moon, and I had a terrific attack of fever.

SIXTH. When you travel, travel rapidly. Do not lag and drag. Be quick and spry, "gang your ain gait" and require everybody accompanying you to behave in the same fashion. Accept no gratuitous interpreters. Pay the men who interpret for you, so that you may control them and be under no obligations to consult them concerning methods of travel. It is highly important to avoid companions who constantly agitate you by some petty disagreements as to how to travel in Tropical Africa. Get rid of such people. They will give you fever and interfere with your clear thought of local conditions. You had better stop your journey than continue ten days with such a man. Good humour saves time, is absolutely essential in travelling anywhere especially on the Equator. Chamfort says, "The most wasted of all days is that on which one has not laughed" and we all know the difference between a man and a mule is a man can laugh and a mule can't laugh on the very slightest provocation when travelling.

Travel early in the morning. "The morning hours are the wings of the day." Be on the march at four o'clock. If there is no moon, use flambeaux. March very fast and have the travel for the day all done by eleven o'clock. Have good strong porters and do not permit them to control your movements. If you say go fast, see that they obey. They will try your metal and will presume on your good nature just as far as they dare. Indeed black carriers are experts in determining how far they can impose on a white man. Do not expect them to quote Browning's Grammarian: — What's time? Leave "now" to dogs and apes; Man has forever, but expect them to do nothing "to-day" they can put off till "forever." Remember the current Chinese proverb, "There is no difficulty in the world that cannot be overcome by the man who hustles."

SEVENTH. Take a mosquito net which can be put up anywhere at any time. You will come to many places where they will tell you there are no mosquitoes. Put your net up just the same. At one such place I woke in the night and struck a match and on the outside of my net directly opposite my mouth as if sucking in my breath was a huge poisonous spider. A mosquito net is a good thing for mice and all sorts of things that run about when a body is not watching. Elephants and insects should be treated alike in Africa, though a mosquito net will not stop an elephant. Before starting, the voyageur visits a gun shop and selects a rifle of such bore and power of resistance as will "stop a charge" whether of leopard, lion or elephant. It is equally important to stop a charge of insects. If an elephant is seen, it is gone after and killed, or at least it is closely watched lest it "turn and rend" the man. It is important to be as vigilant concerning ants, spiders and mosquitoes, as leopards, lions and elephants.

EIGHTH. Take fire-arms. While it is possible to cross Africa from Mombasa to Banana with no other protection than an umbrella, yet for the sake of game it is wise to take a good rifle, a good shotgun and a revolver. There will be savages all about you, men with cannibal appetites having a taste for the human anatomy; there will be wild beasts and deadly crawling things; take good fire-arms and a thousand rounds of cordite shells. Get fresh meat whenever you can.

NINTH. "Chop." Qiop is a word to which the traveller must at once accustom himself. It means all sorts or any sort of food. Take a few boxes containing canned oatmeal, meat extracts, canned California pears and peaches, some army rations, rice and salt. Do not use canned goods when it is possible to avoid them. A resident in Congo for over fifteen years says, "Shun tinned goods as you would sin. If I eat tinned meat for two days, I find myself with an attack of constipation. I would rather go short than eat tinned meat. I would rather eat native dried fish." Fresh meat is better than meat tinned a year or years ago. Eat fresh vegetables. It is possible to obtain all these things in the country. The chop boxes should be carried as a precaution and as a reserve. It is advisable to drink water, but never unboiled. I seriously question the advisability of using a filter. Miss Kingsley advises that "all water for drinking purposes should be boiled hard for ten minutes. Before boiling the water you can filter it if you like; a good filter is a very fine thing for clearing drinking water of hippopotami, crocodiles, water snakes, cat-fish, etc.; but if you think it is going to stop the microbes of marsh fever, you are mistaken." Take onions. Eat them raw, eat them every day, eat them every meal. The Bedouin first told me to do this. Far off in the land of Moab near Mount Nebo, the chieftain of a tribe dwelling in black tents said that if I would eat at least one large onion each day, change of drinking water would do me no harm. Take a large supply of onions with you and then obtain fresh green ones as often as possible. They will protect you from fever and give you an appetite. Do one thing at a time and do it well; eat onions, not a few hashed up into soup with other equally unfortunate vegetables, but eat them individually, separately, letting the individuality of the onion assert itself. Eat the tops also. Eat them with salt. Not to speak scientifically, I believe that by frequently perspiring, salt is removed from the system. Hence after having fever I have found myself eating three times as much salt as usual. Take along plenty of salt, not only for yourself, but it is always welcomed by the natives.

TENTH. Take small, useful gifts such as knives, safety pins, little mirrors and so forth. Do not fool the natives, do not deceive them, do not give them useless things. On one occasion I was about to trade a shoe to one native and its mate to another, but at the last moment I had not the heart to do it. It would have been fun to have described them walking around, each with one shoe on, and would have made good reading; but the boot might have been on the other leg when they saw my joke. Make small, useful presents.

ELEVENTH. Take plenty of sleep. Take it sensibly, not insanely. A man who has not sense enough to get up very early in the tropics should have a guardian appointed and be under surveillance, for he will harm himself. He may not cut his throat or cast a noose about his neck, but there are slower ways of committing suicide, and one is getting up late in the tropics. A resident in Tropical Africa for a quarter of a century says, "Study your symptoms. If you wake in the early morning and because of drowsiness hesitate about arising, do not lie there and continue to slumber, but get up and retire earlier at night thereafter."

Before midnight is the most valuable time for sleep in the torrid zone. Many people find it advisable to take a short nap after the midday meal, say for twenty or thirty minutes. Longer is not desirable. Do not sleep where a strong reflection of the sun will strike your head or back. Plenty of sleep will preserve the nervous system and make it more comfortable for your fellow voyagers. Retire early. Poor Richard said:

"Early to bed and early to rise Makes a man healthy, wealthy and wise."

And nowhere on this planet can it be better applied than in Tropical Africa. At six P.M. say "I go to tie up my eye-lashes."

LAST. Take a Bible and plenty of good, ordinary, common sense and take yourself out of Tropical Africa as soon as possible.

11

MYSTIC NEDIEF: THE SHIA MECCA

FREDERICK SIMPICH

*Frederick Simpich's obituary concludes that, first as a newspaper corre-
spondent, then as a diplomat, and eventually as an assistant editor of
the National Geographic Society, he had "traveled by almost every
means of transportation and to almost every major city and country in
the world." Overstatement or not, he was indubitably prolific, writing
more than eighty articles for the magazine, the last of which, "So Much
Happens along the Ohio River," was published days before his death.
In this, his first article for the Geographic, he joins the pilgrimage to
Iraq's sacred city of Najaf.*

MYSTIC NEDIEF, THE SHIA MECCA: A VISIT TO ONE OF THE STRANGEST CITIES IN THE WORLD

FEW white men of any race have made the pilgrimage to
mystic Nedjef, the Mecca of Shia Mohammedans and one of the
marvels of inner Arabia.

It is five days by mule or camel caravan from Bagdad to Nedjef, and in the eventful centuries since the Shias founded Nedjef—on the spot where a nephew of the Prophet Mohammed was slain—it is estimated that over 25,000,000 Moslems have made the pilgrimage to this mysterious desert city of golden domes, fabulous treasures, and weird rites.

Thousands of devotees from the Shia hordes of India, Persia, and South Russia flock through Bagdad each year, bringing with them their mummified dead—salted and dried—for burial in the holy ground about the mystic city. By camel caravan and winding mule train the patient pilgrims make the long march; many from distant Turkestan are a whole year making the round trip. To help handle the throng that pours through Bagdad each spring and autumn, enterprising Bagdad Jews have established an "arabanah," or stage line, from Bagdad to Kerbela, the half-way town on the desert route to Nedjef. And for a taste of stage-riding in Arabia, I started my journey by arabanah, a four-wheeled coach drawn by four mules harnessed abreast.

It was 2 o'clock on a starlit morning when I walked over the rude bridge of boats that spans the Tigris at Bagdad, ready for an early start from the west bank. Soon the jolting, noisy coach was in motion, the Arab driver cursing the religion of his four mules and plying his long whip of rhinoceros hide as we whirled away through the still empty streets. Only a few watchmen, shouting occasionally to keep up their courage, and the eternal vagabond dogs of Bagdad were astir.

Through the outlying Sunni cemetery we rolled past the beautiful tomb of Zobeida, favorite wife of Harun-al-Rashid, past the white tents of sleeping Turkish troops, through a gap in the ruined wall, and out onto the gray desert. The mules galloped evenly on, the wheels hummed, and we seemed to float over a sea of haze that lay on the desert, bathed in starlight.

Thus till dawn, when we reached the first relay post. Khan Mahoudieh, a mud-walled desert stronghold, where we got fresh mules, tea, and a few minutes rest. All about was noise and confusion; some 500 Persians, surrounded by their camels, donkeys, dogs, and rolls of baggage, were making up their caravan for the day's march to the Euphrates. Soon we were off again, the fresh mules leaping forward in their collars and jerking the bounding arabanah along at a lively clip.

We passed many caravans of pilgrims, mostly Persians, the bells of their lead animals tinkling musically, the long-legged camels groping through the half light of early day. Women rode in covered boxes, like bird-cages, slung one on each side of a mule or camel. A few upper-class persons rode in swinging palanquins, carried between animals walking tandem. Hundreds of the Persians, their legs wrapped in bandages like puttees, plodded along on foot, driving their baggage-laden donkeys before them. The country we passed through from Bagdad westward comprised a vast, dry plain, barren and desolate and flat as a great floor.

Near noon the fringe of date palms marking the course of the Euphrates lifted from the desert horizon, and an hour later we rode into the river village of A/fussayeb. Here also a bridge of boats is found spanning the Euphrates at the point where some say Alexander and his Ten Thousand crossed on their way to Babylon. On the west bank we got fresh mules, and soon passed through the belt of fig and date gardens that I flourish along the river. Before us the desert reappeared—a barren, treeless plain. Smooth it was, save where we bounced over the banks of ruined canals, remnants of the irrigation system built ages ago by the Babylonians.

Half way to Kerbela, and scattered for a mile along the route, we passed a caravan taking corpses for burial at the holy city of Nedjef. Among the dead was the body of a Persian nobleman. Three hundred paid mourners, who had come all the way from Teheran, sent up their weird chant as we passed.

Strict as are the Turkish quarantine regulations, badly "cured" bodies or bones are often smuggled in from Persia, and on a hot day the wise traveler will stay at a discreet distance from these death caravans. The odor, when noticeable, is peculiarly penetrating and sickening.

It is a month's marching from Teheran to Kerbela, and these dismal persons had wept all the way.

Kerbela, likewise a sacred Shia city, we reached about four in the afternoon.

THE PILGRIM HORDE

Kerbela sucks life from the unending pilgrim horde. Myriads of Shias have come and gone in centuries past, and millions are buried in the plain outside the city. Of its 75,000 permanent residents, nearly all are Shias. Hussein, martyred son of Ali, is buried in the magnificent mosque of Kerbela, and in the vaults about his tomb are stored the priceless offerings of the Shias who have come to pray, and paid tribute to the Mujteheds, or interpreters of the law. These Mujteheds, of whom there are twelve, have long been a thorn in the side of Persia's government. Safe in their retreat at Kerbela, they have hatched many of the political plots that made murder and riot in Teheran.

As early as 1350 Kerbela was known as a retreat for learned Moslem teachers. Shah Namat Ulla studied at Kerbela and lived 40 days on dust, tradition says. Many of his prophecies still live. In her book, "On the Eace of the Waters," Mrs. Steele quotes one of them, as follows:

"Fire worship for a hundred years, A century of Christ and tears; Then the true God shall come again, And every infidel be slain."

Major Sykes, in his work on Persia, says this prophecy was on every one's lips a generation ago and was perhaps the main cause of the Indian mutiny.

The Wahabi marauder, 'Abd-Allah, looted the treasure vaults of Kerbela in the last century, pillaged the tomb of Fatima's son, and slew nearly the whole population of the city. In Zehm's "Arabic" is a list of the booty taken, comprising gold tiles from the dome of the mosque, great quantities of gold coin, rich Kashmir shawls, etc., and many Abyssinian slaves.

Beyond the mosque, however, Kerbela has few attractions for the traveler. The people showed no resentment as I wandered through the narrow bazaar on the evening of our arrival. I slept the night in a mud-walled khan, surrounded by scores of talking, singing, swearing, quarreling Persians. Donkeys, camels, dogs, and chickens were all crowded together with the human element of the caravans; but an hour after dark quiet ensued, for men and beasts who march all day must sleep at night.

At dawn the confusion of, the crowded khan awakened me, and I was glad when my servant said our mules were ready and we might be off. Fortified with a hasty breakfast of dates, Arab bread, and tea, we extricated our mules from the fighting, scrambling horde before the khan gate and moved away. It is two days by caravan from Kerbela to Nedjef, though the distance is less than 60 miles. An hour south of Kerbela we came once more upon the desert, dreary and monotonous. Vast spots appeared covered with a thin, salty crust that crackled as the mules walked over it. After a few miles these spots faded away and we entered on a rolling sea of gray sand, the margin of the great waste that sweeps Arabia from Kerbela and Nedjef to Mecca, Aden, and the Red Sea. Our six mules filed head to tail. Besides my servant, two zaptiehs (soldiers) came also. The governor of Kerbela had sent them as an escort. The Turkish authorities refuse to be responsible for the safety of foreigners who travel in Arabia without a government guard.

All about us lay the flat, empty world. Not a tree, a shrub, a plant, or a bird—not an object, dead or alive—broke the vast stretch of sun, sand, and silence. Only the muflied footfalls of the plodding mules, or the soft, slopping sound of water splashing in the goatskins, came to our ears. At times we rode up and down over billows of gray sand, stretching away to the right and left in endless swells like giant furrows.

THE DESERT TRAIL

I wondered how the zaptiehs kept the trail; often I could see no signs that previous travelers had passed our way, so quickly does the wind obliterate tracks in the shifting sand. Bones of dead camels and mules lay along our path at intervals. The wind plays in tiny eddies about them and prevents their being covered up with sand. For long, still hours we held our way, pushing always south.

The day was well spent when we came upon the mean, mud-walled khan built at the wells marking the half-way resting place. Already others who traversed the desert had reached the friendly spot. They proved a caravan from the busy Euphrates town of Kuffa, and were on their way to the stronghold of the Amir of Nejd. Rumors of fighting between Arab clans on their direct route had sent them on this round-about course. Half a hundred pack-camels laden with bales of Manchester "piece-goods," bags of rice, and Marseilles sugar in blue cones, lay about, chewing contentedly, or nosing among the meager clumps of camel's-thorn which grew about the camp.

The rough, half-clad camel drivers rested on their haunches, talking volubly and plying my servant with questions as to my nationality, destination, wealth, family relations, etc. And I am sure that in his replies the boy, Naomi, allowed my reputation to suffer not at all. To the Bedouins, all foreigners are Ferenghies ("Franks"). These camel men had not heard of America, and asked if it were a part of London.

One camel man watched over a smoky fire of dried camel dung, where coffee was boiling. Water from the well was green and brackish, and I imagined it smelled of camels; but coffee made of it tasted like any other. Naomi got my meal ready—dates, bread, and coffee, with a bowl of lebban, curdled camel's milk. Off to themselves, the two zaptiehs ate, smoked long Bagdad cigarettes, and talked in low, droning voices.

Sleep is sweet in the pure air of the Arab desert, and soon I lay dreaming. Only once I was awakened, when a restless camel came sniffing near. Overhead burned the planets, big and steady in their glare, like near-by arc lights. About rose the snores of tired, sleeping Arabs; the bulk of herded camels loomed large, and I heard the low crunching of their rolling cuds. The glow of the night watch's cigarette came to me from one side; in Bedouin camps no one knows the hour when desert thieves may come.

The gurgling grunt of camels rising stiffly, under unwelcome loads, roused me at dawn. Already the west-bound caravan was astir, making ready for the day's march. The drivers were testing the ropes of twisted palm fiber which held the packs to see that all was fast. Then, urged by sharp blows from the stout sticks and cries of "Ek, oosh, ek, oosh!" the clumsy beasts rose reluctantly, their odd, thoughtful faces stuck high in the air. Soon our own mules were ready, and we mounted to ride away southward to Nedjef. The rude, blaspheming camel men of the Amir's caravan shouted us their adieus as they trekked off, miles of waterless plain between them and Nejd. But their goat-skins were tight full of water; as for the camels, they would not need to drink.

All day we followed our course, as on the day previous, through seas of sand. Toward noon we met hundreds of Persians returning from the pilgrimage. All the men could now dye their beards red and enjoy the title of Hahji—one who has made the Hahj, or pilgrimage. Soon I, too, would become a Hahji, for Nedjef was now near at hand.

NEDJEF, THE MYSTIC

The sun was nearly down, sliding like a fire ball from the copperish sky, when, we caught the first glimpse of holy Nedjef. First the great gold dome of its; mosque, burning in the sun rays; then, as we drew nearer, the high, frowning walls that surround the sacred city came into view. It was a gorgeous spectacle, mirage-like vision, as of a mighty city floating in the air. The high, sharp walls shut it off abruptly from the desert, and it seemed a mighty thing apart from the surrounding sea of sand. In a few moments we were passing through the acres of graves outside the walls and soon arrived at the city gate.

The sight of a white man riding into Nedjef upset the guards at the gate very noticeably; they seized the rein of Naomi's donkey, gestured wildly in my direction, and quickly drew a copious flow of potent Arabic profanity from the zaptiehs. These latter worthies, now suddenly become very important, abused the lowly guards to perfection, and demanded that we be conducted immediately to the Kaimakam (a sort of subgoverner). Followed by hundreds of Arabs—as many as could crowd into the plaza about us—we were taken to the Belladieh, where I met the Kaimakam (a Turk). It was now quite dark, and I was pleased to follow the Kaimakam's advice, that we turn in and "see Nedjef" next day.

We spent the night in a fairly comfortable khan, sleeping on its flat mud-roof Moorish fashion. From the house-tops about came the dull rattle of tom-toms and the sound of Arab women's voices, singing to the accompaniment of their jangling tambourines. Two captive desert lions, caged on a roof near the khan, roared at intervals during the night, and each time they roared I awakened, startled by the unusual sound.

A FREAK CITY

Nedjef is a freak city. Not a green thing—a plant, shrub, or tree—lives within its dry, hot limits. It is built on a high plain of soft sandstone. The narrow, crooked streets, in many places mere passages 3 or 4 feet wide, wind about like jungle paths. But for the four zaptiehs sent with me as a guard by the friendly Kaimakam, I must soon have lost my way when I set forth to see Nedjef.

For more than an hour we followed these narrow passages that lead through the Arab quarter. The mud-plastered houses were all two stories high and, odd as it sounds, had no windows facing the street. Only a wooden door, massive and bolt-studded, but so low that one must stoop to enter, opened to the street. As we threaded the cramped, crooked paths we came frequently on small Arab children playing before these doorways. Invariably they took one look at me, doubtless the first white man they had seen, and fled screaming through the low door-ways. An instant later I would hear the startled voices of women, and then the hurried sliding of the great door bars.

Three or four times, in turning a sharp curve in the warped gloomy street, I came face to face with veiled Arab women. At sight of me through the odd peep-holes, in their black veils they whirled about and dashed hastily into the first friendly doorway with many exclamations of surprise. Often, when we had passed a little beyond these women, I heard them burst into shrieks of hysterical laughter.

One of the strange features of this strange city is its cellars. In summer the fierce heat drives the panting people deep down into the earth, like rats in a hole. Beneath every house is a cellar, burrowed mine-like to amazing depths; one I explored reached an astoundingly low level, being more than 100 feet below the street. Down into these damp, dark holes the Shias flee when the scorching desert air sizzles above and imported German thermometers stand at 130 Fahrenheit. Some of the cellars (serdabs) are arranged in a tier of cells or rooms, one below the other; the upper room is used in the first hot months, the family going lower down as the heat increases.

So many of these vast underground retreats have been dug that the excavated material, carried from the city on donkeys' backs and dumped on the desert outside, forms a young mountain over 100 feet high, from the top of which a fine view of the city may be had. I was told that many of these serdabs are connected by means of underground corridors, and that criminals, who swarm in Nedjef, easily elude capture by passing through these tunnels from house to house, finally emerging at a point in the city remote from their place of disappearance.

In the heart of Nedjef, its great dome visible for miles on the surrounding desert, stands the magnificent mosque of Abbas, the shrine that draws the teeming throng from all the Middle East.

TILES OF GOLD

Turning from the native quarter, we came to the long straight bazaar leading to the mosque. I was struck with the difference in the looks of the Nedjef people and the crowds at Kerbela. Few Persians were about; the folk seemed all Arabs. Many uncouth, swaggering desert men were among them, their long hair, faded dress, and camel sticks, or oversupply of guns and side-arms, marking them as from the wild places. There was a spirit of crude, barbaric primitiveness in the crowd that surged past. The little touches of outside influence one sees at Bagdad, like an occasional European hat or an imported overcoat, were all lacking at Nedjef. Here was old Arabia in original bindings.

The mosque we came on suddenly, for the crowded bazaar street ends in an open plaza before this dazzling structure.

In amazement I gazed on its wonderful facade; golden tiles and fancy silver-work rise above and about the great portal, and across the wide entrance is hung a giant chain of brass, worn smooth and shiny from contact with the millions of turbans, tarbooshes, and keffeyehs which have brushed under it in centuries gone by. This chain is so hung that all who enter the mosque must bow.

Through this open gate, from where we stood, some 20 yards back, I could see the base of the great mosque itself. To my profound surprise, the great gold tiles which cover the dome also run to the very base of the mosque! And on the inside of the walls about the court were more gold tiles. Above the outer portal, too, on the outside, were sprawling Arabic characters 20 inches high, seemingly cut from sheets of gold! What must this barbaric splendor have cost!

The cost of the wonderful temple itself is but a bagatelle compared with the value of the treasure in its vault. For ages, be it known, Indian princes, shahs, and nobles of the Shia faith have made precious gifts to this temple at Nedjef, pouring into it a priceless stream of jewels, gold, and plate. A British Indian army officer told me that the looting of the Nedjef mosque was a favorite dream of soldiers in the Middle East, who looked forward to the day when war may sweep an army of invasion into Nedjef. The true enormity of the treasure at Nedjef was only brought to light in recent years, when the Shah of Persia made the Hahj and the pent-up wealth was revealed to his royal gaze by its zealous official keeper, the "Kilitdar."

But no Christian has ever seen the inner glories of the great mosque of Abbas at Nedjef. The contrast between two faiths is striking: a Moslem walking into a Christian church is made welcome; a Christian who walked into the Moslem mosque at Nedjef would be slain as a defiler; yet both claim the same God!

Lost in admiration of the splendid structure before me, I had failed to note the gathering crowd of Shias who now packed the plaza about us. It was the anxious voice of the zaptieh urging that I move away that finally roused me. In an instant, it seemed, fully 200 people had gathered in the small square before the mosque and were glaring at me and asking why and whence I had come.

One zaptieh, feeling my dignity assailed, foolishly struck or pushed a Shia who had cursed my religion and spat at me. A serious disturbance seemed about to break out, but we managed to slip away through a narrow side passage and thus avoid the crowd. As it was, a hundred or more men and boys followed, nor left off until we passed through the south gate of Nedjef and out onto the desert for safety.

More human bodies are buried in the plain outside the walls of Nedjef, it is said, than in any other one spot on earth. Myriads of fancy tombs, terminating at the top in little blue-tiled domes, rise from the plain. I asked how many might be buried there. "Allah knows all their names," said a zaptieh, simply. And all the millions of pilgrims who have come in ages past with corpses for burial have also brought money to spend. The richer the man who brings the body, the greater the toll taken. Twenty thousand dollars was spent on one funeral.

Burial sites within view of the great mosque bring a high price. The Turks put a tax on every corpse imported from India, Persia, etc. Many bodies are smuggled in. It is told of one astute Persian pilgrim that he divided his grandfather's skeleton and sent it in separate parcels by mail to save freight and tax.

When a death caravan reaches the outskirts of Nedjef, they unpack their gruesome baggage and prepare the various bodies for burial. The crude methods of embalming or mummifying would expose Nedjef to disease were it not for the dry desert air. The very few folk of Nedjef who work for a living make money manufacturing fancy shrouds, stamped with Koranic sentiments, for the burial of corpses brought in by the pilgrims.

Others turn out prayer-bricks ("Tor-ba"), which every Shia uses in his daily prayers. These are made from holy clay, scooped up from the great cemetery and pressed into tiny odd-shaped bricks, and also stamped with an inscription from the Koran. When a Shia prays, he lays this torba on the ground, faces Nedjef, and prostrates himself, touching his forehead against the sacred brick.

Near the mosque in Nedjef lives a colony of what might be called perennial brides; they are legally married many times each year. When a caravan of pilgrims come in from a distant land, the men in the company seek out this colony of professional marrying women. An authorized priest performs a fixed cere-mony, and the pilgrim is comfortably settled as a married man during his visit and period of prayer at holy Nedjef.

As crooks prey on the crowds that throng our "world's fairs," so a large criminal element thrives in Nedjef, living off the timid pilgrims. Gamblers, thieves, and sharpers abound, and few pilgrims leave Nedjef with money. Many fall by the wayside and eke out the life of beggars on the streets of Ker-bela, Bagdad, etc.

In all of this unnatural city I saw not a tree or shrub; not even a potted plant. It is a dry, prison-like place of somber gray stones and mud-plastered walls. Remove its mosque, its one priceless possession, and Nedjef, with its horde who live on those that come to pray, would perish from the earth. In the 1,200 years of its eventful life, not one useful article has been manufactured within its fanatical precincts.

Yet in all Islam, Shias turn to Nedjef to say their prayers. To Nedjef every good man must make the pilgrimage once in his life, and at Nedjef he hopes to be buried when he dies.

12

A SECOND ATTEMPT ON HUASCARÁN

ANNIE S. PECK

When Brown University refused her admission on the basis of her gender, Annie Peck entered one of the first coed classes at the University of Michigan. When, in her 40s, she joined the male-dominated world of alpinism, she bucked convention and notched the first ascent of a major world peak (Peru's 22,205-foot Huascarán; see Fanny Bullock Workman). When women still fought for suffrage, she planted a "Votes for Women" flag on the summit of Peru's Coropuna. And when, at nearly 80, commercial airlines started flying internationally, she shirked retirement for a 7-month journey, mostly by plane, across South America. Here she makes a second attempt on Huascarán.

CHAPTER XVI: A SECOND ATTEMPT ON HUASCARÁN

The west side of the mountain, it was now evident, afforded the better route to the summit, since on account of its different outline it presented no danger from avalanches. Though I could not expect, in the present condition of the ice, to reach a great height, it seemed desirable to learn whether the indians would be willing to go upon the glacier, and if so whether the labyrinth of crevasses was as bad as it looked.

I now dismissed Peter, who had proved of no real service, declaring everything to be impossible and groaning over his discomforts; he hadn't slept, he had a headache, he couldn't eat this, he didn't like that; in no respect amenable to my wishes, and tiresome with his voluble protestations. He was a strong, well-meaning fellow, but more accustomed to swearing at the members of a gang of workmen than to the society of ladies. So I sent him on his way back to Lima without hinting that I thought of making a second attempt. His enthusiasm for this sort of employment may be judged from the fact that I learned after his departure that he had declared that he would not take such a trip again for a million dollars. Evidently a person in that frame of mind would not be a very helpful assistant.

For my next expedition I decided upon a smaller and select party of four indians only, recommended by Señor Jaramillo as being capable and thoroughly reliable. Although I did not speak Spanish very well, I could make the indians understand all that was necessary, and I thought I should get on better with them alone. The indians here, as a class, are of more prepossessing appearance than the Aymarás in Bolivia, generally faithful and trustworthy. Two of those I had before were going again and two new ones. Never having the opportunity to train for my mountain climbing as I should like, I felt that I needed every particle of my strength for absolutely necessary work. I have had none to waste in carrying things. Though I had a pretty little

82-calibre revolver which weighed but a trifle, I had no desire to burden myself with it unnecessarily. Accordingly, I inquired of Senor Jaramillo, "Shall I carry my revolver?"

"No," he said, "you don't need it," so I left it behind at the Vinatéas.

The indians had no suitable footgear or underwear, and neither could be purchased in the place. One or two had poor shoes, the rest none at all. After some inquiries as to what was possible, I purchased some skins which were to be put over their feet when they went on the ice, also some woollen cloth in which their feet would previously be wrapped. Additional climbing irons had been made which would go over the skins, also ice axes or alpen-stocks, so that each man could have one. As for clothing, I urged them to wear the warmest they had and to bring as many ponchos as possible.

Five days after our return from my first expedition I quietly set out on the second. The porters leaving on foot earlier in the day, I went in the afternoon, accompanied by Señor Jaramillo, to a mine, Matarao, 2,000 feet above the town, from which Mr. Enock had set out for his climb. Riding south for an hour along the valley to a village called Mancos, we then turned to the left following a very poor and stony bridle path up the mountain side, on which were many cultivated fields and here and there a cluster of dwellings. It was dusk before we arrived. The Italian engineer was unfortunately absent in Caraz, but the hut which he occupied when there was opened for my benefit, and I had the pleasure of sleeping on a bed of boards above an adobe bench, rather than on the floor. The mine, which was worked for both gold and silver, was the joint possession of three persons, one of whom was Señor César Cisneros, the Sub-prefect of Yungay, the gentleman who had accompanied Mr. Enock a short distance on the glacier. He was much interested in my undertaking, though the present condition of his health prevented his participation in my enterprise. On my visit to Yungay in 1908 I was grieved to learn that his death had occurred in 1907.

One or two indians who lived near the mine joined my company of porters in the morning to direct us by the best way to the snow line. From the edge of the glacier the side of the mountain descends several thousand feet at a very sharp angle, so far as to make a considerable gully between this and the rounded cultivated hillsides that one sees from the valley below. This gully runs down towards the north, the stream at the bottom emptying into the one that flows from the Llanganuco Gorge into the Santa River in the valley. At the south end of the mountain a ridge comes out from the south peak just below the snow line, here higher than in the middle of the west face. A short distance from the mountain, this ridge, turning north, forms the enclosed head of the gully and gradually lowers until a trifle north of Matarao it breaks sharply off down to the rounded hilltops which from this point on remain as the west wall of the gully.

Accompanied by Señor Jaramillo I rode to the top of the ridge and some distance along, until the way was altogether too bad for the animals, when he departed with them. The rest of us with frequent halts for breath continued along the narrow uneven *arête* till near the end we climbed down into a small gully where we had luncheon. From this point we proceeded directly upwards, where bushes and stunted trees grew well toward the ice. The indians who had accompanied Mr. Enock and Señor Cisneros led the way in the direction which they had followed and which I approved, as it seemed wise to go as high as convenient before entering upon the glacier. Moreover, in front of the south peak, the glacier was not so terribly crevassed as farther north below the saddle and the north peak, which made the ascent here still more desirable. It is hard work to climb a steep and rocky slope at this altitude, even when carrying nothing, and it was nearly five o'clock when at length we set up the tent within a few rods of the glacier, on a space as nearly level as we could find, at least 1,000 feet higher than where the ice comes down in the middle and at an altitude of something over 15,000 feet. My aneroid barometer, which was a trifle too low on the pass of the Black Range, indicated 15,800 feet.

Enock gives the height of the snow line as 14,000 feet, which probably means the average line rather than the highest or lowest point of the glacier. This may well be the case in May, at the close of the wet season, for five months of tropical sunshine would probably curtail the lower limit of snow 1,000 feet.

The tent was hardly pitched when a small snow squall warned us of the approach of the rainy season and the possibility of bad weather; but the night was fair and we hoped for nothing worse on the morrow. One man from the mine having begged permission to take the place of one of my porters and another being added, six persons were now crowded into my little tent, only 7×9 feet. Obviously there was not sufficient room for all to lie at full lengthy and after my sleeping bag was stretched by the door the men curled up as best they could. The Indians often sleep sitting, leaning against a wall, so this to them was no hardship, and their snoring soon indicated that some of them were slumbering.

I did not sleep much myself; not that I felt at all afraid, for it was evident that the men would be held responsible for my safety. I of course carried no money, and there could be no possible motive for ill conduct. Indeed, the men seemed to feel a pleasure in their responsibility and the confidence reposed in them, and I have no doubt but that I was much safer than I have been at times in our great cities, although I never happened to meet with any unpleasantness there.

Early in the morning we breakfasted and arranged the loads. At the edge of the ice all put on climbing irons and were tied with the rope. After some discussion, it had been arranged that a little chap named Jacinto Osorio, who had worked in a mine and knew how to wield a pickaxe, should lead the way, that Adrian, a stalwart fellow, major domo of Jaramillo, should go second, and I third; Adrian second, especially because, if Jacinto should fall into a crevasse, he would be better able to hold him or pull him out than I. It was desirable that I should be as far forward as possible in order to give directions about the route. The other three men followed in the rear. I instructed them carefully in the use of the rope, telling them to keep as far apart as they could and hold the rope taut, so that if any one fell into a crevasse there would be the least jerk possible. Thus arranged we began our snow climb at a point below the south peak, a little to the right of its central portion.

It seemed odd to enter upon this enormous glacier, covering the entire west slope of the mountain, with five men none of whom had ever been on the ice before; but the leader seemed intelligent, careful, and courageous, the ice proved less difficult than it had looked from below, and, far from realising the tremendous difficulties of the task before me, I began to feel hopeful of camping that afternoon in the saddle. From my examination of the mountain through a glass, the most practicable route had seemed to be from this point straight up towards the southern peak until beyond the worst crevassed section farther north, then across to the left nearly to the foot of the north peak, and thence up the saddle between the two. But in spite of my advice that this course be followed, once on the ice, the leader pursued the line of the least resistance, that is to say where in the immediate vicinity the fewest and smallest crevasses appeared, so that we presently found ourselves taking a diagonal to the northeast towards the north peak and already in a line with the saddle.

Some distance above us there now appeared a great ice wall extending for a long distance, absolutely impassable to novices, if not to experts. In one place at the left there was a break which might possibly be negotiated, but when we had proceeded thither, Jacinto declared it impossible and chose another route which led down instead of up and proved to be a great mistake. He cut his way around a difficult corner with ice towering thirty feet above and a gulf yawning fifty feet below. By this traverse we hoped to come to easier going, but alas! it was only the beginning of evil.

For the next two hours we turned and twisted among towers and pinnacles in a labyrinth of crevasses far worse than anything I ever saw in Switzerland, up and down, around and about, crossing snow and ice bridges, cutting steps, walking now at the bottom of an ice gully, oftener on a narrow table or bench, with crevasses hundreds of feet deep on either side, most unpleasant of all passing under ice pinnacles, which, like leaning towers, rose twenty or thirty feet above. For the sun was hot, we could see the water dripping and hear it gurgling far beneath, and knew not but these masses might at any moment topple over.

We seemed to proceed from bad to worse, yet having passed so many ugly places we were disinclined to retrace our steps, every moment expecting that a little farther on our difficulties would cease. Several times our valiant little leader declared that there was no way farther. Then I would advance to his side and after carefully scanning the field point out a possible route. He would promptly assent to try it, and on we would go.

After two hours of such exciting labour, during which no one suggested rest or refreshment, on coming once more to a halt, rebellion broke out among the rear guard. They insisted upon going back, declaring farther advance impossible. I represented to them that it was much better to go on than to return over the dreadful way we had come. We were now on a narrow table, ten feet wide or less, with crevasses broad and deep on each side, at the end a perpendicular drop to another shelf or table. I pointed out a place at the comer where we could climb down six or eight feet to this, in spite of yawning crevasses on either hand; an ice bridge led to another table, a snow bridge to a higher plane beyond; these passed, it looked as if we might be pretty well out of the labyrinth, to where it was comparatively smooth sailing. The leaders, Jacinto and Adrian, were willing, but the others refused to advance unless I would double their promised pay. This, perforce, I consented to do, with the proviso that they continue at least to the saddle this same day, the possibility of which I had begun to doubt. All agreeing to this, Jacinto carefully cut his way down while Adrian held the rope so that if the former slipped he would suffer no harm. Following in his footsteps, we then passed with light tread over an ice bridge barely two feet thick from this table to the next, crossed a narrow crevasse to the one following, and soon found ourselves on safer ground or ice, where we could take some needed rest and food, as it was already one o'clock.

In the early afternoon when again on our way a snow squall reached us, but so quickly passed that we did not pause in our course. Soon, however, the indians urged fatigue and a wish to stop for the night where there was a fairly good place for the tent. As yet we were not more than half way to the saddle, so much time had been lost in that terrible labyrinth of crevasses into one of which Jacinto's hat had disappeared from view. Not heeding their suggestion I urged them onward, but presently observing the rapid approach of a very black cloud from around the cormer of the south peak, seeing no good camping place ahead, I decided that it was the part of prudence to retreat to a nearly level spot below. The tent was pitched but not well fastened when, about four in the afternoon, the storm burst upon us, a genuine snow storm, which made us thankful to be under cover. It seemed almost as if the snow *poured* down, faster and thicker than I had ever seen in my life before. This continued for hours until several inches had fallen. It was cold, too. With two suits of all wool underwear, other garments, and my sleeping bag, I was chilly. It is not strange that the men, with their ponchos only, suffered from the freezing temperature.

During the night I meditated upon the morrow. What should we do? A whole day would be required to reach the top of the saddle, another to attain the summit: at the least, two nights more on the ice, with the probability of success small, in view of what we had encountered already. I could endure the hardship well enough, but could the men? It seemed cruel to ask the indians, thinly clad as they were, to proceed farther; probably they would not have gone if I had.

In the morning, therefore, after a sleepless night on my part, and a little snoring from some of the men, I decided to abandon the attempt. I put my name and the date, according to custom, in a bottle, though as a memorial it was useless. It would soon be buried in the snow, and if ever it came to light, it would be at the edge of the glacier 2,000 feet below, which might lead some persons to suppose that that was as far as I had been.

Our camp, according to the aneroid, was at an altitude of about 17,600 feet. Desiring to avoid the dreadful maze of crevasses on the descent, I suggested going higher towards the south, which we did for several hundred feet, so that we may have reached a height of approximately 18,000 feet. We were very near the foot of the south peak. My idea was to go some distance farther south until we were beyond the labyrinth, then straight down to the point where we had entered upon the ice. Jacinto and Adrian, however, thought we should do better to go down on the north side of the labyrinth, to which I consented, so we turned about face. Half way down there were a good many crevasses and some step cutting, but the worst of the maze was avoided. When we paused for luncheon, Jacinto was too tired to eat. Besides cutting all the steps, he carried a small pack. I tried to induce him to let one of the others take this, but he resolutely refused. He was a faithful little chap, with valour enough for a man twice his size. With a few more like him, much could have been accomplished; but, as I discovered when at last the mountain was climbed, it would have been suicidal to have gone much farther without skilled assistants. Then I did not fully appreciate the difficulties that lay above.

By the time we left the glacier for the rocks, it was in the neighbourhood of three o'clock. A few articles, deposited near our first camp, were hunted up. Meanwhile I proposed descending to the mine. Though tired, the prospect of a roof over my head, and an ordinary evening meal, was attractive enough to enable me to brace up for the long walk down. Jacinto first agreed to accompany me, then one or two others, while those who wished I allowed to remain in the tent over night. It was a weary way, but having taken a short rest we made good progress, better I think than I ever did again. By dark we were once more at the mine, returning to Yungay the day following.

On the whole I was fairly well pleased with this venture; I had been 1,000 or 2,000 feet higher than Mr. Enock, though still lacking at least 2,000 feet to the top of the saddle, above which the twin peaks rose several thousand feet more. My idea of the mountain's height at this time was vague, merely from 22,000 to 26,000 feet, as it had been estimated by others. It seemed probable that it might turn out higher than Aconcagua, and thus gain the distinction of being the loftiest mountain on this hemisphere. In any event I felt sure that it exceeded Sorata, hence the summit of Huascarán, rather than that of the Bolivian peak, became for the future the goal of my ambition.

Furthermore, I had discovered that some Indians were bold enough to venture upon the ice and had no superstitious prejudice against climbing the mountain. If suitably equipped with warm clothing, proper foot gear, and ice axes, it appeared that these men would prove valuable assistants and might even render Swiss guides unnecessary, especially if one had not the funds to obtain these. At a better time of the year, early in the dry season, May or June, when the sun is far to the north, the heat in the middle of the day not so great, the crevasses fewer in number, and the glacier well covered with snow, the ascent to the saddle, I thought, would be a comparatively easy matter, the *arêtes* above could probably be climbed with care. Now with daily recurring, snow storms, it was folly to think of another attempt, so I prepared to return home feeling that, if I had not accomplished all I desired, I had done enough to show that I was not insane in believing that I was personally capable, with proper assistance, of making the ascent of a great mountain. I should bring to the attention of Alpinists a new and accessible territory, worth visiting not merely to make a record, but to behold a glorious collection of mountain peaks, some of which will long defy their would-be conquerors.

13

THE TRAP IS SPRUNG

MARGUERITE E. HARRISON

When her husband died suddenly, leaving her burdened with debt, Marguerite Harrison turned to her family connections to pick up a job as a reporter at the Baltimore Sun. Initially assigned to cover the social calendar, she eagerly switched trajectories to join the World War I effort. Using language skills gleaned from childhood summers in Europe, she was dispatched to Germany as a spy—Harrison was one of America's first female intelligence officers—and later Russia and Japan. In 1919, when she snuck into Russia via Poland, the country was in the throes of a civil war after its recent revolution. In Moscow, she reported on the social and political climate and mingled with revolutionaries— until she found herself bound for the famed Russian prison, Lubyanka.

CHAPTER XXII: THE TRAP IS SPRUNG

There is a current saving in Russia that every citizen "has sat, is sitting or will sit in prison." After eight months in Moscow I had ample proof of the relative accuracy of this statement, so that when I was arrested on the night of the twentieth of October I was not taken unawares by any means. Indeed, for some time, as I have already stated, I had had reason to suspect that my turn was coming, and I often used to lie in bed at night listening to passing automobiles, wondering when one would stop at the door of the government guest house in the Mali Horitonévski Pereoulak. A motor in a quiet street at night in Moscow nearly always means a "Zosad," or raid, or an arrest, for none but official personages on official business use cars and the few commissars who work at night have no business to transact in the residential sections.

On this particular night I had come home very late, about two o'clock as usual, from the Foreign Office, where everyone, including Chichérin, works all night, the news bulletin being given to press correspondents at twelve o'clock, and I was just preparing to go to bed when I heard a motor stop outside. In a few minutes there was a knock at my door. "It's all up," I thought, calmly, and without getting up from the sofa where I was sitting I called out in as cheerful a tone as I could muster, "Come in."

The door opened and a young, exceedingly well dressed, rather pretty woman came in, followed by two soldiers wearing the pointed caps of the Checka and carrying the rifles which have almost entirely taken the place of revolvers even with the city militia. They were nice looking boys, not at all fierce or formidable, and they seemed rather reticent about stating their errand, so I thought I would help them out.

"I suppose you have come to arrest me," I remarked.

Without replying the elder of the two boys handed me a small slip of paper. It was an order for my arrest, accompanied by a search warrant, written with a red pencil, and signed by Piatt, executive head of the "Secret Operative Section" of the Extraordinary Commission, which is the correct title in English for the Checka.

At the same moment the Commandant of the house arrived, rubbing his eyes, and looking very sleepy indeed. This was strictly in accord with the prescribed legal routine which requires the presence of the Commandant or the chairman of the house committee whenever a search warrant is served.

The two men then began a thorough overhauling of everything in the room, and nothing escaped them. They were evidently experts at the job. All my personal belongings were gone over, my bags turned inside out and the space between the cover and the lining thoroughly examined. The bed was subjected to a rigid search, as was each piece of upholstered furniture, the carpet was turned up and the space behind the radiator received particular attention.

All my papers were collected down to the smallest scrap of writing — blank sheets were held to the light to detect possible invisible characters and my books were gone over page by page. As I had collected a number of books and pamphlets, made innumerable notes, kept copies of all my newspapers, articles and telegrams for eight months, there was much to be inspected. And then my money had to be counted. I had quite a lot of it, a million and a half roubles, for I was at that time supplying weekly food packages to eight Americans and a number of British prisoners and had to keep considerable cash on hand for my purchases in the market. The money was counted twice, I was asked to verify the amount, then money and papers were made into two packages to accompany me to the Checka.

Meanwhile I had been subjected to a personal search by the woman who had been sent for that purpose. She examined my pockets, felt in my corsets, my stockings and my hair, went over every inch of my fur-lined coat to see if it concealed any papers, but, much to my surprise, I was not compelled to undress, and I was treated most courteously throughout.

I asked permission to pack the necessary articles to take to prison with me, and this was immediately granted. Although warned that there was not room for much luggage in the automobile, I managed to take a bag containing toilet articles, a change of underwear, some chocolate and cigarettes, an army bedding roll with a pillow and a steamer rug and my big fur coat.

When the search was over I was asked to sign a document, witnessed by the Commandant, certifying that the search had been conducted in a proper manner, my room was closed, locked and sealed with a large red seal. I was then taken to the waiting motor, a fine English car, and driven through the silent moonlit streets to the prison of the secret section of the Checka, which is in a building on the Lubianka, in the heart of Moscow's business district, formerly the property of the "Rossia" Life Insurance Company. From the outside it looks like anything but a prison. On the ground floor a row of unoccupied shops, divided by temporary unpainted wooden partitions, serve as offices for the Checka. The car stopped outside one of these, and I was taken into a small dingy room, with a railed space at one end, behind which were sitting two Checkists in front of a large deal table covered with documents and papers. Lined up along the railing were a number of other people who had evidently been arrested, all men except myself. I was the last in the line, and it was more than an hour before my turn came to fill out the questionnaire presented to me by the men behind the table. It was a most elaborate affair, evidently intended only for Russians, for among the questions to be answered were whether I had any relatives in the Red or White Armies. When this was over my money was again counted, my valuables were all taken, including my wedding ring, and I was given a receipt for them, as well as for my typewriter and kodak.

This done, the commissars behind the table yawned, locked up their books and disappeared, and I was left alone with half a dozen soldiers. Then I was subjected to the only personal indignity I experienced during my ten months' imprisonment.

One of the soldiers, who was what we would call a fresh guy at home, proceeded to search me on his own account, accompanying the proceedings with a number of witticisms which, fortunately, I did not know enough Russian to understand, but which sent his companions into roars of laughter. They seemed to think it especially funny when I protested on the ground that I was an American.

"Much good being an American will do you here, citizenness," returned my tormentor scornfully.

Finally they had enough, and I was taken through a labyrinth of ground floor passages and up three flights of stairs to the office of the Commandant, where I surrendered my receipts, and was searched again, this time in a perfectly correct manner. The commandant, whom I afterwards got to know quite well from his daily visits, was the living image of "Kaiser Bill," and my Russian companions always called him "Vilgelm" behind his back. Officially we addressed him as Citizen Commandant. He was a rigid disciplinarian, but absolutely just, and was always willing to listen to any reasonable complaints or requests.

By this time it was nearly six o'clock. I was desperately tired, and very thankful when I was taken to my room on the floor below. Here again the first impression was not that of a prison, though as a matter of fact the "Lubianka 2" is the strictest prison in Moscow. Except for the armed sentinel at the door, the winding corridor into which I was taken might have been the hall of any second-class hotel anywhere in Europe. On both sides were numbered rooms. We stopped opposite number 39, the door was unlocked, the light turned on "for five minutes, so that you can undress if you want to," my guard informed me, the door was banged and locked, and I found myself in a small single room already occupied by three women.

Two were lying on the floor, and one on a bed of three boards laid across wooden horses and covered by a thin straw pallet. The only other articles of furniture were a deal table, and the "parashka," a large iron garbage can, which is unpleasant but indispensable considering the fact that prisoners are permitted to go to the toilet but twice a day.

On hearing the key turn in the lock all three of my companions, who had evidently been "playing 'possum," sat bolt upright and began deluging me with questions as is always the custom in prison. Where was I from, why had I been arrested? I retaliated with a cross-fire in French and Russian, which resulted in the discovery that I was already acquainted with one of the prisoners, a pretty Jewish woman whom I had last seen at "The Bat," *Lietuscha Muisch*, one of Moscow's best known vaudeville theaters, with Mr. Michael Farbmann, the correspondent of the *Chicago Daily News*. The second was a young girl employed in the Foreign Office. Both had been arrested a few hours before I was and professed to be ignorant of the charges against them, though I suspected that my acquaintance was probably in for what is known as "international speculation," which means that she had had illegal business transactions with foreigners. The third woman, a young Russian girl, had been for six weeks in solitary confinement until our advent, which explained why she was the proud possessor of the bed. Hers was a most romantic story.

She had fallen in love with a Hungarian prisoner of war, a near relative of Count Széchenyi, who married Miss Gladys Vanderbilt of New York some years ago, and was accused of being implicated in a plot for his escape, together with a number of Hungarian officers.

For more than a year she had been taxing her slender resources to provide him with food and other comforts in prison, and I never told her that I had already heard that this same faithless Szechenyi was at the same time receiving food packets from a certain Princess Galitzin. She was what we would call in America a good sport. Though facing charges which might mean the death penalty if they were proved against her, she was always in the best of spirits, and made light of our hardships in the most delightful manner.

When our herring soup was served at noon she assured me that it was fine for the digestion, and she told me that the six weeks in solitary confinement had been wonderfully soothing to her nerves. During all this time she had had no books and no amusements, except conversation through a small hole in the wall near the steam pipe, with the man in the next room, a well known theosophist.

The morning passed without any incident except our matutinal trip to the bathroom, where we all performed our ablutions together in a big tin trough with cold water. In the afternoon,

I was taken to be photographed, full face, left and right profile, against a white screen on which my serial number was printed — as nearly as I can remember it was 3041.

That night, curled up in my bedding roll on the floor, for there had been so many arrests recently that there were not enough beds to go around, I slept well. Strange to say I was not in the least nervous. After many weeks of suspense the worst had happened, and my first feeling was one of relief, for it must be remembered that my status in Russia had always been illegal, I had been arrested once before, and I knew that I was subject to rearrest at any time.

The next day, shortly after dinner, a soldier appeared.

"Garrison," he demanded. "Here," I answered.

"Na dopros," he said, shortly. I was puzzled, for it was a new word to me. "That means," said my Russian friend, "that you are summoned to a hearing. You are lucky. Sometimes people wait for weeks before they are questioned by one of the judges."

I followed my guard out into the hall, up and down a maze of stairways and passages, until I reached a familiar room, the office of Moghilevski, a member of the prsesidium of the Checka, who had questioned me in the spring when I was detained for forty-eight hours on account of the fact that I had come to Russia from Poland, an enemy country, without the permission of the authorities.

Moghilevski is a tall, slender, dark man, tremendously earnest and intensely fanatical in his Communistic beliefs, utterly unsparing of himself and others in his work, but he has his human side, as I discovered when I noticed a beautifully bound copy of Rabelais lying on his desk. I remarked about this and he told me that he had a weakness for old French literature.

Our conversation in general, however, was not about literary subjects. I was put through a rigid cross-examination, lasting nearly three hours about my acquaintances in Moscow, my relations with foreigners, my relations with the prisoners to whom I had been sending food packages, and other matters, during which, while perfectly courteous, he made it quite plain to me that my position was exceedingly serious. In the midst of his questions a soldier brought in two glasses of tea with sugar, a box of cigarettes was at my elbow, and I sat in a big luxurious leather arm chair. My answers were not altogether satisfactory, and the examination ended with my being returned to my companions in room 39, with the admonition to think things over and refresh my memory.

I had not been back more than a few minutes, however, when one of the prison guards appeared again.

"Pack your clothes," he ordered.

"Where am I going?" I asked.

"You'll see when you get there," he answered.

I started to put on my fur coat. "You won't need that," he said, and then I realized that I was probably to be transferred to solitary confinement, the thing I dreaded most, and I said good-bye to my new-found friends with a sinking heart, and followed my escort down the passage. It was just as I expected. I was shown into an empty room, the key turned in the lock and I was left alone.

14

ADVENTURES WITH A CAMERA IN MANY LANDS

MAYNARD OWEN WILLIAMS

Maynard Owen Williams was, by all accounts, chronically affable. As a National Geographic *photographer, he easily brushed off concern about travel to unknown lands of unknown people: "When I am abroad, I am the foreigner. I'm the one who has strange speech and strange habits and even strange clothes." During his 40-year tenure with the magazine, including 30 years as the chief of foreign staff, he documented everything from the opening of the tomb of Tutankhamen to an Arctic expedition with Donald MacMillan, using his camera as a lens to convey his message of understanding to his million or so readers. "Adventure, to me, has not been danger, or hardship," he wrote, "but a revealing that men everywhere like what I like, want what I want, and realize that if we are to have it, we must give ourselves the same chance of friendship that we do in distrust."*

ADVENTURES WITH A CAMERA IN MANY LANDS

THE snap-shot photograph is the magic carpet which adds a fairy-tale touch to a routine world. It satisfies man's desire to extend his horizon, to reach out into the unknown, and to identify himself a little more closely with the world of which he is a part.

Photographing the common people of foreign lands is a fascinating pastime. No fisher is forced to use more patience than the man who seeks through photography to show the folks at home how the other half of the world actually lives. No hunter can boast of so satisfactory a bag as falls to him who hunts with the clairvoyant eye of the camera. The focusing knob of a graflex is a more thrilling bit of mechanism than the trigger of a rifle.

THE PHOTOGRAPH IS A BASIS FOR FRIENDLY UNDERSTANDING

But photographing the world is not frivolous, nor is it merely good sport. If people and places are worth writing about, they are worth picturing. Such work is a step in the visualizing of our distant neighbors and the introduction of strangers to those who know no more about them than the camera tells. All the world is watching how the rest of the world lives.

It is habitual to speak of "the mask-like features of the Chinese." Unquestionably, when a Chinese wishes to conceal his emotions, the Sphinx looks vivacious in comparison, but when a casual observer insists that the people of China never smile or laugh, a few photographs reveal such an error of generalization.

The Chinese is unusually clever in disguising his feelings when he wants to disguise them; but a frank show of friendship and a readiness to smile in spite of toil, cold, or hunger are among the most prominent of Chinese characteristics.

When members of a family are separated, they exchange photographs. The same method is applicable to the building up of international relations. Photography, with all its faults, is a social art. It furnishes a basis for friendly understanding.

About once a year we of the Occident hear of little glass or metal bracelets, such as the girl babies of India wear, being found in the stomachs of slaughtered crocodiles. At times I wish that someone would vary the tale by making the reclaimed property a shirt-stud or a collar-button. But when the camera is called in to report on the inhumanity of distant and little-understood peoples it is quite as likely to reveal proud mothers in India as in Indianapolis.

The camera enthusiast often has the same sort of an alibi as the fisherman. The ones that get away are always the best. Nor is this unnatural. Taking pictures requires concentration, and such diversion as a charming subject offers may drive all thought of formulae from the amateur photographer's head.

A QUEEN OF THE HOLY LAND

Coming up through Palestine some years ago I was traveling with an enthusiast who had read somewhere that the habit of carrying heavy jars of water on their heads gave to the women of the Holy Land a queenly carriage. At one of the roadside springs we halted, and after he had looked over a score or so of water-girl candidates for queenly honors, he was the most disappointed man imaginable. Then the cry of "All aboard!" rang out and the party was about to continue the ride to Samaria.

Around a curve of the road there glided a young woman who fitted perfectly the mental picture of my friend. Her raven hair was neatly parted on as fair a forehead as ever carried jet black brows above soft brown eyes. Her oval face was satiny olive. with a flush of red in the cheeks; her teeth were pearls; her nose was finely molded; but the memorable feature was that she really had the form and carriage of an uncrowned queen.

My companion made a grab for his camera, commandeered my slight knowledge of Arabic, and started off in the direction of his vision in a way that would have frightened a less capable woman. She consented to let us snap our cameras at her, and we dashed back to the carriage. A mile farther on, my friend gave a cry of chagrin. He had forgotten to withdraw the dark slide from his camera. I had not shared his enthusiasm to such a disastrous extent, with the result that a picture of our fair model appeared in The Geographic several months ago.

One of the vexing problems for the photographer is the matter of tips ("back-sheesh"). My own rule is never to offer or give tips to those who let me take their photographs unless they are professional beggars, hardened in their vice. The tourist centers of the world have been spoiled by those who have distributed extravagant largesse in return for photographic rights. One can be given privileges that he cannot buy.

You can't ride a high horse or a motor car and get familiar close-ups of common folks. The people of the East are suspicious of those camera hunters who stalk their game from the cushions of an automobile.

CAMERA HUNTING IN BALUCHISTAN

From Quetta to Sibi, in Baluchistan, I rode on the cowcatcher of a locomotive over one of the weirdest scenic routes in the world. A luxurious seat, upholstered in leather, had been placed on the front of the engine for my use, and the station masters whom I encountered were not sure but what I owned the line. At one station I noticed a charming little girl, wearing a lemon-colored scarf with that grace which western women seldom attain, because their drapery is arranged by their dress-makers and not by themselves. But that lovely Hindu child up there in the bleak regions of Baluchistan was afraid of the black box and its Polyphemus eye.

The station master knew that if I had a private lounge attached to the engine I must be a Lieutenant-Governor or a General at least, and he feared that if his daughter balked he might be subjected to censure. He explained and pleaded, but in vain. He even dragged her toward the camera.

BUYING A SMILE WITH A TIN BOX

Now, the first rule of the photographer should be the Golden Rule; and, in any case, I had no desire to picture that lovely child in tears. I gave her the tin container from which a reel of film had been taken. She smiled. I gave her some of the chocolate almonds which constituted my lunch. Again she smiled her thanks. She had no dislike for me personally, but she would not let me point the camera at her, for she feared that it might be loaded, even if I didn't know it.

Then I let her look in at the top and showed her the locomotive and the barren hills and the long-haired Baluchis, with their spinster curls, and the smiling face of her father. If she had been a movie queen, drawing $100 a smile and $1,000 a tear, she could not have been more magnanimous in letting me photograph her after that.

"I PRESS THE BUTTON; YOU DO THE REST"

Time and again I have had to show illiterate people what the mysterious black box really is. One man with whom I traveled suggested that the unwashed people who formed in line to look through my graflex would probably breathe a million different kinds of disease germs into the hood of the machine, and he pictured the possibility of my contracting pink eye, diphtheria, and other dread diseases as the result of my experiment.

But one can't get friendship without giving it, and a portrait is not a mechanical thing, but a collaboration between subject and photographer. "I press the button, but you do the rest" is one of the slogans to be kept in mind when taking pictures of Asiatic peoples, upon whose good will the recorder of pictorial geography must rely.

It is this cooperation with those common folks who cannot speak his language which robs many a photographer's day of loneliness and makes the picturing of foreign peoples a delight such as the lion-hunter never knows. I have never seen a smile on the face of the tiger which has fallen before the rifle of a sportsman, but I have captured many a very friendly smile with my camera.

These smiles of brotherhood flashed half way around the world are the symbols of mutual confidence and understanding.

IN THE RAWALPINDI BAZAAR

The Rawalpindi bazaar, by all the conventions of guide-book emphasis, is a place of no importance at all. In the midst of the busy street, a crude rolling-mill turned by hand transformed sugar-cane from ambrosia to nectar. Sitting on a pile of a thousand suits of cast-off army clothing, the city Solomon Levi figured up his losses on the last sale. Fruit venders had their luscious stock displayed in golden pyramids or ruddy cones touched here and there with bits of tinfoil light. Cattle strolled about at will, and, sitting beside the dusty road, a solemn personage gave such close attention to his chin that he neither saw my camera nor heard it click.

Under a tree whose dense shade lay like a tangible thing in the thoroughfare, two holy men sat beside a smokeless fire which cast a sheen on their naked chests, although beyond the boundary of their leafy shade' the sunlight was intense. Around them sat several novices, bright-eyed lads who had not yet attained that air of detachment which characterized their leaders.

One of the novices had an enormous shock of hair, which looked like a grotesqtte wig. His face was most expressive. As his eyes and teeth flashed out from the dense shadow, the gamut of passions was reflected on his features.

Here was a boy whose life no one of us could understand, across whose features human emotions played with vivid force. As he smiled over his bare brown shoulder, I snapped the camera. Then he turned back to the contemplation of the smokeless fire and the naked religious leader to whom he had attached himself.

I returned to the table d'hote dinner at the English hotel. But for a moment we had smiled into each other's eyes and for a moment we had understood.

GETTING PICTURES OF MOSLEM WOMEN IN EGYPT

It is harder to get a man to pose for a photograph than it is to get a woman's picture. On the other hand, one can take a man's picture without asking permission and run little risk of causing trouble, while it is dangerous to take pictures of some of the women of *harem* or *purdah*, whether they are veiled or not.

In Cairo a Moslem woman with most hypnotic eyes was dictating a letter to a professional letter-writer. She sat perfectly still and looked straight into the camera when I asked her in sign language if I might take her picture. Obviously she was a person to whom I could not offer money, but I thought that such a woman would like to have a copy of the picture sent to her. The letter-writer, it developed, spoke English, and I was so grateful to this fair Egyptian for this unusual opportunity that I asked him to tell her that if she would give her address I would send her a print.

"If her husband know she let you take picture, he beat her," replied the scribe after a hurried consultation.

But out at the Pyramids two women gladly let me take their pictures, both veiled and unveiled, and although neither would tell me where I could send her a picture direct, I did send photographs to the husband of one, while the other had her picture sent to her through her camel-driver!

AN ENCOUNTER ON THE BATHING BEACH AT DELHI

At Delhi there is a long sand-bar beside the River Jumna, where thousands of men and women bathe in the murky water. Here and there are small shelters in which the high-caste women change their *saris*, but the whole riverside is one vast open-air dressing-room, without a trace of immodesty on the part of any one. Food-sellers and hawkers of toys and notions dot the sands and the whole scene is a blaze of color and movement.

A six-foot foreigner wearing a glaring white sun helmet and carrying a camera has about as much chance of hiding in such a crowd as the man who sneezes while the tenor is climbing to his prize note, but I took several photographs of the crowd without anyone showing hostility.

Then there came up a man who, by wearing a spotless turban, a well-pressed Prince Albert, and trousers rolled up to his bare knees, and carrying neat button shoes and ungartered socks in his hand, formed a fit subject for a photograph himself. Strangely enough, it did not occur to me or to him that he would do as a model for an art study.

He told me that I really ought not to be taking pictures of the people. "Especially the women," he said.

"Why not?" I asked, just as though I was accustomed to seeing the outside world changed into a boudoir.

"All these women are in *purdah*. No man must look upon them," was his startling reply.

"How do you know there are any women here, then?" I asked.

At that moment a dusky queen passed us, just as she had emerged from the water, with her gaily colored sari plastered to the lower portion of her body and with her well-built figure doing graceful imitations of a quickened Venus.

"That woman is in *purdah* and no man should see her," he replied, without denying that he did see her.

"I'm afraid she is not quite what I want, anyway," I replied. "But if she really desires seclusion, I think a Mother Hubbard would help a lot."

Women gladly consent to being photographed if they think they are well dressed, but woe to the photographer who attempts to take a picture of a woman in what she considers is not becoming to her!

FEMININE VANITY ON THE BANKS OF THE BRAHMAPUTRA

Our motor bus dropped down from Shillong to the banks of the Brahmaputra and stopped beside the little railway station at Gauhati. It was to wait there for a few minutes before going on to the ferry crossing at Pandnghat. So I shouldered my camera and went off to utilize the time. Seeing a very interesting old woman in the bazaar, I pointed to my camera and asked if I might take her picture. Her reply was to jump up with an alacrity surprising in one of her years and disappear into her home. Once safe in the shadow, however, she turned and signaled me to wait.

Down the village street, the motor bus soon turned the corner with a roar. Knowing that the Assam mails were in the body of the machine, and that time and tide set the tradition for the King's mails, I started away; but out from that doorway stepped my genial friend, proudly bearing up under the greatest weight of jewelry that I ever saw one woman wear.

While the mail waited and the motor horn honked, I took several pictures of the happy old lady, and then, with the last film wound from the roll, I snapped the shutter a half dozen times just to let her know that her kindness and fascination were appreciated.

USING A CAMERA IN JAPAN

Sometimes a photographer is embarrassed by official kindnesses. In Shiraoi, in Hokkaido, the Japanese were making a well-meant but vain attempt to inculcate into the Ainu their own love for bathing. As an aid to this object, they had built a bright new bath-house in the midst of the hovels in which the Ainu dwelt.

I was the guest of a Japanese official, and the right to take the official photograph of this auspicious occasion had been given to a commercial photographer. I had no desire to buy a formal picture of this group, in which the Japanese, clothed in Western dress, mixed with the fine-looking old Ainu chiefs and their wolfish-looking sons. I hinted as broadly as possible that I would like to secure some poses of my own, but all in vain.

One of the Japanese officials might be smiling or frowning or something, or his frock coat might not be buttoned properly, or his silk hat might not be held at the regulation angle, and an uncensored print let loose on the world might bring the Japanese Government and the Mi-kado into disrepute.

Until the ceremony was over, I was not allowed to take a single picture. But afterward I was at liberty to take all the pictures I desired, and secured a portrait of an Ainu Saint Nicholas which satisfied me better than would all the silk hats in Dai Nippon.

THE SMILE TALISMAN IN CEYLON

A smile works in all languages and its power of reflection exceeds that of, many a mirror. If this funny old world is ever to make friends with itself, it will be the face with the smile that wins. And to get a smile onto the face of an unwilling subject is not easy. Sometimes one has to resort to horse-play to get the people in good humor, and even when well-intentioned fun overshoots the mark, it is well to have established an atmosphere of friendliness.

One of the great prizes to the people of Asia is the tin container from which a film has been removed. These can be given away where money would introduce an undesirable element into the relations. But usually there are several claimants to the tin tube.

The tiniest baby is always entitled to first chance, but when the claimants are all of an age, I have had to decide by the ancient "eenie, meenie, miny, mo" method, and the result is usually great amusement and profound satisfaction by all concerned.

In Negombo, Ceylon, one small boy suggested that I throw the tube and let them scramble for it. That worked admirably the first time. But there was a small lad who seemed to lack strength or spirit and he gave signs of thinking that that was not a square deal.

All the boys were barelegged and I stood near the edge of a shallow pool. This small boy was nearer to the water than the rest; so, while pretending to throw the second tube ahead of me, as I had the first, I tossed it over my shoulder into the water. It fell quite near the disconsolate youth, but others were quicker. A more agile boy rushed for it and, stumbling over a guy rope, fell sprawling into the water.

There was nothing for me to do but laugh as loudly as the rest, and when the boy picked himself up with the prize in his hands and a smile on his face, every one was happy. But I was glad that he did not wear a Little Lord Fauntleroy suit and a broad, starched collar, and that I had made friends with the crowd before the accident happened.

WORKING AGAINST SUPERSTITIONS IN THE ORIENT

Throughout the Orient there are innumerable superstitions which make it difficult to secure personal photographs. Not only are Oriental men jealous of their women folk, but there are few places where the illiterates do not have some fear of the evil eye. Many fear misfortune if their picture is taken, and there are still Mohammedans who have a religious objection to lending themselves to the representation of living beings. A people who have made caligraphy their ideal of art do not readily lend themselves to portrait work.

Many fear that if their photographs are taken their bodies will waste away. This belief is especially common among the Ainu, and some photographers have risked their lives because of their indiscretion in photographing those who are obsessed by such fears.

When there is a flat-footed refusal of the right to take pictures, one must desist; but ignorance of the language spoken by the people helps a great deal. Most people are shy about having their pictures taken, but this shyness quickly melts before a sincere smile, and when to apparent friendliness is added the pitiful spectacle of lingual helplessness, there are few who can refuse the respected foreigner's request.

A PHOTOGRAPH THAT REPRESENTS GRATITUDE

Many a Moslem husband has allowed me to photograph his women folk, and the toleration of these people in letting visitors see and photograph their mosque services is worthy of mention; but the most memorable case of Moslem magnanimity of my experience occurred in Ongole, where a Christian missionary had saved the life of an Indian Moslem's son, and this man, out of trust and gratitude, allowed me to photograph his family, with his wife unveiled, because I was a friend of the doctor.

Throughout the East there is a hearty response to genuine friendliness. The native is not accustomed to familiarity with the white man and at first he resents it, because he does not understand the motives, but I have never met with anything other than the utmost politeness among the common people of Asia.

More troublesome than those who resent having their pictures taken are those superactive and ubiquitous imps who insist on being in every picture. One lad bothered me a great deal when I was trying to photograph a street scene in Buddh Gaya, India, though obviously he had as much right to the locality as did I. Since I could not remove him, I tried to get him to loosen up his frame a little and look more like Tom Sawyer and less like a monument. When I had shown him how to do it, and returned to my place, I turned to find him doing a scarecrow dance that would have won plaudits in the "Wizard of Oz" or done credit to Saint Vitus himself.

In the spring of 1919 the Chinese burned millions of dollars' worth of opium, not individually, in small doses, but collectively, in huge incinerators opposite Shanghai. At that time I was in the interior of Fukien, in the bandit-infested region between the Northern and Southern troops, and passed through wide fields of opium poppy which the people had been induced to plant so as to afford quick revenue to the war lords who were then ravaging the province.

A friend, to whom I mentioned my desire to get a photograph of this condition of affairs, said that if I attempted to photograph opium poppies the Chinese would probably try to destroy my camera, as they had no desire to be thus convicted of duplicity. I took a score of pictures in the poppy fields, showing the cultivation of the opium plants and the gathering of the milky juice from the poppy pods, but no one showed the slightest objection.

In Japan I met a man who was roundly condemning the Japanese for preventing foreigners from taking pictures and who was exceedingly surprised to know that, outside a few fortified areas, a camera can be as widely used in Nippon as in the United States.

He had attempted to take forbidden photographs at Nagasaki and had been so badly frightened by the police that he packed away his camera for weeks. Yet even in Nagasaki the government would gladly have furnished him a police officer, under whose surveillance he could have taken any legitimate views.

A RACY ENTERTAINMENT AT BEIRUT

While wandering around the waterfront in Beirut on one occasion, I saw a group of porters paying good money to look at a small peep-show which, judging from the laughter, was not of the most elevating variety. A little shamefacedly, I paid my *metalik* and looked at the exhibition.

I certainly got my money's worth, if side-lights on foreign life are worth anything. Four of the pictures were cover drawings from a popular American weekly magazine, with the full title left on and nothing added. A fifth was a foreign calendar issued by one of the shops of Beirut. It was a very racy entertainment for those barbaric burden-bearers, but there are few American mothers who would not have given such pictures to their five-year-olds.

Throughout northern India there wander Kashmiri musicians, usually with a young boy dressed in girls' clothes to dance to their exotic music. In Rawalpindi the native Christians were holding their Christmas entertainment outdoors on the campus, and a band of these musicians strolled up to watch the games and listen to the recitations and songs, such as a Christmas program produces in every corner of the world.

Their eyes glistened at this ready-made audience and the promise it gave for profit if they could only substitute barbaric music for hymns and sinuous dances for obstacle races; but the missionary tactfully explained that the program was already a long one—the Kashmiri was not familiar with Christmas programs—and that there would be no chance for them to entertain the Sunday-school scholars.

The wistfulness of those poor minstrels, standing outside that gay crowd, with presents being distributed and everybody radiant with the Christmas spirit, and being unable to contribute to the entertainment was a memorable sight. They seemed to feel as badly as a pick-pocket would at not being asked to perform before a millionaire Sunday-school class.

TRAGEDY OF "THE" PICTURE

Out in Beirut, Syria, the day came when I secured THE picture. As soon as the shutter snapped, I knew that I had a wonder. In the dark room the plate surpassed my fondest hopes, and I think I dreamed that night of the wonderful picture which I had put out to dry on the window-sill.

With the coming of daylight I went to look once more at my treasure. The weather at that season was damp and the emulsion was still wet; but the picture was more beautiful in the soft light of early morning than it had been by lamp light. I shaved with a song on my lips. Deborah might have composed the words, if there had been any. Triumph rang from every note.

Then the sun rose over the Lebanon, whose lofty line, punctuated by snow-peaks, faced my window. The quick warmth of the Oriental sun promised to dry the plate quickly after the muggy night. I went back to the window to gloat once more. The dream picture was a black smudge on the limestone ledge. Phoebus had glimpsed the beauty and had melted the emulsion on the plate like the wax on the wings of inordinate Icarus.

15

PASSAGE FROM NUGGOHEEVA TO CANTON, AND DISCOVERY OF SOME NEW ISLANDS

EDMUND FANNING

Edmund Fanning made his fortune in the seal-skin trade with China, but it was his discovery of three South Pacific islands—Washington, Fanning, and Palmyra (collectively known as the Fanning Islands)— in 1798 that earned him the nickname "Pathfinder of the Pacific." Fanning was born in Connecticut in 1769 to a family of eight brothers, all of whom ended up on the ocean, and first took a job as a cabin boy at 14. Here he describes the discovery of Fanning Islands— including a sleepless night that saved the crew from shipwreck but left Fanning reeling and Palmyra shrouded in the mystery that still surrounds it today.

CHAPTER XII: PASSAGE FROM NUGGOHEEVA TO CANTON, AND DISCOVERY OF SOME NEW ISLANDS

June 7th. The trade wind, with which we have been favored for the last few days, has blown a moderate breeze during the same, varying from the E. to the N. N. E. with occasionally, heavy showers of rain. Boobies, man-of-war hawks, small white gulls, fern, or egg-birds, in great numbers, always in company, together with many flying-fish, of a larger size than ordinary; these were a favorite fish with us, and came very opportunely just now, by adding to the variety of our dishes. At 4 A.M. crossed the equator for the second time, being in longitude 154 ° 43 ° west.

June 11th. Had the trade wind light from the E. S. E. with passing clouds; at intervals light showers of rain. At 3 A.M. soon after one of these showers, the seamen at the mast-head on the lookout, gave the cry of "Land ho!" and in reply to the demand of the officer, then in charge, of "where away?" replied, "direct ahead, and close aboard;" the ship under full sail, with steering sails set below and aloft, was at this time going before the wind. The orders for the officers having charge of the deck, while sailing across this extensive ocean, were, in case land, or any dangers should be discovered during the night time, for them not to leave the deck to report the same to myself, but to give their immediate attention to the helm and the sails, have all hands called, while at the same time by stamping on the deck, over my head, I should be awaked. In the present instance, these directions had been promptly complied with, by the officer then in charge, so that in a few seconds I reached the deck, just at the moment that the lookout again called out, "breakers close aboard;" the helm was then a lee, at port, and the ship coming fast to the wind on her starboard tacks, the studding sails were coming in, and yards bracing up, when stepping to the larboard rail, the land was seen stretching along in a direction seemingly about north and south, with the surf in the western board, as a rain shower passed over, and its clearing up enabled us to see it, appearing to be one continued sheet of white foam along the horizon, breaking high, with a tremendous noise, on the coral reef that bound the coast, and about one mile distant from the ship, as seen from the deck. After trimming every sail upon the wind, the ship looked about two points of the land, moving to the north-east at the rate of two and a half miles per hour, a heavy swell or sea from the eastward heaving her to the leeward, as she ranged along the land.

After an hour passed in great anxiety, a point or cape was discovered off the fore-beam, while as the day began to dawn upon us, it was observed that we had fallen in with the land, about four miles to the south of the North-east Cape, from which we were now gaining an offing to the north, and whence the land tended away to the westward. The ship had not gained over two miles to the northward of this cape, when it became suddenly calm, and by 8 A.M. the leeward swell or sea had hove her much more than a mile along the coast to the westward of this cape.

In this instance, we narrowly escaped shipwreck, as on sounding with the boat, for the purpose of ascertaining if such would probably have been the case, we were led to infer as much from our not being able, with fifty fathoms of line, to obtain bottom at a cable's length from the coral reef which binds the shore; so that had the calm happened only two hours sooner, it would unquestionably have taken place. At 10 A.M. a sea breeze from the north-east sprang up, whereupon we bore away, and sailed along the northern coast to the westward: this island appeared to be one of some extent, and the group to consist of three, nil within sight at the same time, and laying in such position to each other, as in some measure to form a triangle. The north and south islands were each about nine miles in length; the other, the easternmost one, stretching to the northward and southward, and adjacent to the eastern ends of the two first mentioned, was about six miles in length, the whole three forming a most spacious bay with good anchorage and good harbors. At noon, being off the north-west port, we hauled in under easy sail, over a bank which lays off the western end of the islands, where a ship, abreast of a passage into the bay, may anchor under their lee.

On gaining this position we hove to, hoisted out the boat, manned her, and pulled up through the passage. The landing we found perfectly smooth, and effected by resting the bows of the boat on a small sandy beach, at the starboard hand, as we passed into the bay. On the south island, and near by a grove of cocoa-nut trees, whose fruit then lay strewed around, covering the ground from one to three feet deep, and seemed to have ripened and thus fallen for many years past, our boat's crew, having formed themselves in a line from these to the boat, very quickly loaded her from the upper course of those nuts which had fallen last, by passing them briskly from one to another; meanwhile, I employed myself in taking a kind of fish, much like the striped bass. Of these there were great quantities continually crowding against the boat, so that it was an easy matter to spear and take them, without letting the shaft of the grains go out of the hand. After getting upwards of fifty, weighing from five to twelve pounds each, I desisted, supposing that this number would be fall as many as we could consume on board ship before they should spoil: when cooked, they were found to be very finely flavored, and good eating. The sharks here are very numerous, and while the boat was on her passage into the bay, before she entered the pass they became so exceedingly ravenous around her, and so voracious withal, as frequently to dart at, and seize upon her rudder and the oars, leaving thereon many marks of their sharp teeth and powerful jaws; but so soon as she left the pass and entered within the bay, they deserted her, their stations being instantly occupied by multitudes of fish, less rapacious, yet infinitely more valuable. When the boat was loaded, accompanied by an officer, the steward going along, we took a stroll into the interior for a few minutes, among the upland grass and groves of various kinds of trees, without being able to discover any of the valuable bread-fruit tree. At the barren spots, the birds, boobies, knoddies, and the like, were quietly setting on their nests, so fearless and gentle, as to be easily taken by the hand; yet in self defense, sometimes pecking sufficiently hard to draw blood. Amongst the birds, was one species about the size of our robbin; with a breast of scarlet colored feathers, the under portion of the body being finished off with bright red, the neck of a golden color, back a lively green, with a yellow beak, except the very points, which were of a light dun color, the wings and tail being both of a jet black, and the last tipped off with white: it was a most beautiful and lovely bird, with its brilliant and richly variegated plumage. We were much chagrined, while observing these, to see a man-of-war hawk flying by with one in his mouth, apparently having just caught it. At 6 P.M. returned to the ship, with the result of our afternoon's operations.

There were no signs nor vestige of habitation discovered by us during our perambulations, from which we could infer that mortal ever had placed his foot upon these shores, previous to the date of our arrival; still Captain Donald Mackay, in a vessel under the agency of the author, a few years after their discovery, being at anchor some weeks at Fanning's Island, while procuring a cargo of beach la mer, turtle shell, &c. for the China market, reported on his return home, that during this stay he frequently walked into the interior, and in one of these walks had come across some heaps of stones, which, to all appearance, from their order and regularity, were thus placed by the hands of men, although from the coat or crust of weather moss with which they were covered, it must have been at some very remote date. Being prompted by curiosity, and a desire for further information upon this subject, he caused one of these piles to be removed, and found it to contain, a foot or two under the surface of the ground, a stone case, filled with ashes, fragments of human bones, stone, shell, and bone tools, various ornaments, spear and arrow heads of bone and stone, &c.

These islands are situated in latitude 3° 51' 30" north, longitude 159° 12' 30" west, and as before stated, are three in number, exclusive of the islets. We gave them the name of Fanning's Islands, and by this they have been recorded, and remain on the charts in use. There is sufficient depth of water through the passage for any merchant ship to pass in, and on the inner or bay side is smooth and convenient anchoring, which, together with the abundance of wood and water, the tropical fruits, best of fresh fish, and excellent turtle, here to be obtained, make this a very desirable place, for the refitting of a ship, and refreshing a crew. The soil, generally speaking, as it appeared throughout the interior, was rich and luxuriant. The anchoring, on the bank off the western ends, and under the lee of the islands, is from twenty to thirty fathoms, over a sandy bottom: this, as the trade winds here prevail, will be found to be a smooth and easy roadstead; in the ebb and flow of the tide, the current runs in and out of this bay.

Having recruited our stock of fire wood, as well as a goodly quantity of cocoa-nuts, at 7 P.M. we weighed anchor, and sailed from Fanning's Islands, then steered under a moderate trade breeze, to the N. W. by W. the weather fair and pleasant, attended by a smooth swell of the sea from the eastward.

A little before noon, June 12th, the seaman at the mast-head again called out, "Land ho!" adding, that the same was half a point off the lee-bow. At meridian, this newly discovered island bore west by north four leagues distance. This, was of a much greater elevation than Fanning's Island, and was, moreover, covered with plants or grass, presenting to our eyes a beautiful, green, and flourishing appearance. With the unanimous approbation of every individual on board, both officers and seamen, and with feelings of pride for our country, we named this, Washington Island, after President Washington, the father of his country.

Having but recently obtained a bounteous supply of refreshments, there was no necessity for our making a landing here, although the trees and green foliage, among which we plainly saw the tall cocoa-nut tree, presented a very strong inducement for us so to do, but passed it to the south, we then steering to the west. At 2 P.M. our ship was abreast of the island, having it between one and two miles distant, off the starboard beam. The waters now, were filled with a vast many fish of different kinds: of these we caught with the grains several excellent well-fed fellows, much resembling the king fish taken in the West India seas.

There can be no doubt but that at this island a vessel might obtain an abundant supply of excellent refreshments for her crew. As at Fanning's Islands, so here, we could perceive no tokens of its being at all inhabited. Washington Island is in latitude 4° 45' north, longitude 160° 8' west, and lies in a N. W. by W. direction from Fanning's Island, at a distance of some twenty-seven leagues. As we passed it, we discovered a coral or sand bank off its western side, extending a mile and a half from the shore, where it appeared a ship might come to anchor: from the south-west point, a coral reef, on which the sea breaks, puts out into the sea about a quarter of a mile, we left this beautiful island under a whole sail breeze, and at 6 P.M. it bore E. S. E. at a distance of about six leagues. From the many flocks of birds hovering over and around us at this time, particularly a small dark brown bird, with a white crown, which had not before been seen so far from the land, we were inclined to think that still more land existed in our vicinity; yet were not able to discover any other, notwithstanding we had remarkably fine weather, and kept constantly a sharp lookout aloft for the purpose.

June 14th. Although somewhat foggy around the horizon, yet we had the weather quite pleasant, with a brisk trade breeze, nor has there been any necessity, while sailing over or across the western part of this extensive Pacific ocean, to lay the ship by a single night, through fear of running her upon any hidden danger, the weather having been remarkably fine all the time, with moderate trade winds, ever keeping a good look-out, and believing ourselves perfectly secure from this precaution; as usual attended by a great many of the feathered race, our constant companions. In this manner prosecuting our voyage, it seemed more like a sailing excursion, or party of pleasure, at least this portion of it, than what it in fact was.

The following occurrence, although bordering upon, and seemingly partaking of the miraculous, did nevertheless, actually take place. At nine o'clock in the evening, my customary hour for retiring, I had as usual repaired to my berth, enjoying perfect good health, but between the hours of nine and ten found myself, without being sensible of any movement or exertion in getting there, on the upper steps of the companion-way. I suddenly awoke, and after exchanging a few words with the commanding officer, who was walking the deck, returned to my berth, thinking how strange it was, for I never before had walked in my sleep. Again I was occupying the same position to the great surprise of the officer (not more so than to myself), after having slept some twenty minutes or the like: here, upon observing the glittering stars overhead, and feeling the night air, I was preparing to return to the cabin, after answering in the affirmative his inquiry whether Captain Fanning was well; why, or what it was, that had thus brought me twice to the companion way, I was quite unable to tell, but lest there should be any portion of vigilance unobserved by those then in charge, I inquired how far he was able to see. around the ship; he replied, that although a little hazy, he thought he could distinctly see land or danger a mile or two, adding, that the lookout was regularly relieved every half hour, in reply to my question if such was the case. There was something very singular in all this, and with a strange sensation upon my mind, after what had passed, I again returned to my berth. What was my astonishment on finding myself the third time in the same place! yet with this addition: I had now, without being aware of it, put on my outer garments, and hat; it was then I conceived some danger was nigh at hand, and determined me upon laying the ship to for the night; she was at this time under full sail, going at the rate of five or six miles per hour; all her light sails were accordingly taken in, the topsails were single reefed, and the ship brought to forthwith on a wind: leaving directions with the officer in charge to tack every hour, and the same to be passed to the officer who should relieve him at twelve o'clock, so that by these means we might maintain our present station as near as possible until morning; I added a request that he would call me at day light, since himself would then be on the watch. He was surprised, and looking at me in astonishment, appeared half to hesitate whether to obey, in all probability supposing me to be out of my mind. I observed to him, however, that I was perfectly well, and possessed of my right senses, but that something, what it was I could not tell, required that these precautionary measures should be studiously observed. After leaving these necessary directions, a few minutes before eleven I once more retired, and remained undisturbed, enjoying a sound sleep, until called at day light by the officer. He reported the weather then to be, as it had been during the night, much the same as the evening previous, with a fine trade wind from E. N. E. Giving him directions to keep the ship off her course and make all sail, after attending to some little duties, I followed to the deck just as the topmost rays of the sun came peering above a clear eastern horizon.

The officers and watch were busily engaged in the washing of decks, and attending to those various duties which claim attention at this portion of the twenty-four hours. All was activity and bustle, except with the helmsman: even the man on the lookout was for a moment called from his especial charge, and was then engaged in reeving and sending down on deck the steering sail haulyards. This induced me to walk, after taking a few turns back and forth on the weather side of the quarter-deck, over to the lee quarter, not expecting, however, to make any discovery, but solely to take a look ahead; in a moment the whole truth flashed before my eyes, as I caught sight of breakers, mast high, directly ahead, and towards which our ship was fast sailing.

Instantly the helm was put a lee, the yards all braced up, and sails trimmed by the wind, as the man aloft, in a stentorian voice, called out, "Breakers! breakers ahead!" This was a sufficient response to the inquiring look of the officer, as perceiving the manoeuvre, without being aware of the cause, he had gazed upon me to find if or no I was crazed; now, however, casting a look at the foaming breakers, his face, from a flush of red, had assumed a death-like paleness. Still no man spake: all was silence, except the needed orders as promptly executed, every man moved, and every operation was performed in the manner, and with the precision that necessarily attends the conduct of an orderly and correct crew.

The ship was now sailing on the wind, and the roaring of the herculean breakers under her lee, at a short mile's distance, was distinctly heard, as the officer to whom the events of the past night were familiar, came aft to me, and with the voice and look of a man deeply impressed with some solemn convictions, said, "Surely, sir. Providence has a care over us, and has kindly directed us again in the road of safety. I cannot speak my feelings, for it seems to me, after what has passed during the night and now also appears before my eyes, as if I had just awaked in another world. "Why, sir," continued he, "half an hour's farther run from where we lay by in the night, would have cast us on that fatal spot, where we must all certainly have been lost. If we have, because of the morning base around the horizon, got so near this appalling danger in broad daylight, what, sir, but the hand of Providence, has kept us clear of it through the night." With him I perfectly agreed, and answered, that we should now be truly thankful to that Heavenly and protecting Being. But urgent and imperative calls for attention to our perilous situation, forbade at present any farther remarks; the officer forth-with took the glass, and went aloft for the purpose of ascertaining whether the ship was nearest to the north or south end of the reef, as also whether we were likely to weather and clear it on this tack.

I freely confess, that this premonition, so unusual, and the transactions therewith connected, are deeply impressed upon my mind, as an evidence of the Divine superintendence, and there, ever will remain so firmly imprinted,—how could they otherwise be?—as never to be erased. All hands, by this time made acquainted with the discovery, and the danger they had so narrowly escaped, were gathered on deck; gazing upon the breakers with serious yet thoughtful countenances. We were so fortunate as to weather the breakers on our stretch to the north, and had a fair view and overlook of them from aloft. It was a coral reef or shoal, in the form of a crescent, about six leagues in extent from north to south; under its lee, and within the compass of the crescent, there appeared to be white and shoal water. We did not discover a foot of ground, rock, or sand, above water, where a boat might have been hauled up; of course had our ship run on it in the night, there can be no question but we should all have perished.

16

SOME WONDERFUL SIGHTS IN THE ANDEAN HIGHLANDS

HARRIET CHALMERS ADAMS

Harriet Chalmers Adams's love affair with South America began in 1904 when she and her husband Franklin set off for a nearly 3-year trip across the continent, eventually covering more than 40,000 miles via boat, train, and horseback. This trip would lead to the first of twenty-one bylines in National Geographic *and launch a career in journalism that would, among other things, see her retrace the routes of Spanish colonialism and serve as the first female correspondent to visit the frontline trenches of World War I. In a 1912* New York Times *profile, she reflected on her still burgeoning career, saying, "I managed on all my trips to get along well; and I've wondered why men have so absolutely monopolized the field of exploration. Why did women never go to the Arctic, try for one pole or the other, or invade Africa, Thibet, or some unknown wildernesses? I've never found my sex a hinderment; never faced a difficulty which a woman, as well as a man, could never* surmount; never felt a fear of danger; never lacked courage to protect myself."

SOME WONDERFUL SIGHTS IN THE ANDEAN HIGHLANDS

AS the train steamed away, leaving us in the little Andean village of thatched mud huts, I pinched myself to make sure I was awake. We were in Tiahuanaco, an Indian hamlet, situated on that bleak upland plain of Bolivia which the traveler must cross in each La Paz, the capital. From Lake Titicaca we had journeyed in a modern railway coach, but with the departure of the train seemed to have dropped back five hundred years. "No trace here of Spanish invasion," I said; but just then we came upon a street shrine and a stone cross, and were reminded that these high-land Indians are no longer sun-worshipers.

Passing through the village, we cached the ruins of Tiahuanaco, pre-Incasic "beyond the reach of history and tradition" even in those clays when the ancient Inca Fortress of Sacsahuaman was erected on a hill overlooking Cuzco. These ruins mark the site of the oldest city in the New World, and from under the drifting sand of centuries a civilization still more remote than that of Tiahuanaco may yet be brought to light on the Andean plateau.

Tiahuanaco is in the very heart of the region known as the Tibet of the Western World. It lies on a plain which is over twelve thousand feet above the level of the sea, a plain from which rises the lofty *Cordillera*, the third and great range of the Andes. Journeying eastward from Lake Titicaca, we crossed an open, unprotected country, wind-swept, barren. The thatched villages and adobe-walled corrals looked as dreary and colorless as the desolate *Puna* itself. Yet here, archaeologists tell us, flourished the most advanced of the ancient American civilizations.

In the Tiahuanaco of today beautifully cut stones brought from the nearby ruins form a part of the church built by the early Spaniards. To neighboring villages and even as far as to La Paz, the capital, these great stones were carried to be used as foundations of churches erected in the faith of the conquerors.

The ruins lie on a level part of the plain where the soil is firm and dry. They consist of rows of stones, sections of foundations, carved doorways, portions of stairways, vast masses of rock, but partially hewn. No mortar was used in the construction, yet these stones were so skillfully cut and fitted that the foundations have outlived the centuries. They are of red sandstone, slate-colored trachyte, and dark basalt transported from quarries many miles away. Later, in the ancient Peruvian fortresses, we saw wonderfully cut and massive stones, but none with the carved ornamentation found here.

The most remarkable monument is the monolithic gateway which, although broken at the time of our visit three years ago, was still standing. A friend who visited the ruins last year tells me that the Mighty is now fallen. As we saw it, a doorway about four and a half feet high and two and a half feet wide was cut out of a great block of stone over seven feet high, thirteen feet wide, and eighteen inches thick. Above the doorway, four rows of carving, a central figure sculptured in high relief. It is claimed by students of antiquity that no better piece of stone-cutting exists. The figures in the rows of carving have human bodies, feet, and hands, but are winged, and some have the heads of condors; others, with human heads, wear crowns and carry scepters. All of these smaller figures seem to be kneeling in worship of the large raised figure, which also is crowned and sceptered, and decorated with the heads of condors and tiger, symbolic of strength and power.

As I gazed on this quaint doorway, unique on this continent, a picture came to me of the metropolis which it once raced. The massive wall of which it formed a part rose before me, a wall surrounding a populous city, contemporaneous with the ancient capitals of Egypt and the East. I did not feel as confident of our triumphant modern civilization as I stood in the shadow of this hoary gateway. "History repeats itself," the thought came to me; "civilizations rise and fall." Which of the mighty edifices now standing in America will testify to our nation's greatness in the centuries to come?

I still felt that we were linked with the past as we walked back to the village of Tiahuanaco. In fact, throughout the Andean highlands the traveler feels transported to centuries gone by. The coast cities of Peru are progressing rapidly; in Lima one can now live quite as comfortably as in New York. In the uplands, however, wander a bit off the beaten path and there are only the village church towers to remind one of the years that have passed since Pizarro sailed south from Panama. The mountaineers of Peru are still, in greater part, full-blooded *Quichuas*, descendants of the Inca tribes. After crossing Lake Titicaca, we found the *Aymarás*, descendants of a people conquered by the Incas shortly before the coming of the Spaniards.

In the Andean country the head-dress changes with the locality. In Tiahuanaco the belles exhibit a remarkable head-gear, reminding me of that worn by pictured, top-heavy, ill-fated British queens. The hat consists of a stiff, coffin-shaped piece of pasteboard covered with red or blue cloth and tinsel; hung around this is a deep valance as a protection from sun and wind.

The men here are not to be outdone, and on feast days come forth in head covering that would put even this season's "Merry Widows" to shame. Multi-colored macaw feathers, colored cloth, and tinsel combine to dazzle the beholder, and as the revelers march down the village street, blowing on reed pipes and beating drums, they are accompanied by a score of half-naked children and a few dozen barking dogs. The children are always dirt-covered, the dogs always lean and savage, and the players always imbibe too freely of *chicha*, ending the day in a drunken carouse. I always worried about the hats, fearing they wouldn't be in good condition for the next feast day.

It is bitterly cold in Tiahuanaco, but the natives, both men and women, are scantily clad, and go bare-legged, believe in keeping the head warm, however, and tie bands of cloth, woven from llama wool, over their hair underneath; their hats. They sleep on the ground in unfurnished huts, and live principally on *chuño*, the frozen potato, and *cholona*, dried goat or mutton. As we returned to Lake Titicaca, we looked out on the highway which parallels the railroad, and saw Aymarás driving their llama trains and laden burros. In the fields were the shepherds, often mere lads, playing on reed pipes as they watched their flocks of sheep, goats, or alpacas. Glorifying the dreary landscape, the *Cordillera de los Andes* towered to the northward, the jagged peaks of Illampu rising to twenty-three thousand feet above the sea.

THE LAKE OF THE CLOUDS

Lake Titicaca is in many respects the most extraordinary body of water in the world. It is the highest lake on earth which is steam navigated, and the grandeur of the mountains which surround it and the romantic legends which encircle it combine to make this Lake of the Clouds most interesting to the traveler. In shape it is long and irregular; its extreme length is one hundred and twenty miles; its width sixty miles, and its elevation twelve thousand five hundred feet above the sea. The lake is of great depth and never freezes over, although ice forms in places near the shore where the water is shallow.

In color it is dark blue, shimmering in the sunlight, and its brown islands look like a topaz necklace on a sapphire-colored gown. Titicaca is a border lake between Peru and Bolivia, and it is on the Bolivian shore that the Andes sweep in a crescent across the horizon. Illampu, or Sorata, is the most majestic of the peaks, but in crossing the lake we saw an uninterrupted chain of mighty *nevados* stretching from Illampu to the graceful Illimani, the beautiful White Lady which overlooks the picturesque city of La Paz.

Of the eight large islands in the lake, Titicaca and Coati are the most historic. To the ancient Peruvians they were sacred islands in the worship of the sun and the moon. To Titicaca, Island of the Sun, the Peruvians traced their origin – the same Adam and Eve story which we find the world over. From Titicaca the first Inca and his wife – so runs the legend – started forth to the northwest to found Cuzco, Sacred City of the Sun. There are ruins on a number of the islands, and tombs of Inca chiefs near by on the mainland. The hill sides bordering the lake are barren, except for a few cultivated patches, but reeds and lake-weed form an emerald fringe around the shore. It is a pretty sight to see the cattle wading into water to feed on the lake-weed, their principal food at a certain season of the year. The reeds are of great value the natives, since out of them the *balsas* or lake boats are woven.

The rush balsa is the most picturesque feature of the landscape. The sail as well as the boat is built of woven reeds and the balsa can be used for six months, when it becomes water-soaked, and must be abandoned. Sailing in this queer little craft proved an exciting pastime. The boat is simply a big basket made of bundles of grass tied together and shaped a little like a canoe. One is in danger of becoming very wet and very seasick, I decided that the boats are most attractive *when seen from the shore*. The Titicaca Indians wear homespun, as in years long past, and as I watched a fleet of balsas sailing out to the fishing grounds I realized that in the people, crafts, and lake itself there is little change since prehistoric days.

On our return to Peru from Bolivia we boarded a small steamer at Guaqui and were a day crossing the lake to Puno. In the crossing to Bolivia we had been passengers on the *Cuyo*, a fairly comfortable little vessel, but on the return trip embarked on the *Yavari*, which certainly was built "when Columbus was a little boy." It was a rough and disagreeable voyage, and a number of passengers suffered from seasickness and from soroche. This mountain illness affects people differently. Some suffer from pain in the head, others from nausea, and the most dangerous form is heart failure. We escaped the trouble altogether, probably because we ascended to high altitudes gradually, first remaining a week at seven thousand feet, then stopping at twelve thousand, and finally reaching nineteen thousand two hundred feet without difficulty.

From Lake Titicaca we journeyed by rail to Sicuani, then the terminus of the road which is now well on to Cuzco; but when I visit Peru again, I shall journey once more by coach beyond Sicuani. By this method one can better study the life of the natives in this most romantic part of the Andean country. In a recent story I told of our journey over the old Inca highway, and in the future will write of life in Cuzco, the ancient Mecca of the New World.

"THE SWEETEST VALLEY IN PERU"

While in Cuzco we decided to make a journey to the Valley of Yucay, to visit the old fortresses of Ollantaytambo and Pisac. This is one of my most delightful memories of Andean travel. It was in the Valley of Yucay, "the sweetest valley in Peru," that the Incas are supposed to have built their summer palaces. We made this journey in the saddle, with only our blankets and saddle-bags, unhampered by guide or cargo mule. Starting out very early one June morning, we rode over the rocky streets of Cuzco, the city of all others in the Americas rich in its legends and history, its charming situation, and unpleasant odors. The road led up to a hilltop where we had a comprehensive view of the red-roofed town, with its many church towers and ancient plazas, overshadowed by the Fortress of Sacsahuaman, which looks down on the *bolsone*, the mountain valley, in which Cuzco lies. Facing in the opposite direction, we saw our trail leading to the Cordillera, the same snowy chain we had known as the Bolivian Andes. Now we were many miles to the north.

All day we traveled over the high plateau, at times on a trail, again over a portion which still remains of the Inca highway, formerly connecting Cuzco with Quito. The Inca road was formed of rough stones set into the ground, bordered by low stone walls, through which passages were cut at intervals to carry off the water. As between Sicuani and Cuzco, we met many pilgrims and llama trains, and now there were burros heavily laden with produce from the Valley of Yucay and from the more tropical valleys beyond. We had food in our saddle-bags, and went without water, observing that the passing brooks serve for all village household purposes. In the late afternoon we reached Chinchero where there are Inca ruins near a few dilapidated huts and an old Spanish chapel. Riding on, we faced the Andes, and were wondering where Yucay could be hidden, when we suddenly reached the edge of the plateau and saw the canyon-like valley four thousand feet below.

One who has stood on the heights overlooking the Yosemite Valley, in California, can form a mental picture Yucay as seen from this elevated table land. Through the valley flows the River Yucay, which we had known above Cuzco as the Vilcanota, and which, father on, as it flows to the king of river, is called the Ucayali. It is the longest formative branch of the Amazon. As in the Yosemite Valley, fertile banks mark the shores of the river, but instead of waterfalls the steep mountain walls of Yucay are covered in many places with graceful terraces of the ancients. Broad at the base, narrowing as they rise, the terraces are one thousand feet in height. So the Inca's subjects gained area for agriculture, irrigating by means of aqueducts which started at the verge of the snows.

Although the floor of the valley is elevated eight thousand feet above the sea, it is so sheltered that the climate is mild and delightful. The coast, sierras, and highlands of Peru are without rain or natural verdure. It is as though Nature gave her all to the forest-covered eastern slope of the Andes. It is only when rivers break through the mountain wall and cross the deserts that the barren country to the west of the Cordillea blooms. To travelers long on the bleak *Puna* the Valley of Yucay seems an enchanted vale. As we descended from the heights of Chinchero by the steep, narrow, winding trail the wonderful scenery put me into an exalted mood. I was a Quichua princess carried by my willing slaves down to the beautiful summer palace of my father, the Inca; only just then my tiredhorse stumbled, and I came back to earth a dusty little Andean traveler longing for any moth-eatcn *posada* where I could rest my weary head.

We found the *posada* in the village of Urubamba every other name ends in "bamba" or "tambo" in the Quichua country and it broke all records for uncleanliness. It wasn't an expensive resort, however; we paid something like seventy cents for our bed, a day's board, and fodder for our animals. On the trails many of the natives speak only the Quichua tongue, but in Urubamba Spanish is spoken. There are a number of merchants in the village who buy the produce as it comes up from the Lower Yucay Valley and the tropical Valley of Santa Ana, sending it on to Cuzco and to other parts of the highlands. When the tired little burros jogged into town, I was always interested in their cargo. They brought coffee beans, cacao, coco-coca leaves, and tropical fruits. We saw few llamas in Yucay; the little mountain cousins of the camel are better suited to the highlands.

From Urubamba we rode down the valley over a trail which follows the winding river, a charming trail bordered by fragrant yellow Spanish broom and many varieties of the cactus plant, shaded by giant willows and pepper trees in ruddy blossom. Passing through peaceful villages, we came upon curving terraces and moss-hung ruins, but saw no remains of the wonderful summer palaces. I irreverently suggested that perhaps the

Inca kings also yearned at times for "the simple life," and, leaving scepters and *llautus* behind, "camped out" in the restful Valley of Yucay.

Without palaces the ancients could exist, but not without fortresses, especially in this frontier country near the Andean passes leading to the vast forest which, in other days as now, was inhabited by savage tribes. A day's journey from Urubamba is the Fortress of Ollantaytambo, which guards the lower entrance of Yucay. A pretty legend is attached to the old place. Ollantay, a brave chieftain, was in love with the ruler's daughter, Cusi Coyllur, the Joyful Star. Ollantay was not of royal blood, and, being denied his lady love, made war against the Inca. He is said to have built this fortress, which he held for many years. The story ends in the good old way. At the death of the king the lovers were united, and lived happily forever after. In truth, the fort was built to safeguard the Inca's domain against the wild tribes of the Montaña.

Ollantaytambo was erected on a spur of a mountain at the meeting place of the Yucay and Patacancha valleys. The outer walls of the fortress zigzag up the hillside, and on the summit are the remains of cyclopean walls, beautifully hewn doorways, niched corridors, and great slabs of porphyry supporting a terrace. There are six of these giant slabs in an upright position, and half way up the mountain side others weighing many tons, which fell by the wayside. These abandoned slabs are called "The Tired Stones."

With all other travelers who have seen the Inca fortifications, I have never ceased to marvel at these enormous rocks carried to great mountain heights from far-away quarries. I cannot content myself with the explanation given by a Yankee whom we met at a *posada* in Sicuani. Four of us, speaking English, brought up the old question, "How were the mighty stones carried great distances, to great heights?" and "Uncle Si" slapped his hand on his knee, hitched up his trousers, spat, and declared, "They done it with a yerb." Artificial stone mixed on the spot with a magic herb, I suppose he meant. Well, he was a wise old Yank! He was traveling around South America trying to sell a patent green paint to cover blackboards a noble endeavor to save the eyesight of the little Latin Americans.

There is no posada in the village of Ollantaytambo. The Gobernador, chief magistrate, took us in, but he had no extra beds in his house, and we were obliged to sleep on the dining-room table. At the witching hour of three in the morning we were awakened by the crowing of roosters, and found that the pet fighting cocks of the family were tied to the table legs – the Peruvian alarm clock! In the early dawn we were on our way up the valley, and, passing Urubamba, rode on toward Pisac, the fortress which guards another mountain pass.

Before visiting Peru I had been impressed, in reading, with the monumental greatness of the Incas, but in the Upper Yucay Valley saw evidences of their agricultural and engineering skill as well. There are many terraces, aqueducts, well-planned fields, and the river has been straightened for miles from its serpentine course.

A number of the bridges spanning the river are of *mimbres*—woven branches fastened to cables with thongs of hide or vines. This makes a very picturesque bridge, but I have crossed rivers on safer ones. The mimbres, which we nicknamed "monkey bridges," are often lopsided and sway with the breeze. The question with us was whether to risk our lives in crossing the bridges or in fording the river.

Pisac is the most imposing of the fortresses. It is built on a mountain top, and looks down on the meeting of the Yucay and a lesser canyon which leads to the Paucartambo region, across the Andes. It is the most complete of the fortifications, has the most commanding situation, and contains a fairly well preserved temple built to hold the famous Inti-huatani, the astronomical stone. In the Quichua language, "Inti-huatana" means "where the sun's rays are gathered." Within the fortress are many agricultural terraces and aqueducts, an evidence that the garrison was not dependent on the valley below, but self-supporting in days of siege. Looking across the canyon we saw ancient tombs built high in the rocks, seeming accessible only to birds. In a quarry within the fort I found an instrument, a wedge of *chumpe*, the Peruvian bronze, left there by a Quichua workman many centuries ago. Comparatively few students or relic hunters visit Pisac, and we found a number of fine old *chica* jars in village. From Pisac we crossed Andes to the Paucartambo country, but "that's quite another story." Returning to the Yucay Valley some weeks later we reached Cuzco by a new trail.

Those were long days in the saddle with little food and less water. We knew the river water to be impure, as the sewage of Cuzco flows into it, and the brooks are also contaminated as they pass through the villages. At night we slept on the ground, wrapped in our blankets, at times finding shelter in a ruined temple, as there are many lesser ruins throughout the Valley of Yucay. We met no travelers save the highland Indians, and picked up a few words of their tongue. I felt that we had left civilization far behind. Even the Spanish colonial days faded. We were in the old Peru.

To know a country and a people, one must leave the highway and live near to Nature. We traveled much in the saddle on this great elevated plateau—over a thousand miles on a single journey—and gradually my standpoint changed. I started as an outsider, having little sympathy for the Quichuas and Aymarás, little understanding of the history and environment which has made them the sullen, lifeless folk they are. In time I grew, through study and observation, but more through sharing the life, half-Andean myself, and find, in looking back over years of travel in South America – years in which we visited every country – that my greatest heart interest lies in the highlands of Peru and Bolivia.

17

DOG-DRIVING

GEORGE KENNAN

George Kennan was barely 20 when he boarded a ship in San Francisco bound for Russia's Kamchatka Peninsula. Having worked as a telegrapher in the Civil War, he had signed on to an expedition to scout a route for an overland telegraph line across Siberia. Although the venture was aborted—an undersea cable was laid beneath the Atlantic first—Kennan's insightful and surprisingly funny account of his 2 years in Siberia captured American interest in the Russian Far East. Upon returning home, he worked as a war correspondent and journalist for the Associated Press *but continued to travel back and forth from Russia to report on the budding revolution—until his harsh criticisms of the Russian prison and exile system led to a ban on returning in 1901. His knowledge of Russia—including the little-known severity of the crushing tsarist rule—and his skill as a writer and orator cut a powerful figure, and, on a January night in 1888, he was one of thirty-three men, and the only journalist, to found the National Geographic Society. Here he tries his hand at dog sledding in Siberia.*

CHAPTER XXII: DOG-DRIVING

WE left Meekina early, November 23rd, and started out upon another great snowy plain, where there was no vegetation whatever except a little wiry grass and a few meagre patches of trailing-pine.

Ever since leaving Lesnoi I had been studying attentively the art, or science, whichever it be, of dog-driving, with the fixed but unexpressed resolution that at some future time, when everything should be propitious, I would assume the control of my own team, and astonish Dodd and the natives with a display of my skill as a "kiour."

I had found by some experience that these unlettered Koraks estimated a man, not so much by what he knew which they did not, as by what he knew concerning their own special and peculiar pursuits; and I determined to demonstrate, even to their darkened understandings, that the knowledge of civilization was universal in its application, and that the white man, notwithstanding his disadvantage in color, could drive dogs better by intuition than they could by the aggregated wisdom of centuries; that in fact he could, if necessary, "evolve the principles of dog-driving out of the depths of his moral consciousness." I must confess, however, that I was not a thorough convert to my own ideas; and I did not disdain therefore to avail myself of the results of native experience, as far as they coincided with my own convictions, as to the nature of the true and beautiful in dog-driving. I had watched every motion of my Korak driver; had learned theoretically the manner of thrusting the spiked stick between the-uprights of the runners into the snow, to act as a brake; had committed to memory and practiced assiduously the guttural monosyllables which meant, in dog-language, "right" and "left," as well as many others which meant something else, but which I had heard addressed to dogs; and I laid the flattering unction to my soul that I could drive as well as a Korak, *if* not better. To my inexperienced eye it was as easy as losing money in California mining stocks. On this day, therefore, as the road was good and the weather propitious, I determined to put my ideas, original as well as acquired, to the test of practice. I accordingly motioned my Korak driver to take a back seat and deliver up to me the insignia of office. I observed in the expression of his lips, as he handed me the spiked stick, a sort of latent smile of ridicule, which indicated a very low estimate of my dog-driving abilities; but I treated it as knowledge should always treat the sneers of ignorance—with silent contempt; and seating myself firmly astride the sledge back of the arch, I shouted to the dogs, "Noo! Pashol!" My voice failed to produce the startling effect that I had anticipated. The leader—a grim, bluff Nestor of a dog—glanced carelessly over his shoulder and very perceptibly slackened his pace. This sudden and marked contempt for my authority on the part of the dogs did more than all the sneers of the Koraks to shake my confidence in my own skill. But my resources were not yet exhausted, and I hurled monosyllable, dissyllable, and polysyllable at their devoted heads, shouted "Akh! Te shelma! Proclataya takaya! Smatree! Ya tibi dam!" but all in vain; the dogs were evidently insensible to rhetorical fireworks of this description, and manifested their indifference by a still slower gait. As I poured out upon them the last vial of my verbal wrath, Dodd, who understood the language that I was so recklessly using, drove slowly up, and remarked carelessly, "You swear pretty well for a beginner." Had the ground opened beneath me I should have been less astonished. "Swear! I swear! You don't mean to say that I've been swearing?"—"Certainly you have, like a pirate." I dropped my spiked stick in dismay. Were these the principles of dog-driving which I had evolved out of the depths of my *moral* consciousness? They seemed rather to have come from the depths of my *immoral unconsciousness*. "Why, you reckless reprobate!" I exclaimed impressively, "didn't you teach me those very words yourself?"—"Certainly I did," was the unabashed reply; "but you didn't ask me what they meant; you asked how to pronounce them correctly, and I told you. I didn't know but that you were making researches in comparative philology—trying to prove the unity of the human race by identity of oaths, or by a comparison of profanity to demonstrate that the Digger Indians are legitimately descended from the Chinese. You know that your head (which is a pretty good one in other respects) always *was* full of such nonsense."—"Dodd," I observed, with a solemnity which I intended should awaken repentance in his hardened sensibilities, "I have been betrayed unwittingly into the commission of sin; and as a little more or less won't materially alter my guilt, I've as good a notion as ever I had to give you the benefit of some of your profane instruction." Dodd laughed derisively and drove on. This little episode considerable dampened my enthusiasm, and made me very cautious in my use of foreign language. I feared the existence of terrific imprecations in the most common dog-phrases, and suspected lurking profanity even in the monosyllabic "Khta" and "Hoogh," which I had been taught to believe meant "right" and "left." The dogs, quick to observe any lack of attention on the part of their driver, now took encouragement from my silence and exhibited a doggish propensity to stop and rest, which was in direct contravention of all discipline, and which they would not have dared to do with an experienced driver. Determined to vindicate my authority by more forcible measures, I launched my spiked stick like a harpoon at the leader, intending to have it fall so that I could pick it up as the sledge passed. The dog however dodged it cleverly, and it rolled away ten feet from the road. Just at that moment three or four wild reindeer bounded out from behind a little rise of ground three or four hundred yards away, and galloped across the steppe toward a deep precipitous ravine, through which ran a branch of the Mikina River. The dogs, true to their wolfish instincts, started with fierce, excited howls in pursuit. I made a frantic grasp at my spiked stick as we rushed past, but failed to reach it, and away we went over the tundra toward the ravine, the sledge half the time on one runner, and rebounding from the hard *sastrugi* (sas-troo'-gee) or snow-drifts with a force that suggested speedy dislocation of one's joints. The Korak, with more common sense than I had given him credit for, had rolled off the sledge several seconds before, and a backward glance showed a miscellaneous bundle of arms and legs revolving rapidly over the snow in my wake. I had no time, however, with ruin staring me in the face, to commiserate his misfortune. My energies were all devoted to checking the terrific speed with which we were approaching the ravine. Without the spiked stick I was perfectly helpless, and in a moment we were on the brink. I shut my eyes, clung tightly to the arch, and took the plunge. About half-way down, the descent became suddenly steeper, and the lead-dog swerved to one side, bringing the sledge around like the lash of a whip, overturning it, and shooting me like a huge living meteor through the air into a deep soft drift of snow at the bottom. I must have fallen at least eighteen feet, for I buried myself entirely, with the exception of my lower extremities, which, projecting above the snow, kicked a faint signal for rescue. Encumbered with heavy furs, I extricated myself with difficulty; and as I at last emerged with three pints of snow down my neck, I saw the round, leering face of my late driver grinning at me through the bushes on the edge of the bluff. "Ooma," he hailed. "Well," replied the snowy figure standing waist-high in the drift.—"Amerikanski nyett dobra kaiur, eh?" [American no good driver]. "Nyett sofsem dobra" was the melancholy reply as I waded out. The sledge, I found, had become entangled in the bushes near me, and the dogs were all howling in chorus, nearly wild with the restraint. I was so far satisfied with my experiment that I did not desire to repeat it at present, and made no objections to the Korak's assuming again his old position. I was fully convinced, by the logic of circumstances, that the science of dog-driving demanded more careful and earnest consideration than I had yet given to it; and I resolved to study carefully its elementary principles, as expounded by its Korak professors, before attempting again to put my own ideas upon the subject into practice.

As we came out of the ravine upon the open steppe I saw the rest of our party a mile away, moving rapidly toward the Korak village of Kooeel. We passed Kuil late in the afternoon, and camped for the night in a forest of birch, poplar, and aspen trees, on the banks of the Paren River.

We were now only about seventy miles from Geezhega. On the following night we reached a small log yurt on a branch of the Geezhega River, which had been built there by the government to shelter travellers, and Friday morning, November 25th, about eleven o'clock, we caught sight of the red church-steeple which marked the location of the Russian settlement of Geezhega. No one who has not travelled for three long months through a wilderness like Kamchatka, camped out in storms among desolate mountains, slept for three weeks in the smoky tents, and yet smokier and dirtier *yurts* of the Koraks, and lived altogether like a perfect savage or barbarian—no one who has not experienced this can possibly understand with what joyful hearts we welcomed that red church steeple, and the civilization of which it was the sign. For almost a month we had slept every night on the ground or the snow; had never seen a chair, a table, a bed, or a mirror; had never been undressed night or day; and had washed our faces only three or four times in an equal number of weeks! We were grimy and smoky from climbing up and down Korak chimneys; our hair was long and matted around our ears; the skin had peeled from our noses and cheek-bones where it had been frozen; our cloth coats and trousers were grey with reindeer hairs from our fur "koohlánkas;" and we presented, generally, as wild and neglected an appearance as men could present, and still retain any lingering traces of better days. We had no time or inclination, however, to "fix up;" our dogs dashed at a mad gallop into the village with a great outcry, which awakened a responsive chorus of howls from two or three hundred other canine throats; our drivers shouted "Khta! khta! hoog! hoog!" and raised clouds of snow with their spiked sticks as we rushed through the streets, and the whole population came running to their doors to ascertain the cause of the infernal tumult. One after another our fifteen sledges went careering through the village, and finally drew up before a large, comfortable house, with double glass windows, where arrangements had been made, Kerrillof said, for our reception. Hardly had we entered a large, neatly swept and scrubbed room, and thrown off our heavy frosty furs, than the door again opened, and in rushed a little impetuous, quick-motioned man, with a heavy auburn moustache, and light hair cut short all over his head, dressed in neat broadcloth coat and trousers and a spotless linen shirt, with seal rings on his fingers, a plain gold chain at his vest button, and a cane. We recognized him at once as the 'Ispravnik," or Russian governor. Dodd and I made a sudden attempt to escape from the room, but we were too late, and saluting our visitor with "zdrastvuitia," [Footnote: "Good health," or "Be in health," the Russian greeting.] we sat down awkwardly enough on our chairs, rolled our smoky hands up in our scarlet and yellow cotton handkerchiefs, and, with a vivid consciousness of our dirty faces and generally disreputable appearance, tried to look self-possessed, and to assume the dignity which befitted officers of the great Russian-American Telegraph Expedition! It was a pitiable failure. We could not succeed in looking like anything but Wandering Koraks in reduced circumstances. The Ispravnik, however, did not seem to notice anything unusual in our appearance, but rattled away with an incessant fire of quick, nervous questions, such as "When did you leave Petropavlovsk? Are you just from America? I sent a Cossack. Did you meet him? How did you cross the tundras; with the Koraks? Akh! those proclatye Koraks! Any news from St. Petersburg? You must come over and dine with me. How long will you stay in town? You can take a bath now before dinner. Ay! lòodee! [very loud and peremptory]. Go and tell my Ivan to heat up the bath quick! Akh Chort yeekh! vazmee!" and the restless little man finally stopped from sheer exhaustion, and began pacing nervously across the room, while the Major related our adventures, gave him the latest news from Russia, explained our plans, the object of our expedition, told him of the murder of Lincoln, the end of the Rebellion, the latest news from the French invasion of Mexico, the gossip of the Imperial Court, and no end of other news which had been old with us for six months, but of which the poor exiled Ispravnik had never heard a word. He had had no communication with Russia in almost eleven months. After insisting again upon our coming over to his house immediately to dine, he bustled out of the room, and gave us an opportunity to wash and dress.

Two hours afterward, in all the splendor of blue coats, brass buttons, and shoulder-straps, with shaven faces, starched shirts, and polished leather boots, the "First Siberian Exploring Party" marched over to the Ispravnik's to dine. The Russian peasants whom we met instinctively took off their frosty fur hoods and gazed wonderingly at us as we passed, as if we had mysteriously dropped down from some celestial sphere. No one would have recognized in us the dirty, smoky, ragged vagabonds who had entered the village two hours before. The grubs had developed into blue and golden butterflies! We found the Ispravnik waiting for us in a pleasant, spacious room furnished with, all the luxuries of a civilized home. The walls were papered and ornamented with costly pictures and engravings, the windows were hung with curtains, the floor was covered with a soft, bright-colored carpet, a large walnut writing-desk occupied one corner of the room, a rosewood melodeon the other, and in the centre stood the dining-table, covered with a fresh cloth, polished china, and glittering silver. We were fairly dazzled at the sight of so much unusual and unexpected magnificence. After the inevitable "fifteen drops" of brandy, and the lunch of smoked fish, rye bread, and caviar, which always precedes a

Russian dinner, we took seats at the table and spent an hour and a half in getting through the numerous courses of cabbage soup, salmon pie, venison cutlets, game, small meat pies, pudding, and pastry, which were successively set before us, and in discussing the news of all the world, from the log villages of Kamchatka to the imperial palaces of Moscow and St. Petersburg. Our hospitable host then ordered champagne, and over tall, slender glasses of cool beaded Cliquot we meditated upon the vicissitudes of Siberian life. Yesterday we sat on the ground in a Korak tent and ate reindeer meat out of a wooden trough with our fingers, and today we dined with the Russian governor, in a luxurious house, upon venison cutlets, plum pudding, and champagne. With the exception of a noticeable but restrained inclination on the part of Dodd and myself to curl up our legs and sit on the floor, there was nothing I believe in our behavior to betray the barbarous freedom of the life which we had so recently lived, and the demoralizing character of the influences to which we had been subjected. We handled our knives and forks, and leisurely sipped our champagne with a grace which would have excited the envy of Lord Chesterfield himself. But it was hard work. No sooner did we return to our quarters than we threw off our uniform coats, spread our bearskins on the floor and sat down upon them with crossed legs, to enjoy a comfortable smoke in the good old free-and-easy style. If our faces had only been just a little dirty we should have been perfectly happy!

The next ten days of our life at Geezhega were passed in comparative idleness. We walked out a little when the weather was not too cold, received formal calls from the Russian merchants of the place, visited the Ispravnik and drank his delicious "flower-tea" and smoked his cigarettes in the evening, and indemnified ourselves for three months of rough life by enjoying to the utmost such mild pleasures as the little village afforded. This pleasant, aimless existence, however, was soon terminated by an order from the Major to prepare for the winter's campaign, and hold ourselves in readiness to start for the Arctic Circle or the west coast of the Okhotsk Sea at a moment's notice. He had determined to explore a route for our proposed line from Bering Strait to the Amur River before spring should open, and there was no time to be lost. The information which we could gather at Geezhega with regard to the interior of the country was scanty, indefinite, and unsatisfactory. According to native accounts, there were only two settlements between the Okhotsk Sea and Bering Strait, and the nearest of these—Penzhina—was four hundred versts distant. The intervening country consisted of great moss "toondras" impassable in summer, and perfectly destitute of timber; and that portion of it which lay north-east of the last settlement was utterly uninhabitable on account of the absence of wood. A Russian officer by the name of Phillippeus had attempted to explore it in the winter of 1860, but had returned unsuccessful, in a starving and exhausted condition. In the whole distance of eight hundred versts between Geezhega and the mouth of the Anadyr River there were said to be only four or five places where timber could be found large enough for telegraph poles, and over most of the route there was no wood except occasional patches of trailing-pine. A journey from Geezhega to the last settlement, Anadyrsk, on the Arctic Circle, would occupy from twenty to thirty days, according to weather, and beyond that point there was no possibility of going under any circumstances. The region west of Geezhega, along the coast of the Okhotsk Sea, was reported to be better, but very rugged and mountainous, and heavily timbered with pine and larch. The village of Okhotsk, eight hundred versts distant, could be reached on dog-sledges in about a month. This, in brief, was all the information we could get, and it did not inspire us with very much confidence in the ultimate success of our enterprise. I realized for the first time the magnitude of the task which the Russian-American Telegraph Company had undertaken. We were "in for it," however, now, and our first duty was obviously to go through the country, ascertain its extent and nature, and find out what facilities, if any, it afforded for the construction of our line.

18

THE RIVER OF DOUBT

THEODORE ROOSEVELT

Theodore Roosevelt was a rough rider, trustbuster, Nobel Peace Prize winner, champion of conservation, and the twenty-sixth—and youngest—president of the United States. After losing the 1912 presidential race (for what would have been his third term) to Woodrow Wilson, he added "Amazon explorer" to the résumé. Upon arrival, the group—including indispensable Brazilian guide Cândido Rondon and Roosevelt's son Kermit—tempted fate with a perhaps ill-advised decision to run "an unknown river." And though they made it down the nearly 1,000-mile River of Doubt (with the new maps to prove it), they were terrorized along the way by hostile tribes, murder, bloodthirsty mosquitoes, churning rapids, starvation, and disease. (Roosevelt himself was nearly killed by malaria and infection.) The Amazon tributary was later renamed Rio Roosevelt in his honor, but the president paid in blood, conceding in a letter to a friend that "the Brazilian wilderness stole away 10 years of my life."

CHAPTER VIII: THE RIVER OF DOUBT

ON February 27, 1914, shortly after midday, we started down the River of Doubt into the unknown. We were quite uncertain whether after a week we should find ourselves in the Gy-Paraná, or after six weeks in the Madeira, or after three months we knew not where. That was why the river was rightly christened the Duvida.

We had been camped close to the river, where the trail that follows the telegraph line crosses it by a rough bridge. As our laden dugouts swung into the stream, Amilcar and Miller and all the others of the Gy-Parana party were on the banks and the bridge to wave farewell and wish us good-by and good luck. It was the height of the rainy season, and the swollen torrent was swift and brown. Our camp was at about 12° 1' latitude south and 60° 15' longitude west of Greenwich. Our general course was to be northward toward the equator, by waterway through the vast forest.

We had seven canoes, all of them dugouts. One was small, one was cranky, and two were old, waterlogged, and leaky. The other three were good. The two old canoes were lashed together, and the cranky one was lashed to one of the others. Kermit with two paddlers went in the smallest of the good canoes; Colonel Rondon and Lyra with three other paddlers in the next largest; and the doctor, Cherrie, and I in the largest with three paddlers. The remaining eight camaradas—there were sixteen in all— were equally divided between our two pairs of lashed canoes. Although our personal baggage was cut down to the limit necessary for health and efficiency, yet on such a trip as ours, where scientific work has to be done and where food for twenty-two men for an unknown period of time has to be carried, it is impossible not to take a good deal of stuff; and the seven dugouts were too heavily laden.

The paddlers were a strapping set. They were expert rivermen and men of the forest, skilled veterans in wilderness work. They were lithe as panthers and brawny as bears. They swam like waterdogs. They were equally at home with pole and paddle, with axe and machete; and one was a good cook and others were good men around camp. They looked like pirates in the pictures of Howard Pyle or Maxfield Parrish; one or two of them were pirates, and one worse than a pirate; but most of them were hard-working, willing, and cheerful. They were white,—or, rather, the olive of southern Europe,—black, copper-colored, and of all intermediate shades. In my canoe Luiz the steersman, the headman, was a Matto Grosso negro; Julio the bowsman was from Bahia and of pure Portuguese blood; and the third man, Antonio, was a Parecis Indian.

The actual surveying of the river was done by Colonel Rondon and Lyra, with Kermit as their assistant. Kermit went first in his little canoe with the sighting-rod, on which two disks, one red and one white, were placed a metre apart. He selected a place which commanded as long vistas as possible up-stream and down, and which therefore might be at the angle of a bend; landed; cut away the branches which obstructed the view; and set up the sighting-pole—incidentally encountering maribundi wasps and swarms of biting and stinging ants. Lyra, from his station up-stream, with his telemetre established the distance, while Colonel Rondon with the compass took the direction, and made the records. Then they moved on to the point Kermit had left, and Kermit established a new point within their sight. The first half-day's work was slow. The general course of the stream was a trifle east of north, but at short intervals it bent and curved literally toward every point of the compass. Kermit landed nearly a hundred times, and we made but nine and a third kilometres.

My canoe ran ahead of the surveying canoes. The height of the water made the going easy, for most of the snags and fallen trees were well beneath the surface. Now and then, however, thc swifl water hurried us toward ripples that marked ugly spikes of sunken timber, or toward uprooted trees that stretched almost across the stream. Then the muscles stood out on the backs and arms of the paddlers as stroke on stroke they urged us away from and past the obstacle. If the leaning or fallen trees were the thorny, slender-stemmed boritana palms, which love the wet, they were often, although plunged beneath the river, in full and vigorous growth, their stems curving upward, and their frond-crowned tops shaken by the rushing water. It was interesting work, for no civilized man, no white man, had ever gone down or up this river or seen the country through which we were passing. The lofty and matted forest rose like a green wall on either hand. The trees were stately and beautiful. The looped and twisted vines hung from them like great ropes. Masses of epiphytes grew both on the dead trees and the living; some had huge leaves like elephants' ears. Now and then fragrant scents were blown to us from flowers on the banks. There were not many birds, and for the most part the forest was silent; rarely we heard strange calls from the depths of the woods, or saw a cormorant or ibis.

My canoe ran only a couple of hours. Then we halted to wait for the others. After a couple of hours more, as the surveyors had not turned up, we landed and made camp at a spot where the bank rose sharply for a hundred yards to a level stretch of ground. Our canoes were moored to trees. The axemen cleared a space for the tents; they were pitched, the baggage was brought up, and fires were kindled. The woods were almost soundless. Through them ran old tapir trails, but there was no fresh sign. Before nightfall the surveyors arrived. There were a few piums and gnats, and a few mosquitoes after dark, but not enough to make us uncomfortable. The small stingless bees, of slightly aromatic odor, swarmed while daylight lasted and crawled over our faces and hands; they were such tame, harmless little things that when they tickled too much I always tried to brush them away without hurting them. But they became a great nuisance after a while. It had been raining at intervals, and the weather was overcast; but after the sun went down the sky cleared. The stars were brilliant overhead, and the new moon hung in the west. It was a pleasant night, the air almost cool, and we slept soundly.

Next morning the two surveying canoes left immediately after breakfast. An hour later the two pairs of lashed canoes pushed off. I kept our canoe to let Cherrie collect, for in the early hours we could hear a number of birds in the woods near by. The most interesting birds he shot were a cotinga, brilliant turquoise-blue with a magenta-purple throat, and a big woodpecker, black above and cinnamon below with an entirely red head and neck. It was almost noon before we started. We saw a few more birds; there were fresh tapir and paca tracks at one point where we landed; once we heard howler monkeys from the depth of the forest, and once we saw a big otter in midstream. As we drifted and paddled down the swirling brown current, through the vivid rain-drenched green of the tropic forest, the trees leaned over the river from both banks. When those that had fallen in the river at some narrow point were very tall, or where it happened that two fell opposite each other, they formed barriers which the men in the leading canoes cleared with their axes. There were many palms, both the burity with its stiff fronds like enormous fans, and a handsome species of bacaba, with very long, gracefully curving fronds. In places the palms stood close together, towering and slender, their stems a stately colonnade, their fronds an arched fretwork against the sky. Butterflies of many hues fluttered over the river. The day was overcast, with showers of rain. When the sun broke through rifts in the clouds, his shafts turned the forest to gold.

In mid-afternoon we came to the mouth of a big and swift affluent entering from the right. It was undoubtedly the Bandeira, which we had crossed well toward its head, some ten days before, on our road to Bonofacio. The Nhambiquaras had then told Colonel Rondon that it flowed into the Dúvida. After its junction, with the added volume of water, the river widened without losing its depth. It was so high that it had overflowed and stood among the trees on the lower levels. Only the higher stretches were dry. On the sheer banks where we landed we had to push the canoes for yards or rods through the branches of the submerged trees, hacking and hewing. There were occasional bays and ox-bows from which the current had shifted. In these the coarse marsh grass grew tall.

This evening we made camp on a flat of dry ground, densely wooded, of course, directly on the edge of the river and five feet above it. It was fine to see the speed and sinewy ease with which the choppers cleared an open space for the tents. Next morning, when we bathed before sunrise, we dived into deep water right from the shore, and from the moored canoes. This second day we made sixteen and a half kilometres along the course of the river, and nine kilometres in a straight line almost due north.

The following day, March 1, there was much rain—sometimes showers, sometimes vertical sheets of water. Our course was somewhat west of north and we made twenty and a half kilometres. We passed signs of Indian habitation. There were abandoned palm-leaf shelters on both banks. On the left bank we came to two or three old Indian fields, grown up with coarse fern and studded with the burned skeletons of trees. At the mouth of a brook which entered from the right some sticks stood in the water, marking the site of an old fish-trap. At one point we found the tough vine hand-rail of an Indian bridge running right across the river, a couple of feet above it. Evidently the bridge had been built at low water. Three stout poles had been driven into the stream-bed in a line at right angles to the current. The bridge had consisted of poles fastened to these supports, leading between them and from the support at each end to the banks. The rope of tough vines had been stretched as a hand-rail, necessary with such precarious footing. The rise of the river had swept away the bridge, but the props and the rope hand-rail remained. In the afternoon, from the boat, Cherrie shot a large dark-gray monkey with a prehensile tail. It was very good eating.

We camped on a dry level space, but a few feet above, and close beside, the river—so that our swimming-bath was handy. The trees were cleared and camp was made with orderly hurry. One of the men almost stepped on a poisonous coral-snake, which would have been a serious thing, as his feet were bare. But I had on stout shoes, and the fangs of these serpents—unlike those of the pit-vipers—are too short to penetrate good leather. I promptly put my foot on him, and he bit my shoe with harmless venom. It has been said that the brilliant hues of the coral-snake when in its native haunts really confer on it a concealing coloration. In the dark and tangled woods, and to an only less extent in the ordinary varied landscape, anything motionless, especially if partially hidden, easily eludes the eye. But against the dark-brown mould of the forest floor on which we found this coral-snake its bright and varied coloration was distinctly revealing; infinitely more so than the duller mottling of the jararaca and other dangerous snakes of the genus lachecis. In the same place, however, we found a striking example of genuine protective or mimetic coloration and shape. A rather large insect larva—at least we judged it to be a larval form, but we were none of us entomologists—bore a resemblance to a partially curled dry leaf which was fairly startling. The tail exactly resembled the stem or continuation of the midrib of the dead leaf. The flattened body was curled up at the sides, and veined and colored precisely like the leaf. The head, colored like the leaf, projected in front.

We were still in the Brazilian highlands. The forest did not teem with life. It was generally rather silent; we did not hear such a chorus of birds and mammals as we had occasionally heard even on our overland journey, when more than once we had been awakened at dawn by the howling, screaming, yelping, and chattering of monkeys, toucans, macaws, parrots, and parakeets. There were, however, from time to time, queer sounds from the forest, and after nightfall different kinds of frogs and insects uttered strange cries and calls. In volume and frequency these seemed to increase until midnight. Then they died away and before dawn everything was silent.

At this camp the carregadores ants completely devoured the doctor's undershirt, and ate holes in his mosquito-net; and they also ate the strap of Lyra's gun-case. The little stingless bees, of many kinds, swarmed in such multitudes, and were so persevering, that we had to wear our head-nets when we wrote or skinned specimens.

The following day was almost without rain. It was delightful to drift and paddle slowly down the beautiful tropical river. Until mid-afternoon the current was not very fast, and the broad, deep, placid stream bent and curved in every direction, although the general course was northwest. The country was flat, and more of the land was under than above water. Continually we found ourselves travelling between stretches of marshy forest where for miles the water stood or ran among the trees. Once we passed a hillock. We saw brilliantly colored parakeets and trogons. At last the slow current quickened. Faster it went, and faster, until it began to run like a mill-race, and we heard the roar of rapids ahead. We pulled to the right bank, moored the canoes, and while most of the men pitched camp two or three of them accompanied us to examine the rapids. We had made twenty kilometres.

We soon found that the rapids were a serious obstacle. There were many curls, and one or two regular falls, perhaps six feet high. It would have been impossible to run them, and they stretched for nearly a mile. The carry, however, which led through woods and over rocks in a nearly straight line, was somewhat shorter. It was not an easy portage over which to carry heavy loads and drag heavy dugout canoes. At the point where the descent was steepest there were great naked flats of friable sandstone and conglomerate. Over parts of these, where there was a surface of fine sand, there was a growth of coarse grass. Other parts were bare and had been worn by the weather into fantastic shapes—one projection looked like an old-fashioned beaver hat upside down. In this place, where the naked flats of rock showed the projection of the ledge through which the river had cut its course, the torrent rushed down a deep, sheer-sided, and extremely narrow channel. At one point it was less than two yards across, and for quite a distance not more than five or six yards. Yet only a mile or two above the rapids the deep, placid river was at least a hundred yards wide. It seemed extraordinary, almost impossible, that so broad a river could in so short a space of time contract its dimensions to the width of the strangled channel through which it now poured its entire volume.

This has for long been a station where the Nhambiquaras at intervals built their ephemeral villages and tilled the soil with the rude and destructive cultivation of savages. There were several abandoned old fields, where the dense growth of rank fern hid the tangle of burnt and fallen logs. Nor had the Nhambiquaras been long absent. In one trail we found what gypsies would have called a "pateran," a couple of branches arranged crosswise, eight leaves to a branch; it had some special significance, belonging to that class of signals, each with some peculiar and often complicated meaning, which are commonly used by many wild peoples. The Indians had thrown a simple bridge, consisting of four long poles, without a hand-rail, across one of the narrowest parts of the rock gorge through which the river foamed in its rapid descent. This sub-tribe of Indians was called the Navaïté; we named the rapids after them, Navaite Rapids. By observation Lyra found them to be (in close approximation to) latitude 11° 44' south and longitude 60° 18' west from Greenwich.

We spent March 3 and 4 and the morning of the 5th in portaging around the rapids. The first night we camped in the forest beside the spot where we had halted. Next morning we moved the baggage to the foot of the rapids, where we intended to launch the canoes, and pitched our tents on the open sandstone flat. It rained heavily. The little bees were in such swarms as to be a nuisance. Many small stinging bees were with them, which stung badly. We were bitten by huge horse-flies, the size of bumblebees. More serious annoyance was caused by the pium and boroshuda flies during the hours of daylight, and by the polvora, the sand-flies, after dark. There were a few mosquitoes. The boroshudas were the worst pests; they brought the blood at once, and left marks that lasted for weeks. I did my writing in head-net and gauntlets. Fortunately we had with us several bottles of "fly dope"—so named on the label—put up, with the rest of our medicine, by Doctor Alexander Lambert; he had tested it in the north woods and found it excellent. I had never before been forced to use such an ointment, and had been reluctant to take it with me; but now I was glad enough to have it, and we all of us found it exceedingly useful. I would never again go into mosquito or sand-fly country without it. The effect of an application wears off after half an hour or so, and under many conditions, as when one is perspiring freely, it is of no use; but there are times when minute mosquitoes and gnats get through head-nets and under mosquito-bars, and when the ointments occasionally renewed may permit one to get sleep or rest which would otherwise be impossible of attainment. The termites got into our tent on the sand-flat, ate holes in Cherrie's mosquito-net and poncho, and were starting to work at our duffel-bags, when we discovered them.

Packing the loads across was simple. Dragging the heavy dugouts was labor. The biggest of the two water-logged ones was the heaviest. Lyra and Kermit did the job. All the men were employed at it except the cook, and one man who was down with fever. A road was chopped through the forest and a couple of hundred stout six-foot poles, or small logs, were cut as rollers and placed about two yards apart. With block and tackle the seven dugouts were hoisted out of the river up the steep banks, and up the rise of ground until the level was reached. Then the men harnessed themselves two by two on the drag-rope, while one of their number pried behind with a lever, and the canoe, bumping and sliding, was twitched through the woods. Over the sandstone flats there were some ugly ledges, but on the whole the course was down-hill and relatively easy. Looking at the way the work was done, at the good-will, the endurance, and the bull-like strength of the camaradas, and at the intelligence and the unwearied efforts of their commanders, one could but wonder at the ignorance of those who do not realize the energy and the power that are so often possessed by, and that may be so readily developed in, the men of the tropics. Another subject of perpetual wonder is the attitude of certain men who stay at home, and still more the attitude of certain men who travel under easy conditions, and who belittle the achievements of the real explorers of, the real adventures in, the great wilderness. The impostors and romancers among explorers or would-be explorers and wilderness wanderers have been unusually prominent in connection with South America (although the conspicuous ones are not South Americans, by the way); and these are fit subjects for condemnation and derision. But the work of the genuine explorer and wilderness wanderer is fraught with fatigue, hardship, and danger. Many of the men of little knowledge talk glibly of portaging as if it were simple and easy. A portage over rough and unknown ground is always a work of difficulty and of some risk to the canoe; and in the untrodden, or even in the unfrequented, wilderness risk to the canoe is a serious matter. This particular portage at Navaïté Rapids was far from being unusually difficult; yet it not only cost two and a half days of severe and incessant labor, but it cost something in damage to the canoes. One in particular, the one in which I had been journeying, was split in a manner which caused us serious uneasiness as to how long, even after being patched, it would last. Where the canoes were launched, the bank was sheer, and one of the water-logged canoes filled and went to the bottom; and there was more work in raising it.

We were still wholly unable to tell where we were going or what lay ahead of us. Round the camp-fire, after supper, we held endless discussions and hazarded all kinds of guesses on both subjects. The river might bend sharply to the west and enter the Gy-Paraná high up or low down, or go north to the Madeira, or bend eastward and enter the Tapajos, or fall into the Canumá and finally through one of its mouths enter the Amazon direct. Lyra inclined to the first, and Colonel Rondon to the second, of these propositions. We did not know whether we had one hundred or eight hundred kilometres to go, whether the stream would be fairly smooth or whether we would encounter waterfalls, or rapids, or even some big marsh or lake. We could not tell whether or not we would meet hostile Indians, although no one of us ever went ten yards from camp without his rifle. We had no idea how much time the trip would take. We had entered a land of unknown possibilities.

We started down-stream again early in the afternoon of March 5. Our hands and faces were swollen from the bites and stings of the insect pests at the sand-flat camp, and it was a pleasure once more to be in the middle of the river, where they did not come, in any numbers, while we were in motion. The current was swift, but the river was so deep that there were no serious obstructions. Twice we went down over slight riffles, which in the dry season were doubtless rapids; and once we struck a spot where many whirlpools marked the presence underneath of boulders which would have been above water had not the river been so swollen by the rains. The distance we covered in a day going down-stream would have taken us a week if we had been going up. The course wound hither and thither, sometimes in sigmoid curves; but the general direction was east of north. As usual, it was very beautiful; and we never could tell what might appear around any curve. In the forest that rose on either hand were tall rubber-trees. The surveying canoes, as usual, went first, while I shepherded the two pairs of lashed cargo canoes. I kept them always between me and the surveying canoes—ahead of me until I passed the surveying canoes, then behind me until, after an hour or so, I had chosen a place to camp. There was so much overflowed ground that it took us some little time this afternoon before we found a flat place high enough to be dry. Just before reaching camp Cherrie shot a jacu, a handsome bird somewhat akin to, but much smaller than, a turkey; after Cherrie had taken its skin, its body made an excellent canja. We saw parties of monkeys; and the false bellbirds uttered their ringing whistles in the dense timber around our tents. The giant ants, an inch and a quarter long, were rather too plentiful around this camp; one stung Kermit; it was almost like the sting of a small scorpion, and pained severely for a couple of hours. This half-day we made twelve kilometres.

On the following day we made nineteen kilometres, the river twisting in every direction, but in its general course running a little west of north. Once we stopped at a bee-tree, to get honey. The tree was a towering giant, of the kind called milk-tree, because a thick milky juice runs freely from any cut. Our camaradas eagerly drank the white fluid that flowed from the wounds made by their axes. I tried it. The taste was not unpleasant, but it left a sticky feeling in the mouth. The helmsman of my boat, Luiz, a powerful negro, chopped into the tree, balancing himself with springy ease on a slight scaffolding. The honey was in a hollow, and had been made by medium-sized stingless bees. At the mouth of the hollow they had built a curious entrance of their own, in the shape of a spout of wax about a foot long. At the opening the walls of the spout showed the wax formation, but elsewhere it had become in color and texture indistinguishable from the bark of the tree. The honey was delicious, sweet and yet with a tart flavor. The comb differed much from that of our honey-bees. The honey-cells were very large, and the brood-cells, which were small, were in a single instead of a double row. By this tree I came across an example of genuine concealing coloration. A huge tree-toad, the size of a bullfrog, was seated upright—not squatted flat—on a big rotten limb. It was absolutely motionless; the yellow brown of its back, and its dark sides, exactly harmonized in color with the light and dark patches on the log; the color was as concealing, here in its natural surroundings, as is the color of our common wood-frog among the dead leaves of our woods. When I stirred it up it jumped to a small twig, catching hold with the disks of its finger-tips, and balancing itself with unexpected ease for so big a creature, and then hopped to the ground and again stood motionless. Evidently it trusted for safety to escaping observation. We saw some monkeys and fresh tapir sign, and Kermit shot a jacu for the pot.

At about three o'clock I was in the lead, when the current began to run more quickly. We passed over one or two decided ripples, and then heard the roar of rapids ahead, while the stream began to race. We drove the canoe into the bank, and then went down a tapir trail, which led alongside the river, to reconnoiter. A quarter of a mile's walk showed us that there were big rapids, down which the canoes could not go; and we returned to the landing. All the canoes had gathered there, and Rondon, Lyra, and Kermit started down-stream to explore. They returned in an hour, with the information that the rapids continued for a long distance, with falls and steep pitches of broken water, and that the portage would take several days. We made camp just above the rapids. Ants swarmed, and some of them bit savagely. Our men, in clearing away the forest for our tents, left several very tall and slender accashy palms; the bole of this palm is as straight as an arrow and is crowned with delicate, gracefully curved fronds. We had come along the course of the river almost exactly a hundred kilometres; it had twisted so that we were only about fifty-five kilometres north of our starting-point. The rock was porphyritic.

The 7th, 8th, and 9th we spent in carrying the loads and dragging and floating the dugouts past the series of rapids at whose head we had stopped.

The first day we shifted camp a kilometre and a half to the foot of this series of rapids. This was a charming and picturesque camp. It was at the edge of the river, where there was a little, shallow bay with a beach of firm sand. In the water, at the middle point of the beach, stood a group of three burity palms, their great trunks rising like columns. Round the clearing in which our tents stood were several very big trees; two of them were rubber-trees. Kermit went down-stream five or six kilometres, and returned, having shot a jacu and found that at the point which he had reached there was another rapids, almost a fall, which would necessitate our again dragging the canoes over a portage. Antonio, the Parecís, shot a big monkey; of this I was glad because portaging is hard work, and the men appreciated the meat. So far Cherrie had collected sixty birds on the Dúvida, all of them new to the collection, and some probably new to science. We saw the fresh sign of paca, agouti, and the small peccary, and Kermit with the dogs roused a tapir, which crossed the river right through the rapids; but no one got a shot at it.

Except at one or perhaps two points a very big dugout, lightly loaded, could probably run all these rapids. But even in such a canoe it would be silly to make the attempt on an exploring expedition, where the loss of a canoe or of its contents means disaster; and moreover such a canoe could not be taken, for it would be impossible to drag it over the portages on the occasions when the portages became inevitable. Our canoes would not have lived half a minute in the wild water.

On the second day the canoes and loads were brought down to the foot of the first rapids. Lyra cleared the path and laid the logs for rollers, while Kermit dragged the dugouts up the bank from the water with block and tackle, with strain of rope and muscle. Then they joined forces, as over the uneven ground it needed the united strength of all their men to get the heavy dugouts along. Meanwhile the colonel with one attendant measured the distance, and then went on a long hunt, but saw no game. I strolled down beside the river for a couple of miles, but also saw nothing. In the dense tropical forest of the Amazonian basin hunting is very difficult, especially for men who are trying to pass through the country as rapidly as possible. On such a trip as ours getting game is largely a matter of chance.

On the following day Lyra and Kermit brought down the canoes and loads, with hard labor, to the little beach by the three palms where our tents were pitched. Many pacovas grew round about. The men used their immense leaves, some of which were twelve feet long and two and a half feet broad, to roof the flimsy shelters under which they hung their hammocks. I went into the woods, but in the tangle of vegetation it would have been a mere hazard had I seen any big animal. Generally the woods were silent and empty. Now and then little troops of birds of many kinds passed—wood-hewers, ant-thrushes, tanagers, flycatchers; as in the spring and fall similar troops of warblers, chickadees, and nuthatches pass through our northern woods. On the rocks and on the great trees by the river grew beautiful white and lilac orchids, the sobralia, of sweet and delicate fragrance. For the moment my own books seemed a trifle heavy, and perhaps I would have found the day tedious if Kermit had not lent me the Oxford Book of French Verse. Eustache Deschamp, Joachim du Bellay, Ronsard, the delightful La Fontaine, the delightful but appalling Villon, Victor Hugo's "Guitare," Madame Desbordes-Valmore's lines on the little girl and her pillow, as dear little verses about a child as ever were written—these and many others comforted me much, as I read them in head-net and gauntlets, sitting on a log by an unknown river in the Amazonian forest.

On the 10th we again embarked and made a kilometre and a half, spending most of the time in getting past two more rapids. Near the first of these we saw a small cayman, a jacare-tinga. At each set of rapids the canoes were unloaded and the loads borne past on the shoulders of the camaradas; three of the canoes were paddled down by a couple of naked paddlers apiece; and the two sets of double canoes were let down by ropes, one of one couple being swamped but rescued and brought safely to shore on each occasion. One of the men was upset while working in the swift water, and his face was cut against the stones. Lyra and Kermit did the actual work with the camaradas. Kermit, dressed substantially like the camaradas themselves, worked in the water, and, as the overhanging branches were thronged with crowds of biting and stinging ants, he was marked and blistered over his whole body. Indeed, we all suffered more or less from these ants; while the swarms of biting flies grew constantly more numerous. The termites ate holes in my helmet and also in the cover of my cot. Every one else had a hammock. At this camp we had come down the river about 102 kilometres, according to the surveying records, and in height had descended nearly 100 metres, as shown by the aneroid—although the figure in this case is only an approximation, as an aneroid cannot be depended on for absolute accuracy of results.

Next morning we found that during the night we had met with a serious misfortune. We had halted at the foot of the rapids. The canoes were moored to trees on the bank, at the tail of the broken water. The two old canoes, although one of them was our biggest cargo-carrier, were water-logged and heavy, and one of them was leaking. In the night the river rose. The leaky canoe, which at best was too low in the water, must have gradually filled from the wash of the waves. It sank, dragging down the other; they began to roll, bursting their moorings; and in the morning they had disappeared. A canoe was launched to look for them; but, rolling over the boulders on the rocky bottom, they had at once been riven asunder, and the big fragments that were soon found, floating in eddies, or along the shore, showed that it was useless to look farther. We called these rapids Broken Canoe Rapids.

It was not pleasant to have to stop for some days; thanks to the rapids, we had made slow progress, and with our necessarily limited supply of food, and no knowledge whatever of what was ahead of us, it was important to make good time. But there was no alternative. We had to build either one big canoe or two small ones. It was raining heavily as the men started to explore in different directions for good canoe trees. Three—which ultimately proved not very good for the purpose—were found close to camp; splendid-looking trees, one of them five feet in diameter three feet from the ground. The axemen immediately attacked this one under the superintendence of Colonel Rondon. Lyra and Kermit started in opposite directions to hunt. Lyra killed a jacu for us, and Kermit killed two monkeys for the men. Toward night fall it cleared. The moon was nearly full, and the foaming river gleamed like silver.

Our men were "regional volunteers," that is, they had enlisted in the service of the Telegraphic Commission especially to do this wilderness work, and were highly paid, as was fitting, in view of the toil, hardship, and hazard to life and health. Two of them had been with Colonel Rondon during his eight months' exploration in 1909, at which time his men were regulars, from his own battalion of engineers. His four aides during the closing months of this trip were Lieutenants Lyra, Amarante, Alencarliense, and Pyrineus. The naturalist Miranda Ribeiro also accompanied him. This was the year when, marching on foot through an absolutely unknown wilderness, the colonel and his party finally reached the Gy-Parana, which on the maps was then (and on most maps is now) placed in an utterly wrong course, and over a degree out of its real position. When they reached the affluents of the Gy-Parana a third of the members of the party were so weak with fever that they could hardly crawl. They had no baggage. Their clothes were in tatters, and some of the men were almost naked. For months they had had no food except what little game they shot, and especially the wild fruits and nuts; if it had not been for the great abundance of the Brazil-nuts they would all have died. At the first big stream they encountered they built a canoe, and Alencarliense took command of it and descended to map the course of the river. With him went Ribeiro, the doctor Tanageira, who could no longer walk on account of the ulceration of one foot, three men whom the fever had rendered unable longer to walk, and six men who were as yet well enough to handle the canoe. By the time the remainder of the party came to the next navigable river eleven more fever-stricken men had nearly reached the end of their tether. Here they ran across a poor devil who had for four months been lost in the forest and was dying of slow starvation. He had eaten nothing but Brazil-nuts and the grubs of insects. He could no longer walk, but could sit erect and totter feebly for a few feet. Another canoe was built, and in it Pyrineus started downstream with the eleven fever patients and the starving wanderer. Colonel Rondon kept up the morale of his men by still carrying out the forms of military discipline. The ragged bugler had his bugle. Lieutenant Pyrineus had lost every particle of his clothing except a hat and a pair of drawers. The half-naked lieutenant drew up his eleven fever patients in line; the bugle sounded;

every one came to attention; and the haggard colonel read out the orders of the day. Then the dugout with its load of sick men started down-stream, and Rondon, Lyra, Amarante, and the twelve remaining men resumed their weary march. When a fortnight later they finally struck a camp of rubber-gatherers three of the men were literally and entirely naked. Meanwhile Amilcar had ascended the Jacyparaná a month or two previously with provisions to meet them; for at that time the maps incorrectly treated this river as larger, instead of smaller, than the Gy-Paraná, which they were in fact descending; and Colonel Rondon had supposed that they were going down the former stream. Amilcar returned after himself suffering much hardship and danger. The different parties finally met at the mouth of the Gy-Paraná, where it enters the Madeira. The lost man whom they had found seemed on the road to recovery, and they left him at a ranch, on the Madeira, where he could be cared for; yet after they had left him they heard that he had died.

On the 12th the men were still hard at work hollowing out the hard wood of the big tree, with axe and adze, while watch and ward were kept over them to see that the idlers did not shirk at the expense of the industrious. Kermit and Lyra again hunted; the former shot a curassow, which was welcome, as we were endeavoring in all ways to economize our food supply. We were using the tops of palms also. I spent the day hunting in the woods, for the most part by the river, but saw nothing. In the season of the rains game is away from the river and fish are scarce and turtles absent. Yet it was pleasant to be in the great silent forest. Here and there grew immense trees, and on some of them mighty buttresses sprang from the base. The lianas and vines were of every size and shape. Some were twisted and some were not. Some came down straight and slender from branches a hundred feet above. Others curved like long serpents around the trunks. Others were like knotted cables. In the shadow there was little noise. The wind rarely moved the hot, humid air. There were few flowers or birds. Insects were altogether too abundant, and even when travelling slowly it was impossible always to avoid them—not to speak of our constant companions the bees, mosquitoes, and especially the boroshudas or bloodsucking flies. Now while bursting through a tangle I disturbed a nest of wasps, whose resentment was active; now I heedlessly stepped among the outliers of a small party of the carnivorous foraging ants; now, grasping a branch as I stumbled, I shook down a shower of fire-ants; and among all these my attention was particularly arrested by the bite of one of the giant ants, which stung like a hornet, so that I felt it for three hours. The camarades generally went barefoot or only wore sandals; and their ankles and feet were swollen and inflamed from the bites of the boroshudas and ants, some being actually incapacitated from work. All of us suffered more or less, our faces and hands swelling slightly from the boroshuda bites; and in spite of our clothes we were bitten all over our bodies, chiefly by ants and the small forest ticks. Because of the rain and the heat our clothes were usually wet when we took them off at night, and just as wet when we put them on again in the morning.

All day on the 13th the men worked at the canoe, making good progress. In rolling and shifting the huge, heavy tree-trunk every one had to assist now and then. The work continued until ten in the evening, as the weather was clear. After nightfall some of the men held candles and the others plied axe or adze, standing within or beside the great, half-hollowed logs, while the flicker of the lights showed the tropic forest rising in the darkness round about. The night air was hot and still and heavy with moisture. The men were stripped to the waist. Olive and copper and ebony, their skins glistened as if oiled, and rippled with the ceaseless play of the thews beneath.

On the morning of the 14th the work was resumed in a torrential tropic downpour. The canoe was finished, dragged down to the water, and launched soon after midday, and another hour or so saw us under way. The descent was marked, and the swollen river raced along. Several times we passed great whirlpools, sometimes shifting, sometimes steady. Half a dozen times we ran over rapids, and, although they were not high enough to have been obstacles to loaded Canadian canoes, two of them were serious to us. Our heavily laden, clumsy dugouts were sunk to within three or four inches of the surface of the river, and, although they were buoyed on each side with bundles of burity-palm branch-stems, they shipped a great deal of water in the rapids. The two biggest rapids we only just made, and after each we had hastily to push ashore in order to bail. In one set of big ripples or waves my canoe was nearly swamped. In a wilderness, where what is ahead is absolutely unknown, alike in terms of time, space, and method—for we had no idea where we would come out, how we would get out, or when we would get out—it is of vital consequence not to lose one's outfit, especially the provisions; and yet it is of only less consequence to go as rapidly as possible lest all the provisions be exhausted and the final stages of the expedition be accomplished by men weakened from semi-starvation, and therefore ripe for disaster. On this occasion, of the two hazards, we felt it necessary to risk running the rapids; for our progress had been so very slow that unless we made up the time, it was probable that we would be short of food before we got where we could expect to procure any more except what little the country in the time of the rains and floods, might yield. We ran until after five, so that the work of pitching camp was finished in the dark. We had made nearly sixteen kilometres in a direction slightly east of north. This evening the air was fresh and cool.

The following morning, the 15th of March, we started in good season. For six kilometres we drifted and paddled down the swift river without incident. At times we saw lofty Brazilnut trees rising above the rest of the forest on the banks; and back from the river these trees grow to enormous proportions, towering like giants. There were great rubber-trees also, their leaves always in sets of threes. Then the ground on either hand rose into boulder-strewn, forest-clad hills and the roar of broken water announced that once more our course was checked by dangerous rapids. Round a bend we came on them; a wide descent of white water, with an island in the middle, at the upper edge. Here grave misfortune befell us, and graver misfortune was narrowly escaped.

Kermit, as usual, was leading in his canoe. It was the smallest and least seaworthy of all. He had in it little except a week's supply of our boxed provisions and a few tools; fortunately none of the food for the camaradas. His dog Trigueiro was with him. Besides himself, the crew consisted of two men: João, the helmsman, or pilot, as he is called in Brazil, and Simplicio, the bowsman. Both were negroes and exceptionally good men in every way. Kermit halted his canoe on the left bank, above the rapids, and waited for the colonel's canoe. Then the colonel and Lyra walked down the bank to see what was ahead. Kermit took his canoe across to the island to see whether the descent could be better accomplished on the other side. Having made his investigation, he ordered the men to return to the bank he had left, and the dugout was headed up-stream accordingly. Before they had gone a dozen yards, the paddlers digging their paddles with all their strength into the swift current, one of the shifting whirlpools of which I have spoken came down-stream, whirled them around, and swept them so close to the rapids that no human power could avoid going over them. As they were drifting into them broadside on, Kermit yelled to the steersman to turn her head, so as to take them in the only way that offered any chance whatever of safety. The water came aboard, wave after wave, as they raced down. They reached the bottom with the canoe upright, but so full as barely to float, and the paddlers urged her toward the shore. They had nearly reached the bank when another whirlpool or whirling eddy tore them away and hurried them back to midstream, where the dugout filled and turned over. João, seizing the rope, started to swim ashore; the rope was pulled from his hand, but he reached the bank. Poor Simplicio must have been pulled under at once and his life beaten out on the boulders beneath the racing torrent. He never rose again, nor did we ever recover his body. Kermit clutched his rifle, his favorite 405 Winchester with which he had done most of his hunting both in Africa and America, and climbed on the bottom of the upset boat. In a minute he was swept into the second series of rapids, and whirled away from the rolling boat, losing his rifle. The water beat his helmet down over his head and face and drove him beneath the surface; and when he rose at last he was almost drowned, his breath and strength almost spent. He was in swift but quiet water, and swam toward an overhanging branch. His jacket hindered him, but he knew he was too nearly gone to be able to get it off, and, thinking with the curious calm one feels when death is but a moment away, he realized that the utmost his failing strength could do was to reach the branch. He reached, and clutched it, and then almost lacked strength to haul himself out on the land. Good Trigueiro had faithfully swum alongside him through the rapids, and now himself scrambled ashore. It was a very narrow escape. Kermit was a great comfort and help to me on the trip; but the fear of some fatal accident befalling him was always a nightmare to me. He was to be married as soon as the trip was over; and it did not seem to me that I could bear to bring bad tidings to his betrothed and to his mother.

Simplicio was unmarried. Later we sent to his mother all the money that would have been his had he lived. The following morning we put on one side of the post erected to mark our camping-spot the following inscription, in Portuguese:

IN THESE RAPIDS DIED POOR SIMPLICIO.

On an expedition such as ours death is one of the accidents that may at any time occur, and narrow escapes from death are too common to be felt as they would be felt elsewhere. One mourns sincerely, but mourning cannot interfere with labor. We immediately proceeded with the work of the portage. From the head to the tail of this series of rapids the distance was about six hundred yards. A path was cut along the bank, over which the loads were brought. The empty canoes ran the rapids without mishap, each with two skilled paddlers. One of the canoes almost ran into a swimming tapir at the head of the rapids; it went down the rapids, and then climbed out of the river. Kermit accompanied by João, went three or four miles down the river, looking for the body of Simplicio and for the sunk canoe. He found neither. But he found a box of provisions and a paddle, and salvaged both by swimming into midstream after them. He also found that a couple of kilometres below there was another stretch of rapids, and following them on the left-hand bank to the foot he found that they were worse than the ones we had just passed, and impassable for canoes on this left-hand side.

We camped at the foot of the rapids we had just passed. There were many small birds here, but it was extremely difficult to see or shoot them in the lofty tree tops, and to find them in the tangle beneath if they were shot. However, Cherrie got four species new to the collection. One was a tiny hummer, one of the species known as woodstars, with dainty but not brilliant plumage; its kind is never found except in the deep, dark woods, not coming out into the sunshine. Its crop was filled with ants; when shot it was feeding at a cluster of long red flowers. He also got a very handsome trogon and an exquisite little tanager, as brilliant as a cluster of jewels; its throat was lilac, its breast turquoise, its crown and forehead topaz, while above it was glossy purple-black, the lower part of the back ruby-red. This tanager was a female; I can hardly imagine that the male is more brilliantly colored. The fourth bird was a queer hawk of the genus *ibycter*, black, with a white belly, naked red cheeks and throat and red legs and feet. Its crop was filled with the seeds of fruits and a few insect remains; an extraordinary diet for a hawk.

The morning of the 16th was dark and gloomy. Through sheets of blinding rain we left our camp of misfortune for another camp where misfortune also awaited us. Less than half an hour took our dugouts to the head of the rapids below. As Kermit had already explored the left-hand side, Colonel Rondon and Lyra went down the right-hand side and found a channel which led round the worst part, so that they deemed it possible to let down the canoes by ropes from the bank. The distance to the foot of the rapids was about a kilometre. While the loads were being brought down the left bank, Luiz and Antonio Correa, our two best watermen, started to take a canoe down the right side, and Colonel Rondon walked ahead to see anything he could about the river. He was accompanied by one of our three dogs, Lobo. After walking about a kilometre he heard ahead a kind of howling noise, which he thought was made by spider-monkeys. He walked in the direction of the sound and Lobo ran ahead. In a minute he heard Lobo yell with pain, and then, still yelping, come toward him, while the creature that was howling also approached, evidently in pursuit. In a moment a second yell from Lobo, followed by silence, announced that he was dead; and the sound of the howling when near convinced Rondon that the dog had been killed by an Indian, doubtless with two arrows. Probably the Indian was howling to lure the spider-monkeys toward him. Rondon fired his rifle in the air, to warn off the Indian or Indians, who in all probability had never seen a civilized man, and certainly could not imagine that one was in the neighborhood. He then returned to the foot of the rapids, where the portage was still going on, and, in company with Lyra, Kermit, and Antonio Parecis, the Indian, walked back to where Lobo's body lay. Sure enough he found him, slain by two arrows. One arrow-head was in him, and near by was a strange stick used in the very primitive method of fishing of all these Indians. Antonio recognized its purpose. The Indians, who were apparently two or three in number, had fled. Some beads and trinkets were left on the spot to show that we were not angry and were friendly.

Meanwhile Cherrie stayed at the head and I at the foot of the portage as guards. Luiz and Antonio Correa brought down one canoe safely. The next was the new canoe, which was very large and heavy, being made of wood that would not float. In the rapids the rope broke, and the canoe was lost, Luiz being nearly drowned.

It was a very bad thing to lose the canoe, but it was even worse to lose the rope and pulleys. This meant that it would be physically impossible to hoist big canoes up even small hills or rocky hillocks, such as had been so frequent beside the many rapids we had encountered. It was not wise to spend the four days necessary to build new canoes where we were, in danger of attack from the Indians. Moreover, new rapids might be very near, in which case the new canoes would hamper us. Yet the four remaining canoes would not carry all the loads and all the men, no matter how we cut the loads down; and we intended to cut everything down at once. We had been gone eighteen days. We had used over a third of our food. We had gone only 125 kilometres, and it was probable that we had at least five times, perhaps six or seven times, this distance still to go. We had taken a fortnight to descend rapids amounting in the aggregate to less than seventy yards of fall; a very few yards of fall makes a dangerous rapid when the river is swollen and swift and there are obstructions. We had only one aneroid to determine our altitude, and therefore could make merely a loose approximation to it, but we probably had between two and three times this descent in the aggregate of rapids ahead of us. So far the country had offered little in the way of food except palm-tops. We had lost four canoes and one man. We were in the country of wild Indians, who shot well with their bows. It behooved us to go warily, but also to make all speed possible, if we were to avoid serious trouble.

The best plan seemed to be to march thirteen men down along the bank, while the remaining canoes, lashed two and two, floated down beside them. If after two or three days we found no bad rapids, and there seemed a reasonable chance of going some distance at decent speed, we could then build the new canoes—preferably two small ones, this time, instead of one big one. We left all the baggage we could. We were already down as far as comfort would permit; but we now struck off much of the comfort. Cherrie, Kermit, and I had been sleeping under a very light fly; and there was another small light tent for one person, kept for possible emergencies. The last was given to me for my cot, and all five of the others swung their hammocks under the big fly. This meant that we left two big and heavy tents behind. A box of surveying instruments was also abandoned. Each of us got his personal belongings down to one box or duffel-bag—although there was only a small diminution thus made; because we had so little that the only way to make a serious diminution was to restrict ourselves to the clothes on our backs.

The biting flies and ants were to us a source of discomfort and at times of what could fairly be called torment. But to the camaradas, most of whom went barefoot or only wore sandals—and they never did or would wear shoes—the effect was more serious. They wrapped their legs and feet in pieces of canvas or hide; and the feet of three of them became so swollen that they were crippled and could not walk any distance. The doctor, whose courage and cheerfulness never flagged, took excellent care of them. Thanks to him, there had been among them hitherto but one or two slight cases of fever. He administered to each man daily a half-gram—nearly eight grains—of quinine, and every third or fourth day a double dose.

The following morning Colonel Rondon, Lyra, Kermit, Cherrie, and nine of the camaradas started in single file down the bank, while the doctor and I went in the two double canoes, with six camaradas, three of them the invalids with swollen feet. We halted continually, as we went about three times as fast as the walkers; and we traced the course of the river. After forty minutes' actual going in the boats we came to some rapids; the unloaded canoes ran them without difficulty, while the loads were portaged. In an hour and a half we were again under way, but in ten minutes came to other rapids, where the river ran among islands, and there were several big curls. The clumsy, heavily laden dugouts, lashed in couples, were unwieldy and hard to handle. The rapids came just round a sharp bend, and we got caught in the upper part of the swift water and had to run the first set of rapids in consequence. We in the leading pair of dugouts were within an ace of coming to grief on some big boulders against which we were swept by a cross current at the turn. All of us paddling hard— scraping and bumping—we got through by the skin of our teeth, and managed to make the bank and moor our dugouts. It was a narrow escape from grave disaster. The second pair of lashed dugouts profited by our experience, and made the run—with risk, but with less risk—and moored beside us. Then all the loads were taken out, and the empty canoes were run down through the least dangerous channels among the islands.

This was a long portage, and we camped at the foot of the rapids, having made nearly seven kilometres. Here a little river, a rapid stream of volume equal to the Duvida at the point where we first embarked, joined from the west. Colonel Rondon and Kermit came to it first, and the former named it Rio Kermit. There was in it a waterfall about six or eight feet high, just above the junction. Here we found plenty of fish. Lyra caught two pacu, good-sized, deep-bodied fish. They were delicious eating. Antonio the Parecis said that these fish never came up heavy rapids in which there were falls they had to jump. We could only hope that he was correct, as in that case the rapids we would encounter in the future would rarely be so serious as to necessitate our dragging the heavy dugouts overland. Passing the rapids we had hitherto encountered had meant severe labor and some danger. But the event showed that he was mistaken. The worst rapids were ahead of us.

While our course as a whole had been almost due north, and sometimes east of north, yet where there were rapids the river had generally, although not always, turned westward. This seemed to indicate that to the east of us there was a low northward projection of the central plateau across which we had travelled on mule-back. This is the kind of projection that appears on the maps of this region as a sierra. Probably it sent low spurs to the west, and the farthest points of these spurs now and then caused rapids in our course (for the rapids generally came where there were hills) and for the moment deflected the river westward from its general downhill trend to the north. There was no longer any question that the Dúvida was a big river, a river of real importance. It was not a minor affluent of some other affluent. But we were still wholly in the dark as to where it came out. It was still possible, although exceedingly improbable, that it entered the Gy-Paraná, as another river of substantially the same size, near its mouth. It was much more likely, but not probable, that it entered the Tapajos. It was probable, although far from certain, that it entered the Madeira low down, near its point of junction with the Amazon. In this event it was likely, although again far from certain, that its mouth would prove to be the Aripuanan. The Aripuanan does not appear on the maps as a river of any size; on a good standard map of South America which I had with me its name does not appear at all, although a dotted indication of a small river or creek at about the right place probably represents it. Nevertheless, from the report of one of his lieutenants who had examined its mouth, and from the stories of the rubber-gatherers, or seringueiros, Colonel Rondon had come to the conclusion that this was the largest affluent of the Madeira, with such a body of water that it must have a big drainage basin. He thought that the Dúvida was probably one of its head streams—although every existing map represented the lay of the land to be such as to render impossible the existence of such a river system and drainage basin. The rubber-gatherers reported that they had gone many days' journey up the river, to a point where there was a series of heavy rapids with above them the junction point of two large rivers, one entering from the west. Beyond this they had difficulties because of the hostility of the Indians; and where the junction point was no one could say. On the chance Colonel Rondon had directed one of his subordinate officers, Lieutenant Pyrineus, to try to meet us, with boats and provisions, by ascending the Aripuanan to the point of entry of its first big affluent. This was the course followed when Amilcar had been directed to try to meet the explorers who in

1909 came down the Gy-Paraná. At that time the effort was a failure, and the two parties never met; but we might have better luck, and in any event the chance was worth taking.

On the morning following our camping by the mouth of the Rio Kermit, Colonel Rondon took a good deal of pains in getting a big post set up at the entry of the smaller river into the Dúvida. Then he summoned me, and all the others, to attend the ceremony of its erection. We found the camaradas drawn up in line, and the colonel preparing to read aloud "the orders of the day." To the post was nailed a board with "Rio Kermit" on it; and the colonel read the orders reciting that by the direction of the Brazilian Government, and inasmuch as the unknown river was evidently a great river, he formally christened it the Rio Roosevelt. This was a complete surprise to me. Both Lauro Müller and Colonel Rondon had spoken to me on the subject, and I had urged, and Kermit had urged, as strongly as possible, that the name be kept as Rio da Dúvida. We felt that the "River of Doubt" was an unusually good name; and it is always well to keep a name of this character. But my kind friends insisted otherwise, and it would have been churlish of me to object longer. I was much touched by their action, and by the ceremony itself. At the conclusion of the reading Colonel Rondon led in cheers for the United States and then for me and for Kermit; and the camaradas cheered with a will. I proposed three cheers for Brazil and then for Colonel Rondon, and Lyra, and the doctor, and then for all the camaradas. Then Lyra said that everybody had been cheered except Cherrie; and so we all gave three cheers for Cherrie, and the meeting broke up in high good humor.

Immediately afterward the walkers set off on their march downstream, looking for good canoe trees. In a quarter of an hour we followed with the canoes. As often as we overtook them we halted until they had again gone a good distance ahead. They soon found fresh Indian sign, and actually heard the Indians; but the latter fled in panic. They came on a little Indian fishing village, just abandoned. The three low, oblong huts, of palm leaves, had each an entrance for a man on all fours, but no other opening. They were dark inside, doubtless as a protection against the swarms of biting flies. On a pole in this village an axe, a knife, and some strings of red beads were left, with the hope that the Indians would return, find the gifts, and realize that we were friendly. We saw further Indian sign on both sides of the river.

After about two hours and a half we came on a little river entering from the east. It was broad but shallow, and at the point of entrance rushed down, green and white, over a sharply inclined sheet of rock. It was a lovely sight and we halted to admire it. Then on we went, until, when we had covered about eight kilometres, we came on a stretch of rapids. The canoes ran them with about a third of the loads, the other loads being carried on the men's shoulders. At the foot of the rapids we camped, as there were several good canoe trees near, and we had decided to build two rather small canoes. After dark the stars came out; but in the deep forest the glory of the stars in the night of the sky, the serene radiance of the moon, the splendor of sunrise and sunset, are never seen as they are seen on the vast open plains.

The following day, the 19th, the men began work on the canoes. The ill-fated big canoe had been made of wood so hard that it was difficult to work, and so heavy that the chips sank like lead in the water. But these trees were araputangas, with wood which was easier to work, and which floated. Great buttresses, or flanges, jutted out from their trunks at the base, and they bore big hard nuts or fruits which stood erect at the ends of the branches. The first tree felled proved rotten, and moreover it was chopped so that it smashed a number of lesser trees into the kitchen, overthrowing everything, but not inflicting serious damage. Hardworking, willing, and tough though the camaradas were, they naturally did not have the skill of northern lumberjacks.

We hoped to finish the two canoes in three days. A space was cleared in the forest for our tents. Among the taller trees grew huge-leafed pacovas, or wild bananas. We bathed and swam in the river, although in it we caught piranhas. Carregadores ants swarmed all around our camp. As many of the nearest of their holes as we could we stopped with fire; but at night some of them got into our tents and ate things we could ill spare. In the early morning a column of foraging ants appeared, and we drove them back, also with fire. When the sky was not overcast the sun was very hot, and we spread out everything to dry. There were many wonderful butterflies round about, but only a few birds. Yet in the early morning and late afternoon there was some attractive bird music in the woods. The two best performers were our old friend the false bellbird, with its series of ringing whistles, and a shy, attractive ant-thrush. The latter walked much on the ground, with dainty movements, curtseying and raising its tail; and in accent and sequence, although not in tone or time, its song resembled that of our white-throated sparrow.

It was three weeks since we had started down the River of Doubt. We had come along its winding course about 140 kilometres, with a descent of somewhere in the neighborhood of 124 metres. It had been slow progress. We could not tell what physical obstacles were ahead of us, nor whether the Indians would be actively hostile. But a river normally describes in its course a parabola, the steep descent being in the upper part; and we hoped that in the future we should not have to encounter so many and such difficult rapids as we had already encountered, and that therefore we would make better time—a hope destined to failure.

19

THE JOYS OF POLAR SLEDGING

WALTER WELLMAN

Walter Wellman was one of many explorers locked in the ferocious battle to claim the North Pole. But after two attempts, Wellman, exhausted by the slog of navigating changing weather and shifting ice, began to consider an attempt by air. Wellman secured the funds for the first of three airships (dubbed America*) among much fanfare in 1906, but the initial attempt self-destructed during engine testing. After a second iteration of the airship was grounded during a trial flight due to high wind, Wellman tested his luck again in 1909, but the third craft suffered mechanical difficulties and had to be rescued by a Norwegian survey ship. Although this would be Wellman's last run for the Arctic (he abandoned the idea after learning of Frederick Cook's—later disputed—claim), he had succeeded in opening the door to future Arctic exploration by air.*

CHAPTER XIII: THE JOYS OF POLAR SLEDGING

Polar sledging is anything but a joy ride. The cold is not the worst part of it, that is, directly: so far as actually feeling the cold was concerned, we had no trouble, and a few frostbites didn't count. Hardest to endure was the indirect effect of the cold, coupled with the absence of a fire to dry things. The camping hour arrives. You have been working hard all day, pulling and tugging in a temperature ranging from twenty-five to forty-five degrees below zero, and perhaps with a nice cool wind blowing from the north. Outside you are a mass of frost, and inside your skin is wet with perspiration.

Be careful in pitching the tent that you do not leave your mittens off more than a few seconds, or you will not only freeze your fingers, but find the mittens frozen so hard you cannot get them on again. The best way is to put them inside your jacket till you want them. When the tent is pitched, one man goes to cut fresh ice—ice that is at the top of the hummocks, fifteen or eighteen feet above the sea—and break it up fine for melting over the petroleum-gas lamp. This is the only way to get water, and it is not an easy way, for the ice is almost as hard as a rock.

Another man feeds the hungry dogs their meager ration of frozen meat. Poor beasts, it is a small bit and swallowed at a single gulp, and then nothing more than snow for them to eat till the next night. It makes one very sad to see the hungry fellows sitting about watching with wide eyes their busy masters, and wagging their tails in expectancy of a crumb or two. But it is a hard life for both man and beast, and rations must be strictly adhered to, no matter how many good dogs go to sleep in the snow with empty stomachs. They'll jump into their work all right in the morning just the same.

Two men get the big sleeping-bag off the sledge and carry it into the tent. There they try to unroll it. Half an hour of tugging, yanking, pounding is needed to accomplish this feat, so fast is it frozen from the moisture of the previous night's use. When it is spread flat in the snow we begin getting in. Preliminary to this we beat and scrape some of the frost from one another's clothing, but it is impossible to get it all off. The remainder goes into the bag with us. We don't take off any clothing, not even our moccasins or our hats. Yes, we do take off our reindeer-skin shoes, but it is only for the purpose of turning them inside out that they may the better dry during the night, and that we may take out the senne grass or hay which we have worn in them to absorb the moisture and keep the feet dry.

The art of keeping warm feet is to keep dry feet, and three or four pairs of woolen stockings and a nicely packed bunch of this hay work to a charm. Whatever else we got in this excursion, we did not get cold feet. Scattered out to freeze, the hay can be shaken entirely free of frost next morning, and so will be fairly dry to put on again. But what a job it is to turn these frozen moccasins night and morning with our frostnipped, tender fingers! More than once have I seen a big, brave fellow shedding tears and swearing together while at this job—it hurt so.

We start kicking our way into the sleeping-bag. It is frosty, icy, hard in there, and it takes a lot of kicking and shoving to straighten it out and work our way well down in. By the time this is done, supper is ready, and this brings in the only glorious hour of the day. Hot soup, hot coffee, biscuits; a piece of cheese; bacon, sometimes, raw, sometimes boiled in the soup; oat-meal porridge; a nice chunk of butter, hard as a rock, but it tastes good in the coffee; and a big drink of ice water when we are lucky enough to have any water left over. If there isn't any left over, we go thirsty, as we can't afford to use more oil.

We sit up in the bag like birdlings in a nest, and eat this supper with voracious appetites, and with mittens on our fingers. The steam is converted into frost and the white particles fall all over us; but we don't mind that as long as there is anything to eat. The saddest moment is when everything is gone and the ration exhausted.

Then a pipe for consolation—a pipe and the pleasant task of writing up one's journal in a temperature of seventy degrees or more below freezing. There was once a time when I didn't believe it possible for a man to write two or three hundred words in half an hour in such cold, with bare hands; but now I know it can be done, and, what is more surprising, the man can actually read what he has written.

The next thing is to push one's self all the way down into the now fairly-well thawed-out sleeping-bag, pull up the flap and button it tight, and get snuggled for the night. All this is easier said than done. The predominant idea of comfort in a sleeping-bag prevailing among my Norwegian comrades was to slide down somewhere near the bottom and telescope themselves together; but I had always to have a smell of fresh air, no matter how cold it was.

There were four of us in one bag, and none of us was small, and we had to lie "spoon-fashion." When one turned over all had to turn. As we were packed in like Smyrna figs in a box, and as I occupied one edge of the bag, where the coverlid was drawn down over me as tight as a drumhead, it sometimes took me a quarter of an hour to turn over. It was quite an athletic feat, but it had its advantage in that it helped one to warm up. The effort to turn about-face usually started perspiration, though the jacket I wore was so stiff with frost that on first getting into bed it was difficult to bend the arms. We always wore our mittens in bed, at least during the first part of the night, when we were struggling to get our blankets straightened out. These were like pieces of sheet metal to start with; but the heat of our bodies and the persistent bending and breaking of them finally licked them into shape.

Surprising, the power of this body heat of a vigorous man! In the course of a couple of hours it thawed most of our clothing into wet compresses, made the blankets limp and soggy, and even softened parts of the sleeping-bag itself. Something like a hundred minutes after buttoning the flaps down over our heads we found ourselves lying with pools of water under our bodies, while frost still adhered to our trousers. By this time two or three of my Norwegian bed-fellows were snoring like threshing-machines, trolley-cars, boiler-shops and batteries of artillery. Then, generally without much loss of time, I suppose I joined in the chorus.

All these and countless other annoyances are small matters when once you get accustomed to them, and as long as one is in full possession of his health and strength. But I cannot conscientiously recommend an Arctic tent as a hospital, nor a dog sledge in rough ice and bad weather as an ambulance.

20

PREPARATIONS FOR VISITING THE RUINS

JOHN LLOYD STEPHENS

When veteran world traveler John Lloyd Stephens and his partner, English illustrator Frederick Catherwood, turned their attention to the lost civilization of Central America, they were tempting the unknown. Starting their search for ancient cities in Honduras, they fought hunger, malaria, suffocating jungle, and unreliable mapping until, on a humid day in November 1839, they entered the ruins of the Mayan site of Copán. Stephens purchased the site for $50 with intentions to ship it to New York (later abandoning the idea), and the two continued to seek out and begin excavation on dozens of sites across Central America and Mexico, including Chichén Itzá, Tulum, and, here, Palenque, which hadn't been seen by Europeans since the Spanish explorers in the sixteenth century. Stephens has since been dubbed the father of American archeology, but he was also critical in communicating the sophistication and dominance of the Mayans. "America, say historians, was peopled by savages," he wrote. "But savages never built these structures, savages never carved these stones."

CHAPTER XVII: PREPARATIONS FOR VISITING THE RUINS

Early the next morning we prepared for our move to the ruins. We had to make provision for housekeeping on a large scale; our culinary utensils were of rude pottery, and our cups the hard shells of some round vegetables, the whole cost, perhaps, amounting to one dollar. We could not procure a water-jar in the place, but the alcalde lent us one free of charge unless it should be broken, and as it was cracked at the time he probably considered it sold. By-the-way, we forced ourselves upon the alcalde's affections by leaving our money with him for safe-keeping. We did this with great publicity, in order that it might be known in the village that there was no "plata" at the ruins, but the alcalde regarded it as a mark of special confidence. Indeed, we could not have shown him a greater. He was a suspicious old miser, kept his own money in a trunk in an inner room, and never left the house without locking the street door and carrying the key with him. He made us pay beforehand for everything we wanted, and would not have trusted us half a dollar on any account.

It was necessary to take with us from the village all that could contribute to our comfort, and we tried hard to get a woman; but no one would trust herself alone with us. This was a great privation; a woman was desirable, not, as the reader may suppose, for embellishment, but to make tortillas. These, to be tolerable, must be eaten the moment they are baked; but we were obliged to make an arrangement with the alcalde to send them out daily with the product of our cow.

Our turn-out was equal to anything we had had on the road. One Indian set off with a cowhide trunk on his back, supported by a bark string, as the groundwork of his load, while on each side hung by a bark string a fowl wrapped in plantain leaves, the head and tail only being visible. Another had on the top of his trunk a live turkey, with its legs tied and wings expanded, like a spread eagle. Another had on each side of his load strings of eggs, each egg being wrapped carefully in a husk of corn, and all fastened like onions on a bark string. Cooking utensils and water-jar were mounted on the backs of other Indians, and contained rice, beans, sugar, chocolate, &c; strings of pork and bunches of plantains were pendent; and Juan carried in his arms our travelling tin coffee-canister filled with lard, which in that country was always in a liquid state.

At half past seven we left the village. For a short distance the road was open, but very soon we entered a forest, which continued unbroken to the ruins, and probably many miles beyond. The road was a mere Indian footpath, the branches of the trees, beaten down and heavy with the rain, hanging so low that we were obliged to stoop constantly, and very soon our hats and coats were perfectly wet. From the thickness of the foliage the morning sun could not dry up the deluge of the night before. The ground was very muddy, broken by streams swollen by the early rains, with gullies in which the mules floundered and stuck fast, in some places very difficult to cross. Amid all the wreck of empires, nothing ever spoke so forcibly the world's mutations as this immense forest shrouding what was once a great city. Once it had been a great highway, thronged with people who were stimulated by the same passions that give impulse to human action now; and they are all gone, their habitations buried, and no traces of them left.

In two hours we reached the River Micol, and in half an hour more that of Otula, darkened by the shade of the woods, and breaking beautifully over a stony bed. Fording this, very soon we saw masses of stones, and then a round sculptured stone. We spurred up a sharp ascent of fragments, so steep that the mules could barely climb it, to a terrace so covered, like the whole road, with trees, that it was impossible to make out the form. Continuing on this terrace, we stopped at the foot of a second, when our Indians cried out "el Palacio," "the palace," and through openings in the trees we saw the front of a large building richly ornamented with stuccoed figures on the pilasters, curious and elegant; trees growing close against it, and their branches entering the doors; in style and effect unique, extraordinary, and mournfully beautiful. We tied our mules to the trees, ascended a flight of stone steps forced apart and thrown down by trees, and entered the palace, ranged for a few moments along the corridor and into the courtyard, and after the first gaze of eager curiosity was over, went back to the entrance, and, standing in the doorway, fired a *feu-de-joie* of four rounds each, being the last charge of our firearms. But for this way of giving vent to our satisfaction we should have made the roof of the old palace ring with a hurrah. It was intended, too, for effect upon the Indians, who had probably never heard such a cannonade before, and almost, like their ancestors in the time of Cortez, regarded our weapons as instruments which spit lightning, and who, we knew, would make such a report in the village as would keep any of their respectable friends from paying us a visit at night.

We had reached the end of our long and toilsome journey, and the first glance indemnified us for our toil. For the first time we were in a building erected by the aboriginal inhabitants, standing before the Europeans knew of the existence of this continent, and we prepared to take up our abode under its roof. We selected the front corridor as our dwelling, turned turkey and fowls loose in the courtyard, which was so overgrown with trees that we could barely see across it; and as there was no pasture for the mules except the leaves of the trees, and we could not turn them loose into the woods, we brought them up the steps through the palace, and turned them into the courtyard also. At one end of the corridor Juan built a kitchen, which operation consisted in laying three stones anglewise, so as to have room for a fire between them. Our luggage was stowed away or hung on poles reaching across the corridor. Pawling mounted a stone about four feet long on stone legs for a table, and with the Indians cut a number of poles, which they fastened together with bark strings, and laid them on stones at the head and foot for beds. We cut down the branches that entered the palace, and some of the trees on the terrace, and from the floor of the palace overlooked the top of an immense forest stretching off to the Gulf of Mexico.

The Indians had superstitious fears about, remaining at night among the ruins, and left us alone, the sole tenants of the palace of unknown kings. Little did they who built it think that in a few years their royal line would perish and their race be extinct, their city a ruin, and Mr. Catherwood, Pawling, and I and Juan its sole tenants. Other strangers had been there, wondering like ourselves. Their names were written on the walls, with comments and figures; and even here were marks of those low, grovelling spirits which delight in profaning holy places. Among the names, but not of the latter class, were those of acquaintances: Captain Caddy and Mr. Walker; and one was that of a countryman, Noah O. Platt, New York. He had gone out to Tobasco as supercargo of a vessel, ascended one of the rivers for logwood, and while his vessel was loading visited the ruins. His account of them had given me a strong desire to visit them long before the opportunity of doing so presented itself.

High up on one side of the corridor was the name of William Beanham, and under it was a stanza written in lead-pencil. By means of a tree with notches cut in it, I climbed up and read the lines. The rhyme was faulty and the spelling bad, but they breathed a deep sense of the moral sublimity pervading these unknown ruins. The author seemed, too, an acquaintance. I had heard his story in the village. He was a young Irishman, sent by a merchant of Tobasco into the interior for purposes of small traffic; had passed some time at Palenque and in the neighbourhood; and, with his thoughts and feelings turned strongly toward the Indians, after dwelling upon the subject for some time, resolved to penetrate into the country of the Caribs. His friends endeavoured to dissuade him, and the prefect told him "You have red hair, a florid complexion, and white skin, and they will either make a god of you and keep you among them, or else kill and eat you;" but he set off alone and on foot, crossed the River Chacamal, and after an absence of nearly a year returned safe, but naked and emaciated, with his hair and nails long, having been eight days with a single Carib on the banks of a wild river, searching for a crossing-place, and living upon roots and herbs. He built a hut on the borders of the Chacamal River, and lived there with a Carib servant, preparing for another and more protracted journey among them, until at length some boatmen who came to trade with him found him lying in his hammock dead, with his skull split open. He had escaped the dangers of a journey which no man in that country dared encounter, to die by the hands of an assassin in a moment of fancied security. His arm was hanging outside, and a book lying on the ground; probably he was struck while reading. The murderers, one of whom was his servant, were caught, and were then in prison in Tobasco. Unfortunately, the people of Palenque had taken but little interest in anything except the extraordinary fact of his visit among the Caribs and his return safe. All his papers and collection of curiosities were scattered and destroyed, and with him died all the fruits of his labours; but, were he still living, he would be the man, of all others, to accomplish the discovery of that mysterious city which had so much affected our imaginations. . . .

But to return to ourselves in the palace. While we were making our observations, Juan was engaged in a business that his soul loved. As with all the mozos of that country, it was his pride and ambition to servir a mano. He scorned the manly occupation of a mule-teer, and aspired to that of a menial servant. He was anxious to be left at the village, and did not like the idea of stopping at the ruins, but was reconciled to it by being allowed to devote himself exclusively to cookery. At four o'clock we sat down to our first dinner. The tablecloth was two broad leaves, each about two feet long, plucked from a tree on the terrace before the door. Our saltcellar stood like a pyramid, being a case made of husks of corn put together lengthwise, and holding four or five pounds, in lumps from the size of a pea to that of a hen's egg. Juan was as happy as if he had prepared the dinner exclusively for his own eating; and all went merry as a marriage-bell, when the sky became overcast, and a sharp thunder-clap heralded the afternoon's storm. From the elevation of the terrace, the floor of the palace commanded a view of the top of the forest, and we could see the trees bent down by the force of the wind; very soon a fierce blast swept through the open doors, which was followed instantaneously by heavy rain. The table was cleared by the wind, and, before we could make our escape, was drenched by the rain. We snatched away our plates, and finished our meal as we could.

The rain continued, with heavy thunder and lightning, all the afternoon. In the absolute necessity of taking up our abode among the ruins, we had hardly thought of our exposure to the elements until it was forced upon us. At night we could not light a candle, but the darkness of the palace was lighted up by fireflies of extraordinary size and brilliancy, shooting through the corridors and stationary on the walls, forming a beautiful and striking spectacle. They were of the description with those we saw at Nopa, known by the name of shining beetles, and are mentioned by the early Spaniards, among the wonders of a world where all was new, "as showing the way to those who travel at night." The historian describes them as "somewhat smaller than Sparrows, having two stars close by then-Eyes, and two more under their Wings, which gave so great a Light that by it they could spin, weave, write, and paint; and the Spaniards went by night to hunt the Utios or little Rabbits of that country; and a-fishing, carrying these Animals tied to their great Toes or Thumbs: and they called them Locuyos, being also of use to save them from the Gnats, which are there very troublesome. They took them in the Night with Firebrands, because they made to the Light, and came when called by their Name; and they are so unwieldy that when they fall they cannot rise again; and the Men streaking their Faces and Hands with a sort of Moisture that is in those Stars, seemed to be afire as long as it lasted."

It always gave us high pleasure to realize the romantic and seemingly half-fabulous accounts of the chroniclers of the conquest. Very often we found their quaint descriptions so vivid and faithful as to infuse the spirit that breathed through their pages. We caught several of these beetles, not, however, by calling them by their names, but with a hat, as schoolboys used to catch fireflies, or, less poetically, lightning-bugs, at home. They are more than half an inch long, and have a sharp movable horn on the head; when laid on the back they cannot turn over except by pressing this horn against a membrane upon the front. Behind the eyes are two round transparent substances full of luminous matter, about as large as the head of a pin, and underneath is a larger membrane containing the same luminous substance. Four of them together threw a brilliant light for several yards around, and by the light of a single one we read distinctly the finely-printed pages of an American newspaper. It was one of a packet, full of debates in Congress, which I had as yet barely glanced over, and it seemed stranger than any incident of my journey to be reading by the light of beetles, in the ruined palace of Palenque, the sayings and doings of great men at home. In the midst of it Mr. Catherwood, in emptying the capacious pocket of a shooting-jacket, handed me a Broadway omnibus ticket:

> "Good to the bearer for a ride,
>
> "A. Brower."

These things brought up vivid recollections of home, and among the familiar images present were the good beds into which our friends were about that time turning. Ours were set up in the back corridor, fronting the courtyard. This corridor consisted of open doors and pilasters alternately. The wind and rain were sweeping through, and, unfortunately, our beds were not out of reach of the spray. They had been set up with some labour on four piles of stones each, and we could not then change their position. We had no spare articles to put up as screens; but, happily, two umbrellas, tied up with measuring rods and wrapped in a piece of matting, had survived the wreck of the mountain-roads. These Mr. C. and I secured at the head of our beds. Pawling swung a hammock across the corridor so high that the sweep of the rain only touched the foot; and so passed our first night at Palenque. In the morning, umbrellas, bedclothes, wearing apparel, and hammocks were wet through, and there was not a dry place to stand on.

Already we considered ourselves booked for a rheumatism. We had looked to our residence at Palenque as the end of troubles, and for comfort and pleasure, but all we could do was to change the location of our beds to places which promised a better shelter for the next night.

A good breakfast would have done much to restore our equanimity; but, unhappily, we found that the tortillas which we had brought out the day before, probably made of half-mouldy corn, by the excessive dampness were matted together, sour, and spoiled. We went through our beans, eggs, and chocolate without any substitute for bread, and, as often before in time of trouble, composed ourselves with a cigar. Blessed be the man who invented smoking, the soother and composer of a troubled spirit, allayer of angry passions, a comfort under the loss of breakfast, and to the roamer in desolate places, the solitary wayfarer through life, serving for "wife, children, and friends."

At about ten o'clock the Indians arrived with fresh tortillas and milk. Our guide, too, having finished cutting up and distributing the hog, was with them. He was the same who had been employed by Mr. Waldeck, and also by Mr. Walker and Captain Caddy, and was recommended by the prefect as the only man acquainted with the ruins. Under his escort we set out for a preliminary survey. Of ourselves, leaving the palace, in any direction, we should not have known which way to direct our steps.

In regard to the extent of these ruins. Even in this practical age the imagination of man delights in wonders. The Indians and the people of Palenque say that they cover a space of sixty miles; in a series of well- written articles in our own country they have been set down as ten times larger than New York; and lately I have seen an article in some of the newspapers, referring to our expedition, which represents this city, discovered by us, as having been three times as large as London! It is not in my nature to discredit any marvellous story. I am slow to disbelieve, and would rather sustain all such inventions; but it has been my unhappy lot to find marvels fade away as I approached them: even the Dead Sea lost its mysterious charm; and besides, as a traveller and "writer of a book," I know that if I go wrong, those who come after me will not fail to set me right. Under these considerations, not from any wish of my own, and with many thanks to my friends of the press, I am obliged to say that the Indians and people of Palenque really know nothing of the ruins personally, and the other accounts do not rest upon any sufficient foundation. The whole country for miles around is covered by a dense forest of gigantic trees, with a growth of brush and underwood unknown in the wooded deserts of our own country, and impenetrable in any direction except by cutting a way with a machete. What lies buried in that forest it is impossible to say of my own knowledge; without a guide, we might have gone within a hundred feet of all the buildings without discovering one of them.

Captain Del Rio, the first explorer, with men and means at command, states in his report, that in the execution of his commission he cut down and burned all the woods; he does not say how far, but, judging from the breaches and excavations made in the interior of the buildings, probably for miles around. Captain Dupaix, acting under a royal commission, and with all the resources such a commission would give, did not discover any more buildings than those mentioned by Del Rio, and we saw only the same; but, having the benefit of them as guides, at least of Del Rio (for at that time we had not seen Dupaix's work), we of course saw things which escaped their observation, just as those who come after us will see what escaped ours. This place, however, was the principal object of our expedition, and it was our wish and intention to make a thorough exploration. Respect for my official character, the special tenour of my passport, and letters from Mexican authorities, gave me every facility. The prefect assumed that I was sent by my government expressly to explore the ruins; and every person in Palenque except our friend the alcalde, and even he as much as the perversity of his disposition would permit, was disposed to assist us. But there were accidental difficulties which were insuperable.

First, it was the rainy season. This, under any circumstances, would have made it difficult; but as the rains did not commence till three or four o'clock, and the weather was clear always in the morning, it alone would not have been sufficient to prevent our attempting it; but there were other difficulties, which embarrassed us from the beginning, and continued during our whole residence among the ruins. There was not an axe or spade in the place, and, as usual, the only instrument was the machete, which here was like a short and wide-bladed sword; and the difficulty of procuring Indians to work was greater than at any other place we had visited. It was the season of planting corn, and the Indians, under the immediate pressure of famine, were all busy with their milpas. The price of an Indian's labour was eighteen cents per day; but the alcalde, who had the direction of this branch of the business, would not let me advance to more than twenty-five cents, and the most he would engage to send me was from four to six a day. They would not sleep at the ruins, came late, and went away early; sometimes only two or three appeared, and the same men rarely came twice, so that during our stay we had all the Indians of the village in rotation. This increased very much our labour, as it made it necessary to stand over them constantly to direct their work; and just as one set began to understand precisely what we wanted, we were obliged to teach the same to others; and I may remark that their labour, though nominally cheap, was dear in reference to the work done.

At that time I expected to return to Palenque; whether I shall do so now or not is uncertain; but I am anxious that it should be understood that the accounts which have been published of the immense labour and expense of exploring these ruins, which, as I before remarked, made it almost seem presumptuous for me to undertake it with my own resources, are exaggerated and untrue. Being on the ground at the commencement of the dry season, with eight or ten young "pioneers," having a spirit of enterprise equal to their bone and muscle, in less than six months the whole of these ruins could be laid bare. Any man who has ever "cleared" a hundred acres of land is competent to undertake it, and the time and money spent by one of our young men in a "winter in Paris" would determine beyond all peradventure whether the city ever did cover the immense extent which some have supposed.

But to return: Under the escort of our guide we had a fatiguing but most interesting day. What we saw does not need any exaggeration. It awakened admiration and astonishment. In the afternoon came on the regular storm. We had distributed our beds, however, along the corridors, under cover of the outer wall, and were better protected, but suffered terribly from moschetoes, the noise and stings of which drove away sleep. In the middle of the night I took up my mat to escape from these murderers of rest. The rain had ceased, and the moon, breaking through the heavy clouds, with a misty face lighted up the ruined corridor. I climbed over a mound of stones at one end, where the wall had fallen, and, stumbling along outside the palace, entered a lateral building near the foot of the tower, groped in the dark along a low damp passage, and spread my mat before a low doorway at the extreme end. Bats were flying and whizzing through the passage, noisy and sinister; but the ugly creatures drove away moschetoes. The dampness of the passage was cooling and refreshing; and, with some twinging apprehensions of the snakes and reptiles, lizards and scorpions, which infest the ruins, I fell asleep.

21

BY MOTOR THROUGH THE EAST COAST AND BATAK HIGHLANDS OF SUMATRA

MELVIN HALL

Colonel Melvin Hall's career spanned time as a spy in World War I, administrator for the American Financial Commission in Persia, and head of a special mission to Indochina to report on the spread of communism, ostensibly confirming his claim that "it is not in my nature to remain static for any considerable stretch of time." His interest in adventure was fanned early when his family purchased one of the country's first commercial automobiles. They motored around the United States and Europe, collecting stories like the time Hall's father used vodka as fuel in Poland and then, when dealing with a flat tire, took to drinking it out of the carburetor. Shortly after his graduation from Princeton, the Halls set off for another road trip, this time leaving from Europe in a Packard touring car bound for Delhi and the

Coronation Durbar of King George V. Hall's father deboarded in India, but he and his mother continued the trip, driving around Ceylon (Sri Lanka), Java, and, in this excerpt, Sumatra.

BY MOTOR THROUGH THE EAST COAST AND BATAK HIGHLANDS OF SUMATRA

THE HIGHWAYS OF SUMATRA

The road was very good, wide, well made, and much better than I had expected. There is practically no rock in this part of the island, and the metaling for the roads must be imported; nevertheless, the chief highways of the coastal plains and the pass over the mountains are all macadamized. In the highlands, where metaling has not yet been attempted, such roads as exist are of a very different type. These are of dirt or clay, well built and maintained, and said to be very good in dry weather.

Unfortunately, we were there when seventeen days of continuous rainfall had reduced them to an almost impassable state of soft mud and slippery clay, and, while our experience is perhaps hardly a fair criterion. I can scarcely believe that with the enormous annual rainfall of Sumatra such is not the condition a large part of the time.

The road from Medan to the interior, however, gave no warning of what was to follow. Leaving the plains and the tobacco plantations, it gradually ascended through wilder country, and presently, with well-engineered zigzags, began to climb into the mountains.

At 3,000 feet altitude we came to the tiny sanatorium of Bandar Baroe, a recuperating station in the clearer atmosphere of the hills for Europeans of the Deli Company enervated by the unhealthy life of the lowlands. It was a wee bungalow of three or four rooms with a wide, pointed roof of thatch, and from its perch on top of the usual piles it looked out between tall tree-ferns over the plain below.

Here we spent the night, having first applied to the *Controleur* for permission. The native in charge had no supplies, so we had recourse to our own for the first of a series of "tinned meals" that continued without interruption until we returned to Medan.

A WAGON TRAIN OF SHIFTING SHADOWS

In the evening, stretched out in comfortable wicker chairs on the bungalow's little veranda, we watched a train of loaded buffalo carts winding stiffly up the hill in a heavy rain. The air was so fresh and cool it was difficult to think of the hot, sultry coast less than forty miles away. The rain pattered gently on the ground and rolled off the over-hanging thatch of the eaves in big drops, while the creaking of wheels and soft cries of the drivers drifted up from the laboring freighters on the road.

For more than an hour the train crept slowly past in a single file of vague, indeterminable shapes, with swaying lanterns casting dim circles of light and queer shifting shadows in the misty darkness. We watched in fascination while the tiny spots appeared out of the jungle below and lengthened into a twin-kling line which wound up past the bungalow and disappeared one by one above us into the night and the forest.

Early the next morning we continued our climb over the pass. The semi-tropical vegetation which had succeeded the coarse grass of the denuded plains gave way in turn to magnificent virgin forests, unbroken except for the narrow, winding path of the road.

THE SUMATRAN JUNGLE

The enormous straight-trunked trees, ensnared by giant creepers, vines, and huge air plants, made so thick a canopy overhead that only a dim twilight filtered in, and that failed to reach the ground through the dense, impenetrable tangle of vegetation.

Little brooks of clear water rushed steeply down the mountainside, hurrying along to the sluggish yellow rivers of the plains their tiny contributions for the extension of Sumatra's coast. Butterflies flitted in the blue-black shadows; jungle fowl, their brilliance all subdued in the obscure half light, vanished silently from the edges of the road as we approached, and other little creeping and fugitive things sought the security of the unbetraying jungle.

Insects with voices out of all proportion to their probable size screamed shrilly from the branches, and the occasional whistle of a bird or the dull boom of a falling tree echoed through the silent, dark recesses of the wood.

Much of the life of the jungle we saw along this little frequented road which opened up the very heart of the virgin forest, but infinitely more were we ourselves observed. Sometimes the crack of a broken branch betrayed the hurried withdrawal of a larger animal, or a whirr of wings that of some startled bird; but only one's own sixth sense told of the hidden watchers who silently followed our progress with wondering, unfriendly eyes.

PURSUED BY HOSTS OF CURIOUS MONKEYS

The swaying of branches overhead as we zigzagged up the pass did not mean wind in the quiet forest; it meant monkeys, and their antics were an unfailing amusement, whether we kept on or stopped to watch them. Some waited in silence until we drew near, then plunged back into the forest with a crash of branches which inevitably produced on us the shock they seemed to have designed. Some tore furiously along beside us through the trees in a desperate attempt to cross in front of the car before we could catch up to them.

When they did cross, far overhead, in a stream of small gray bodies flying through the air between the treetops, they as furiously raced along on the other side and crossed back again. Others clung to swaying branches and bounded up and down in a frenzy of excitement, shrieking gibes in sharp crescendo as we passed.

Often in the midst of their agitation they suddenly lost all interest and forthwith paid no more attention to us; or sat in silence with weazened, whiskered faces peering solemnly down from the trees.

As in Ceylon, it would have been disastrous to leave the motor unguarded anywhere in a Sumatra forest, for everything that prying fingers could unscrew or remove would soon be reposing merrily in the tree-tops.

There were many tribes of the monkey people: little black fellows with very long tails; troops of impudent brown ones; shy black-and-white monkeys with fine silky coats; and hordes of big gray beasts who chased and tweaked each other, evoking shrieks of protest.

Near by, yet aloof from the bands that fed and gamboled together, were a few enormous black bulks which from the distance might have been curious vegetable formations in the trees. But they moved, and I stopped to examine one through the glasses, when my mother suddenly called my attention to something on the other side.

From a leafy branch less than forty feet away a great round head protruded and a solemn black face, comically like a sulky old savage, gazed out upon us. For a few minutes it stared in silence; then with unhurried, deliberate movements returned to a leisurely search for food.

WATCHING THE POWERFUL ORANG-OUTANG

"Orang-outang," I whispered. "Only found here and in Borneo. There are two more on the other side. . . . See him pull that branch down!" He reached up one tremendous, sinewy arm and with the greatest ease drew down a branch that would scarcely have bent beneath the weight of a heavy man. Holding it with one hand, he pawed idly over it with the other, occasionally transferring some morsel to his mouth and promptly spitting it out if it displeased him.

When the branch was duly inspected he released it, and the *swish!* of leaves as it flew back through the air gave some idea of the strength that had bent it.

There was no need of whispering, for although we watched this one for half an hour with the glasses he ignored our presence completely, and except for the first brief inspection not one of the big apes showed a sign of consciousness of our proximity. They were very well aware of it, but were too powerful for fear, and the orang-outang rarely troubles those who do not bother him. We were not inclined to regret this indifference, however, for the "old man of the forest" can be extremely disagreeable when he chooses.

AN UNSOCIABLE JUNGLE BEAST

The other monkeys and apes all moved in troops, but the orang-outangs went alone—severely alone—for their smaller relations seemed to give them a wide berth.

Unlike the monkeys, they appeared conservative of energy, and every movement was carried out with a careful deliberation most amusing to watch. Their huge black bodies were very conspicuous in the trees; their trunks thicker than a man's, with short, heavy legs and arms of extraordinary length and power.

Apparently quite satisfied with the food within reach, the great apes moved lazily along the branches, holding on with their feet and scarcely changing their positions while we watched them. One eventually decided to transfer his operations elsewhere and sauntered off through the trees, swinging his upright body from branch to branch with powerful, far-reaching arms. His movements were still slow and deliberate, but the progress he made was astonishing, though now and then interrupted as he stopped to investigate some delicacy.

The last we saw of him he was hanging serenely by one long arm, indolently exploring a branch with both feet and his other hand.

The Boekit Barisan, a series of mountain ranges running the whole length of the island near the western coast, splits in the north into parallel chains which en-circle the broad Karo-Batak plateau and the vast area of Toba Lake. In these partially explored ranges there have already been discovered ninety volcanoes, twelve of which are now active, the constructive and destructive forces of Sumatra's formation.

The road from Deli crosses over the northeastern part of the parallel chains into the Batak Highlands, as the plateau is called, by a pass between the mountains Sibajak and Baros.

As we neared the summit of the pass a narrow break in the forest revealed a superb view through the trees, over the blue ravine and densely timbered mountainside, to the wide coastal plain shimmering in the heat-haze below; then the foliage again closed in until we reached the height-of-land and looked out on the other side.

A dull, treeless expanse, scarcely lower than the top of the pass, stretched out before us in limitless brown waves, a desolate tangle of grass broken only by detached volcanic heights. Two active volcanoes, the northernmost of the range, towered threateningly above the others—Sibajak guarding the entrance through which crept the highland road; Sinaboeng rising from the plateau in majestic isolation, its smoke-crowned peak and deep purple sides outlined against the heavy white clouds that hung behind it.

A LAND THAT NEEDS PEOPLE

The first strong impression of loneliness and monotonous solitude that the highlands gave was little changed by the few scattered compounds and occasional patches of cultivation later revealed as we progressed.

In common with the greater part of Sumatra, which could easily support twenty-five times its present population, this section is sparsely inhabited and the villages are small and far apart.

The Batak tribes lead a communistic life, and outside of the hedged confines of their compounds—each a little cluster of huts around a large central house—very few buildings are found. The Bataks are mostly peaceful and industrious, occupying themselves with agriculture and farming as well as in hunting and fishing. Their agriculture depends upon the rainfall, which, however, rarely fails; but it consists only of little patches of rice and other grain struggling weakly against the all-encompassing rank growth and is barely sufficient to supply their own modest needs.

Not far from the top of the pass we overhauled the long train of freighters which we had watched in the rain of the evening before creeping up the mountain side past Bandar Baroe. The two-wheeled carts, with low, roughly thatched roofs of branches, extended in a close single file far out across the plain, with the thin legs of their red-turbaned Tamil drivers dangling between the shafts.

The buffaloes were dry and dusty, and by the discouraged droop of their heads seemed to express deep discontent with the wallowless uplands. Among the slate-gray backs of the slow-plodding line, half a dozen light pink albinos—an absurd color on an animal of that size—regarded us suspiciously out of curious white eyes.

THE SIMPLICITY OF THE WOMEN'S ATTIRE

Except for this train, we saw no vehicles in the highlands, but several times passed little groups of pedestrians walking single file along the roadside, on their way to or from one of the markets that are held at intervals in the different Batak villages. Some were even tramping from the other side of the mountain, for since the building of the road the Bataks frequently trade with the nearer compounds of the Deli plain.

Almost all were women, balancing heavily packed baskets of fine matting on their heads, with babies astride their hips, supported by a long scarf tied over one shoulder. The simplicity and similarity of their dress was striking, after the variegated colors favored in Java and Malaya, one dark blue garment— a long *sarong* hung loose from under the arms or around the waist—sufficing in the majority of cases.

Their turban-like head-dresses were of the same dark-blue cloth, peculiarly folded, with drooping corners sometimes used to support part of the weight of enormous coiled silver earrings.

We rarely saw men on the road; the few that accompanied the women strolled along behind, quite unencumbered with either baggage or babies, and saluted us with a friendly courtesy rather unexpected in a tribe once so notorious for cannibalism. Their garments were quite similar to those of the women, with a shorter *sarong* tied around the waist, and often a coat or short pair of breeches in addition.

Both men and women were barefoot, as usual, and although a stripe or a plaid occasionally varied the dark blue of their clothes, exceptions to the general style were very rare.

The earrings worn by many of the women were of extraordinary dimensions. Only the wealthier could afford them, for each pair was worth about one hundred and fifty gulden and must have represented a considerable part of the family treasure. They consisted of long circular rods of solid silver, about three-eighths of an inch in diameter, passed through the upper part of the ear and bent back into the form of double, reversed coils, the coils projecting far forward on the left side, to the rear on the right. Their weight would have torn them from the ears had they not been partially supported by the corners of the headdresses, and there was apparently no way of removal without first uncoiling one side.

THE BATAKS, KINDRED OF THE HEAD-HUNTING DAYAKS

The Batak people are in many ways the most interesting and remarkable of all the tribes of Sumatra, although as yet comparatively little is known of them. Ethnologically they are related to the head-hunting Dayaks of Borneo. Their type has not been modified by contact with the outside world, nor even with the more advanced peoples of the coast, and their state of civilization and development is still quite rudimentary, although it is thought that they were once more advanced than they are today.

The reports of early Arabs trading with the Sumatran coast gave the Bataks their evil notoriety as cannibals, eaters of captives, foreigners, and their own aged and decrepit relatives.

The half million Bataks scattered throughout the mountains and uplands of northern and central Sumatra are roughly divided into groups according to differences in dialect. Over a fifth profess Mohammedanism and about half that number Christianity; but in both cases the faith amounts to little more than a form of superstition, showing only vague traces of those beliefs and hardly affecting the village law of racial customs and traditions.

The remainder, including the Kara-Bataks and the tribes of Toba Lake, are animistic pagans, and the circumcision practiced by the former, although doubtless due to some forgotten Mohammedan influences, is not a religious rite.

It is now general in the case of most of these tribes to refer to cannibalism as a practice of the past and at present non-existent.

CHEATING DEATH BY GIVING ONE'S BODY TO BE EATEN

As to whether or not any tribes continue the practice of eating their aged and decrepit relatives I found a divergence of opinion among the European residents of Sumatra. This form of cannibalism is by no means rare, and usually consists of the ritual killing and consumption of old and infirm males by the younger members of their own tribe.

When the aging warrior feels the waning of his powers, he climbs into a tree encircled by his relations, who dance and chant below. The old man presently drops to the ground, symbolic of the fall of a ripe fruit, and is knocked on the head and promptly eaten. In this both parties are mutually benefited: the consumers in partaking of the wisdom of their late progenitor; the eaten ancestor by finding immortality as a dimly conscious member of the bodies of his strong, young descendants.

To an animistic form of religion which regards the decay of a body in the ground as the end of all existence, this method of cheating death is welcomed alike by the failing tribesman and his younger relations. Not infrequently the practice is extended to the unfortunate strangers falling into the hands of such tribes, who are devoured that their capturers may receive the benefit of whatever wisdom they happen to embody. To this, rather than to a mere partiality for human flesh, cannibalism as practiced by many tribes may probably be attributed.

Dark clouds presaging the usual rain of afternoon had already appeared on the horizon when we stopped for a hasty tiffin by the roadside. The rains of many afternoons had reduced the road to a bottomless morass of mud and clay, for we had left behind the last traces of metaling a few miles after clearing the mountains.

While the average altitude of the plains is about four thousand feet, the level of the rolling surface varies more than a thousand, and the steep clay hills become appallingly slippery when wet. Up these the car barely crawled, moving crab-fashion, with the rear wheels revolving furiously in spite of "non-skid" tire chains, and flinging unbroken streams of clay-mud in all directions, which my boy Joseph vainly tried to dodge while he threw armfuls of cut grass under our track.

On the down grades we tobogganed with hair-raising speed, wheels locked, and the whole road surface sliding with us, frequently finishing up in the ditch if there happened to be curves on the descent. Fortunately the ditches were not very deep, but they were quite enough, in their saturated condition, to call out the shovel before the car could be extricated.

Near the mud-hole in which we elected to stop for tiffin, fifty or sixty Batak women were holding a market, all squatting about on the ground, surrounded by piles of dried palm leaves, rattan, and big woven baskets full of grain, dried fish, and various other comestibles.

As seemed generally to be the case throughout the highlands wherever work was in progress, men were conspicuously absent, and the women bargained and gossiped or waited for some one to come and bargain with them, paying little heed to my intrusion in search of photographs. A few were young and not uncomely in feature, but the vast majority appeared old and hideous, the inevitable results of early marriage, over-work, and, above all, the custom of filing the teeth.

THE PRACTICE OF FILING THE TEETH

This practice is quite common among the tribes of Sumatra, and with the Bataks it is invariable among both sexes. The operation, an extremely painful one, is begun at an early age and continued until maturity, when both sets of teeth have been completely filed away down to the jawbone. Although the Bataks' usual food of rice, syrup, and finely chopped meat and fish is soft and easily digested, their inability to chew must be a serious physical disadvantage.

The custom originated as a form of personal adornment, no more strange than many similar practices among other wild tribes of the tropics; but the reasons for it do not seem to have been inherited with the practice itself. To my repeated inquiries the answer was always the same, the usual native explanation for native customs—"Batak people have always done so."

The afternoon rain came up earlier than usual and caught us on a winding ascent to one of the higher levels of the plain. Our doubts of ever reaching the top grew very acute, but after many futile attempts and the burial of a great deal of grass in the deep ruts made by the whirling rear wheels, the car struggled up and we were saved from another night in the open.

The rain was falling in floods when we finally splashed and skidded into the little compound of Sariboe Dolok and sought the meager protection of a tiny rest-house. It had two dark little rooms with a kitchen house in the rear, and as I groped my way inside I sprawled over the body of a large tiger. It was quite dead, but the encounter was somewhat startling.

The house boasted of little in the way of furniture or supplies and the night was very cold, but we were comparatively dry and were offered the luxury of a chicken for supper.

"Luxury" is perhaps a trifle eulogistic for the rubber-like fowl that was set before us. Had we been able to eat him, we might, like the Batak cannibals, have absorbed the wisdom of his hardy experience; but life had been too long and death too recent to admit of any such liberties with the corpse.

Sariboe Dolok, the capital of Simelungen and Karolanden, is not of the importance that its official title might suggest.

It is a lonely settlement of eight or ten native houses, an opium store, the guest-house, and the bungalow of the Assistant Resident, whose life there must be anything but socially gay. This courteous official spoke excellent English, as do the majority of Dutch in the colonies, and, besides affording a great deal of information, made us a present of six eggs—a welcome addition to our tinned supplies, as we had found eggs an unprocurable commodity, even where chickens were to be had.

I also learned from him that the *Kampong* Kebon Djahe, architecturally the most interesting of the Karo-Batak villages and the one I was most anxious to see, lay about twenty-five miles back by the way we had come, on a hill nearly a mile off, and not visible from, the main road.

So the following morning we retraced our way over the fearful clay-mud track, by no means improved by the evening's downpour, until we came to a half-obliterated trail leading westward toward two isolated little white houses. These formed the "Government Center," or "European Quarter," of Kebon Djahe, and half a mile beyond, perched on the top of a steep clay bank above a small river, the remarkable buildings of the native *kampong* lay hidden away in a clump of trees.

A REMARKABLE BATAK COMMUNITY

In their chief features, all Batak *kampongs* are more or less alike, but in architectural elaboration Kebon Djahe is unique. Confined, as usual, within a rectangular space of smooth-trodden clay hedged by a bamboo thicket, the buildings were all raised on wooden piles, their immense thatched roofs and extraordinary decorations completely dwarfing the low, windowless sides. Clumps of plantains, encircled by fences of woven bamboo, sprung like oases from the hard clay ground, and innumerable evil-looking dogs, chickens, and black pigs scratched or rooted in the rubbish beneath the houses. The buildings ranged in size from little granaries and storehouses of quaint and graceful design to the huge communal house, where the men deliberate and banquet and where the fetishistic treasures of the village are kept and friendly strangers entertained.

Each end of the larger houses terminated in a narrow veranda of bamboo poles, with a bamboo ladder or a notched log leading up to the small opening which it gave into the dark interior.

The immense roofs sloped uniformly on the sides from widely flaring ridges to low, overhanging eaves, but the ends were broken in about half way down, forming great gables beneath the jutting ridge-poles. Brilliantly colored matting woven into artistic designs filled these triangular spaces and closed the similar ends of huge dormer-like projections thrown out from the roofs of the more pretentious buildings.

On the communal house and a few others, the vast roofs had a double over-hang, with gigantic, top-heavy cupolas towering above them, thatched and shaped in miniature of the dormered roofs below. From their corners, and from the ends of all the ridge-poles and the blind dormers carved wooden buffalo heads with arched, white-painted necks and savagely lowered horns, looked fiercely down to challenge the intruder.

The cupolas were surmounted by curious wooden figures, some on foot, some riding Batak ponies, but all, brilliantly colored, facing out over the treetops, with hands raised in supplication toward the little white house of the Dutch Controleur on the plain.

A PIGEON-HOUSE AND A TOMB

Beside the communal house stood two remarkable structures quite similar in design, both gay with colored carving and decoration. One was a pigeon-house; the other a tomb, from within which the upright body of the last head-man looked out on the village he had once directed.

Under the thatched roof of an open building near by, a group of women with long poles were pounding grain in hollowed-out wooden logs, while other blue-garbed figures, bearing flat trays or woven baskets on their heads, moved about the inclosure at their various occupations. A few men idled around, but showed little interest in any work more strenuous than chewing *sirih* or following the various strategies I had to employ to obtain the photographs I wanted.

STRENUOUS OBJECTION RAISED TO THE CAMERA

As was often the case in the highlands, the natives, especially the women, were averse to having a one-eyed devil-box aimed at them, and even my disguised efforts in this direction were regarded with deepest suspicion and not infrequently thwarted. With the additional limitations of low-hanging clouds and lack of direct sunlight, and the penetrating moisture so disastrous to films, photographic results in the Batak country were never wholly dependable.

Kebon Djahe was unlike any other village I have ever seen. For several hours we roamed around, exploring the compound, fascinated by all its singular picturesqueness—the remarkable sky-line of the roofs and their fantastic decorations, the blue-clad figures grouped at their divers tasks below, and the effective blending of brilliant colors with the green of bamboo leaves and grayish brown of the moss-covered thatch.

THE AUTOMOBILE DROWNS IN MUD

The sun had gone down unobserved in the clouds and the early twilight had fallen before we left Kebon Djahe. Vague misgivings of the road from there to Sariboe Dolok in the dark had begun to assail my mind, when the car, which had been rocking and skidding over the rain-soaked trail, suddenly plunged deeper into the mud, stopped short, and began to sink.

There was a little hole in the center of the track, no bigger than a man's hand, which on the way up had scarcely been noticeable, but in passing over it in returning, the whole road seemed to open up and engulf us. A furious effort to clear the chasm, whatever it might be, only succeeded in hastening our doom. When we stopped settling the car was so deep that a list to the right brought the top, which was up, to the level of the road surface, while between the top and the ground on the other side there was barely enough space left to crawl through.

Any further sinking of the car might have permanently imprisoned us, so we hastily crept out on our stomachs through the sticky clay-mud and viewed the catastrophe. It was not encouraging. A careful survey of the car showed it to be hopelessly buried, beyond any possibility of my disinterring it unaided.

The chain falls, in the equipment box on the rear, were completely out of sight some four feet underground; but even had I dug them out there was nothing to which to attach them, and in any case the car was too thoroughly in the grip of the mud to have yielded to single-handed efforts.

With some difficulty I discovered the cause of the accident. A bamboo culvert far under the road, which had rotted peacefully and undisturbed since it had been laid, had finally collapsed from our weight, after being weakened by our first passage over it.

To extricate the car was a task for a first-class train-wrecking crew, and I felt little confidence of being able to raise half a dozen helpers in that country, especially as I had left Joseph in Sariboe Dolok and would be unable to explain our predicament to any natives I might meet.

Kebon Djahe seemed the one light on the situation; but night was falling rapidly, and as my speedometer cable had broken in the morning and there were no noticeable landmarks, I had only a dim idea how far away the compound might be.

EVERY MOTHER IS HER OWN PERAMBULATOR IN SUMATRA

For my mother to be left alone at night in the wilds of a country until recently addicted to cannibalism, while I set out on an indeterminate search for help was an unpleasant prospect; but as Kebon Djahe might have been eight or ten miles away—a nasty walk in the mud and the dark—that seemed the only solution.

NATIVE PRISONERS MARCH TO THE RESCUE

For over an hour I walked, or rather waded, down the road in the utter stillness of the desolate highlands. Then a few barely audible shouts drifted up from across the plain, and I struggled through the grass in their direction to a tiny paddy field on the top of a low hill.

Through the dusk I could see a little bamboo lookout, such as is erected in every grain field, and, squatting on its platform, two blue-clad figures, who stopped their shouting as I approached. But to my weak efforts in Malay they merely stared in silence and continued to jerk on the strings which, tied with fluttering bits of cloth, intersected the field to frighten away feathered marauders.

From the hill, however, I discovered in the twilight two solitary little white houses about a mile away and struck off to investigate. Soon a tiny light sprang out of the darkness, and when I arrived in its cheery glow I found the Dutch Controleur just returning from inspecting a jail which was in course of construction, and I accosted him with my tale of disaster and appeal for help.

"Certainly," he promptly said, as if foreign motorists mired in the interior of Sumatra came to him every day with requests to be dug out, "I will lend you my prisoners."

Although his jail was not yet built, he had a fine collection—thirty-eight Bataks and Achinese in whom respect for Dutch control had not been sufficiently evident. This was my wrecking crew, and joined by a Dutch planter, who was recuperating in the higher altitude of the Batak lands from an assault made on him by two coolies, we marched as if on a night attack back to the buried motor, with two armed native soldiers as a guard.

A "SHIVERY" EXPERIENCE FOR A WOMAN

I had been absent several hours before the lanterns picked out ahead of us the dark outline of the sunken car blocking the road. As we approached I saw the figure of my mother apparently seated in the clay mire of the roadside, with a dozen motionless forms standing in a shadowy row on the bank behind her. She struggled stiffly to her feet, revealing one of the mud-soaked seat cushions that she had succeeded in dragging from the car, and the silent row melted back into the darkness.

"Who are your friends?" I asked, after ascertaining that she had suffered nothing more than an unpleasant wait.

"I don't know," she replied, "but I'm very glad to have you back. I've felt rather 'shivery'; first watching them appear out of the dark, one or two at a time; then hearing them talk in low voices. I didn't know whether they were planning to eat me or simply discussing why I chose this particular place to sit in. But for the last half hour they have stood like a row of vultures and haven't made a sound, and that was the worst of all!"

"These are not bad people around here," said Mr. von der Weide, the Dutch planter; "but they are not always to be trusted. I do not think it well to be alone in the highlands at night."

Armed with native spades, shaped somewhat like a wide-bladed adze, and a small forest of strong cut poles which we had fortunately discovered piled by the roadside, the crew attacked the motor.

The prisoners were strong and willing; my training in the recovery of automobiles from strange places had been varied and thorough, and, aided by the untiring efforts of Mr. von der Weide, we soon had a wide excavation made around the car, supporting it meanwhile with shores to prevent further sinking.

Then with the poles as huge levers we pried up each end of the machine a little at a time, filling the chasm underneath with a cob-house of other poles cut into various lengths, until the car, resting on a wooden pier, rose to the road level and was dragged to comparatively firm ground. I scraped off the worst of the clinging mud from those parts that were completely choked with it, and coaxed the motor into starting.

There seemed to be no damage except for twisted mudguards, and we ran back to Kebon Djahe accompanied by Mr. von der Weide, who insisted on our spending the night there—we did not require much urging—while our army was marched cere-moniously back to jail.

The night was extremely cold, at least for within three degrees of the equator, but we had been spared the usual evening storm and although plastered from head to foot with clay mud when we came in, we were very comfortable.

In the morning, after a very early breakfast of Dutch cheese, brown bread, and delicious cocoa, and another hour or more spent in wandering about the fascinating buildings of the native compound, we ran back to Sariboe Dolok. The road, although still in a wretched condition, had dried considerably, as there had been no rain the previous day, and we reached Sariboe Dolok without difficulty, picked up Joseph, and kept on toward Toba Lake.

HOW THE NATIVE MOTHERS WEAVE

Not far beyond the Assistant Residency was the small compound of Kinalang where we made another long stop. It was concealed by the customary thicket of bamboo, and although the houses were smaller, poorer, and not nearly so elaborate in design as those of Kebon Djahe, the native life was even more interesting.

Scattered about the inclosure were crude bamboo frames, attached to the piles of the houses or to poles driven into the ground and fastened at the corners with straw rope. At these the women of the village were seated—their legs stretched out on the ground before them and one end of the frame in their laps—and with the most primitive kind of equipment were producing the *sarongs* for which Kinalang is noted throughout the highlands.

Their movements seemed in nowise hampered by the babies tied on their backs, nor were the babies themselves in the least disconcerted at having their small heads almost snapped off as their mothers worked.

Large bamboo reels held the yarn to be transferred to the spindles, and in little bamboo pails beside each frame were the strong vegetable dyes which the weavers applied on their work, spreading the color with bunches of chicken feathers, while they kept shooting the spindles from side to side between the separated strands of the warp.

In spite of its thriving industry in *sarongs*, the houses of Kinalang showed none of the neatness and decorative features of those of Kebon Djahe. All, except the huge, oddly shaped communal building, were loosely thrown together, sided with strips of split bamboo or rattan, carelessly thatched, and appearing as if the first strong wind would blow them to pieces.

The interiors were dingy, littered with utensils, and filled with smoke and soot from the open fires that burned in the center of their bamboo floors, while dogs and chickens shared with the owners what little space was left.

SUMATRA'S LARGEST LAKE

About two miles from Kinalang the road descended in a sharp curve, plunged through a narrow cut, and, emerging abruptly on the sheer edge of the plateau, revealed a superb view of Toba Lake, over a thousand feet below.

Toba Meer—the Sea of Toba, as it is called—is the largest inland body of water in the Dutch Indies. It covers an area of nearly eight hundred square miles, entirely hemmed in by the mountains of the Boekit Barisan, at an altitude of about 3,100 feet, and it averages nearly 1,400 feet in depth.

We followed the uncompleted road to its sudden end, about two miles below, and then stopped to eat our tiffin and enjoy the magnificent view. The rugged mountains rising precipitously from the dark water, and the narrow, fjord-like recesses of its winding arms, gave an extraordinary beauty to the great highland lake, which from that point was not unlike the Bocche di Cattaro seen from the Montenegrin Pass.

A cataract tumbled down the mountain side opposite; far below us the fantastic roofs of the village of Harangaul showed picturesquely above a grove of fruit trees in the midst of the green paddy fields of the rich ravine, while out in the lake the long, narrow canoes of the Batak fishermen slipped through the blue shadows, with an occasional glint of wet paddles and dripping nets.

We left reluctantly to return to where the road had branched off, backing up to the plateau again because the unprotected trail was too narrow to enable us to turn the car, then continued down the lake.

The road had dried off rapidly and for more than half the distance was vastly better than above, as well as traversing a more wooded and much prettier country. There were, to be sure, two narrow rain-soaked cuts where the water had not run off, through which the car barely succeeded in struggling; but the highland roads had made us indifferent to anything short of being permanently mired.

A MEETING OF BATAK AND MALAY HEADMEN

We made further stops at two other diminutive compounds. In Poerba Dolok, as at Kinalang, the women were weaving *sarongs* and pounding rice; at Pematang Rajah there was a market, and a meeting of Batak and Malay headmen—gorgeously dressed, with huge golden buttons in their jackets, finely wrought bracelets around their arms, and *kris* with beautifully carved hilts stuck into the brilliant sashes at their waists.

As we left this picturesque group and drove slowly on, a bamboo chair swung high on the shoulders of four bearers appeared hurriedly up the road, and from it, as we passed, a wife of one of the chiefs gazed curiously down at our unfamiliar equipage.

Shortly behind her, preceded by dire shrieks, three men in equal haste to reach the market came trotting around a corner, each carrying two live black pigs tightly bound in split bamboo and protesting volubly, as they were swung at the ends of the shoulder poles.

We ran over a swampy road, gradually working upward, across a desolate, grass-covered plain. Only a few mountains dim in the distance gave any sense of limit to the rolling plateau, and except for the swift-flying wild pigeons, a few of which I shot to add variety to our larder, there was nowhere any sign of life.

Dark, ominous clouds bore down upon us as we splashed over the soft level stretches, skidded down short, slippery descents, and labored on the upgrades among the holes and crevasses of deep washouts.

In one place the road was evidently being lowered, and for several hundred yards more than half of it had been cut away, leaving a shelf on one side too narrow to drive on, and on the other a six-foot trench which was simply a morass of mud and water. As the shelf was quite impossible, I chose the trench, started up it with a rush, and promptly stuck fast.

No efforts could move the car in either direction. The sticky clay formed solid disks about the flying wheels, completely hiding tire-chains and rope under its smooth yellow coating.

After an hour of unavailing labor, Joseph and I abandoned the effort to extricate the machine, and as darkness was rapidly falling we held a hurried consultation to determine what should be done. It was finally decided to desert the car and attempt to flounder through the mud to the nearest native village. It was a desperate decision, but the only alternative was a night in the car.

Detaching one of the side lamps, whose fitful rays would enable us to avoid the deepest pools of water, the three of us began the sliding, splashing tramp.

About a mile beyond where the car was entombed we came to a cut, and at its edge the dull rays of another lantern showed half a dozen natives putting away some tools in a little shed. Joseph and I immediately scrambled over to question them. Only one spoke Malay; the others were part of his gang of road laborers—an evil-looking lot.

I was surprised at finding human beings there, and, feeling consequent misgivings over the security of our abandoned car and luggage, I asked the man in charge if he or one of his men would, for a suitable consideration, spend the night in an automobile about a mile down the road, to guard it from being molested during my absence. To my astonishment he promptly refused, and, asking the question in turn of his men, met with immediate negatives.

THE NATIVES DREAD OF TIGERS

I could not account for their unwillingness. The cushions of the tonneau would surely afford as comfortable quarters as any they were accustomed to; it could not be the storm of which men of the highlands were afraid; and the reward I had offered, though small enough, was probably equivalent to about a week's income.

Then it occurred to me that they were afraid of the automobile itself, and I hastened to assure them that it was not only dry and comfortable, but quite safe; that I had locked it up, and that it could not move until I myself released it.

"Oh, it is not that," said the spokesman, with an air of having slept in automobiles most of his life.

"Well, what is it then?" I was both curious and a trifle annoyed.

"Tigers."

"Tigers?"

"Yes, indeed," said Joseph nervously, translating. "He say plenty of tigers here come down sure and eat him up!"

"But not in the automobile," I objected.

"Oh, no; tiger first take him out."

I readily persuaded the men to help carry our luggage to the village, five miles as he estimated it, but nothing would induce any of those natives to spend the night within reach of the great prowling beasts.

A walk down the mountain to the rest-house on the lake was quite as arduous as we had feared. The trail descended some 1,500 feet in long zigzags. When we finally reached our destination, my mother was nearly exhausted, and we were both too grateful for the shelter to be critical of what we found. But even so, one could hardly have called the accommodations luxurious. The whole building leaked; it was overrun with toads, lizards, spiders, cockroaches, and various other pests.

We rose stiff and unrested in the morning, but when the early mists had lifted from the green island facing us, the beauty of the clear highland lake banished every thought of weariness and discomfort.

Few lakes in all the world can offer such a setting as the Toba Meer. The encircling mountains of the Barisan chain rise sheer from the water's edge, their guttered sides white-flecked with the foam of many rain-fed cataracts.

In the purple shadows along this somber rim, indistinct little villages cling precariously to the steep slopes, checkered with the tiny squares of a few light green or yellow paddy fields.

Overhead the winds of the monsoon may moan and whistle about the peaks, but the deep blue surface of the lake is seldom ruffled, save by the V-shaped wakes of the dug-out canoes, which skim about like tiny water-bugs in the vast dimensions of the silent mountain amphitheater.

Amid such surroundings we lost all count of time until hunger necessitated our return to the motor car, which was salvaged from the mud only with great difficulty.

Many trials and adventures were encountered in making our way down from the heights, but when we reached Pema-tang Siantar we were out of the highlands and back again on the coastal plain, although still at a considerable elevation and a long distance inland. The mountains from this point sloped quite gradually toward the sea. It was again warm at night, warm and soggy, and we returned to sleeping *on* the bedclothes, after the unaccustomed treat in the highlands of sleeping under them.

A MALAY COSMOPOLIS

Siantar forms a trade link between the highlands and the coastal regions, and at its market half the nationalities of the Sundas may be found, beside many from the rest of Malaysia, from India proper, and from the extreme East. There in the morning I wandered for over an hour between rows of women and boys who squatted on their heels behind their trays and baskets, while the stream of different tribes flowed steadily past.

Mostly they were Bataks, hideous with red-stained, toothless mouths; Sumatra Malays in brilliantly flowered *sarongs*; and blue-trousered Chinese wearing the typical broad brown topees, or straw affairs woven in the form of baskets and filled with a kind of lacquer.

Others bargained, gossiped, or wandered aimlessly among them—Malays from far corners of the archipelago; pretty Sundanese girls with white jackets and smoothly combed hair; Tamil women in scarlet *sari*, and Tamil men with white *dhoti* and red turbans; Bandjarese, Sikhs, and even wandering Pathan traders from the Afghan frontier, long-haired and dirty, with heavy, boat-shaped shoes and *lungi* trailing from their rakishly set caps.

THE CHINESE: COOLIE'S GROWING POWER

There were many more, but of every five two were Chinese. Some were nearly naked, half-starved new arrivals peddling trays of small nicknacks hung from poles across their calloused, sweating shoulders. Others, laborers earning high wages on the plantations, squatted about a native restaurant in one corner of the market, talking at high speed with their mouths full of rice or sundry delicacies that no one else would eat.

And there were many, sleek, well dressed, and be jeweled, who had passed in a brief time through both these first stages and now showed the result of indifference to privation and an infinite capacity for overwork, the only assets brought with them from the Middle Kingdom.

The irrepressible Chinese immigrant coolie seems destined to become the financial power of Sumatra, as he already is in Malaya, Java, and elsewhere in the East Indies.

From Siantar we ran back to Medan. The road was hard and dry, a trifle rough at first, but such a transition from the soft ditches we had been following through the highlands that the very steadiness of our progress began to alarm us.

After the conditions of Batak highways, an uninterrupted run of thirty-five miles makes one gravely expectant of dire things to follow; but the road grew better instead of worse, and we drove into Medan early in the afternoon with a ninety-mile run behind us—our longest in Sumatra.

Before we reached Medan we passed a heavy, two-wheeled transport cart on its way to some estate, drawn by the most enormous buffalo I had even seen. A thin, sweating Chinese coolie walked beside it, wearing a battered pair of blue trousers and a round, peaked hat of bamboo, undoubtedly the aggregate of his worldly possessions. Just as we drew alongside, the buffalo got wind of a near-by wallow, stretched his neck, and snapped the extremely simple harness—a piece of rope holding the wooden collar to the shafts.

While the huge beast ambled off to enjoy his mud bath the coolie repaired the harness by unraveling a few lengths of thread from some burlap sacking in the cart, plaiting it into a cord, and then splicing the broken rope. This done, he extracted from the waistband of his trousers what appeared to be a handful of dried peas—probably counted down to the last grain that would support life—ate his meal, and set out to recover his cumbersome charge. But the buffalo was otherwise minded.

For thirty-five minutes the patient Chinaman vainly tried to make the huge animal leave the mud-hole, himself getting plastered with slime and deeply scratched on some dead branches.

At last the relentless yanking on his nose-rope spoiled the buffalo's repose, and he followed his driver to the cart with a fine effect of being very bored. When the collar was again fitted over his neck the oversized animal swung his head fretfully and the harness promptly snapped once more. Without a change in expression the coolie started to make a new repair, and the last we saw of him was a patient figure squatting on the road, laboriously sawing off with his teeth the end of the buffalo's nose-rope.

From Siantar to Tebing Tinggi the road had passed through dense forest, the edges of the right of way choked with wild plantains, "elephant ears," and all the quick-growing plants and vines that the jungle sends out to recover the land stolen from it.

Only a few ambitious tobacco estates broke in on the ranks of the vine-entangled, straight-trunked trees; but from Tebing Tinggi the run to Medan took us through some of the most thriving estates in Sumatra. In that fertile section was represented nearly every variety of plantation found on the island.

THE RUBBER PLANTATIONS OF SUMATRA

Second in extent and in importance to the vast tobacco fields—surpassing them in many cases—were the acres devoted to rubber, both indigenous *Ficus elastica*, many branched and buttress-rooted like a banyan, and *Hervae braziliensis*, enormously popular in Malaya.

Liberian coffee thrived in the shade of the *hervea* or under the protection of vast coco-palm groves; ten-foot pepper vines climbed thickly up the trunks of small trees, clumps of tall areca palms waved their graceful fronds high in the air, and dense forests of teakwood, planted in even rows, overhung and shaded the road.

Other things without end grew in like profusion, and all helped prove what the planter enthusiasts had told of the island's future. With rich alluvial soil, unfailing rainfall, and tremendous natural resources, only the lack of labor and the deterrent influence of warring tribes has held Sumatra practically at a standstill while its sister island, Java, has flourished so greatly.

Sumatra's exploitation has been carried on very slowly and cautiously, it is true, but without the aid of the severe though wonderfully beneficial methods of the Java culture system; and before the close of many years its economic development and wealth will astonish even those familiar with the statistics of Java.

We reached Medan early in the afternoon, and the next morning ran down ten miles to the end of the road and took the Deli railway for two or three miles to the port of Belawan, in the mangrove swamps.

A wearying two-hour struggle ensued in the moist, oppressive heat of the low coast—a contest against heavy odds in the shape of booms that were too short, planks that were too weak, spaces too narrow, and stanchions that interfered, and all the other things that make a nightmare of loading and unloading motor cars on ships unprepared to handle them.

But we won in the end, with the help of a placid Dutch officer, who showed no anxiety over the disruption I was causing the company's sailing schedule; and when the car was at last on board, the *Rumphius* dropped down the river to the Straits, swung southeast for Singapore, and shortly sunk the low east coast of Sumatra in the haze of late afternoon.

22

OUR JOURNEY THROUGH THE WILDERNESS CONTINUED

PAUL DU CHAILLU

Paul Du Chaillu nurtured an early interest in zoology in Gabon, where his father ran a trading company, before emigrating to Philadelphia. Realizing the thirst for information about the Dark Continent and wanting to prove himself as a scientist, he returned to Gabon in 1856, where he journeyed deep into the interior of equatorial Africa, fighting off jungle diseases and poisonous snakes before emerging 4 years later as the first modern European to study gorillas. And though the "hellish dream creature" and "king of beasts" that Chaillu met (and often shot) in the forest stands in contradiction to the social, nonterritorial primates we have since learned gorillas to be, his account of his time kicked off a fiery debate surrounding race and evolution.

CHAPTER VII: OUR JOURNEY THROUGH THE WILDERNESS CONTINUED

I was sitting under a very large tree, when, suddenly looking up, I saw an immense serpent coiled upon the branch of a tree just above me; and I really could not tell whether he was not about to spring upon me and entangle me in his huge folds. You may well believe that I very quickly "stood from under." I rushed out, and taking good aim with my gun, I shot my black friend in the head. He let go his hold, tumbled down with great force, and after writhing convulsively for a time, he lay before me dead. He measured thirteen feet in length, and his ugly fangs proved that he was venomous.

My men cut off the head of the snake, and divided the body into as many pieces as there were people. Then they lighted a fire, and roasted and ate it on the spot. They offered me a piece; but, though very hungry, I declined. When the snake was eaten I was the only individual of the company that had an empty stomach; I could not help reflecting on the disadvantage it is sometimes to have been born and bred in a civilized country, where snakes are not accounted good eating.

We now began to look about the ruins of the village near which we sat. A degenerate kind of sugarcane was growing on the very spot where the houses had formerly stood. I made haste to pluck some of this, and chew it for the little sweetness it had. While thus engaged my men perceived what instantly threw us all into the greatest excitement. Here and there the cane was beaten down or torn up by the roots; and, lying about, were fragments which had evidently been chewed. There were also footprints to be seen, which looked almost like those of human beings. What could this mean? My men looked at each other in silence, and muttered, "Nguyla!" (Gorillas!).

It was the first time I had seen the footprints of these wild men of the woods, and I cannot tell you how I felt. Here was I now, it seemed, on the point of meeting, face to face, that monster, of whose ferocity, strength, and cunning the natives had told me so much, and which no white man before had hunted. My heart beat till I feared its loud pulsations would alarm the gorilla. I wondered how they looked. I thought of what Hanno the Carthaginian navigator said about the wild hairy men he had met on the West Coast of Africa more than two thousand years ago.

By the tracks it was easy to know that there must have been several gorillas in company. We prepared at once to follow them.

The women were terrified. They thought their end had come—that the gorilla would be soon upon them. So, before starting in search of the monster, we left two or three men to take care of them and reassure them. Then the rest of us looked once more carefully at our guns; for the gorilla gives you no time to reload, and woe to him whom he attacks! We were fortunately armed to the teeth.

My men were remarkably silent, for they were going on an expedition of more than usual risk; for the male gorilla is literally the king of the forest—the king of the equatorial regions. He and the crested lion of Mount Atlas are the two fiercest and strongest beasts of that continent. The lion of South Africa cannot be compared with either for strength or courage.

As we left the camp, the men and women left behind crowded together, with fear written on their faces. Miengai, Ngolai, and Makinda set out for the hunt in one party; myself and Yeava formed another. We determined to keep near each other; so that in case of trouble, or in a great emergency, we might be at hand to help one another. For the rest, silence and a sure aim were the only cautions to be given.

As we followed the footprints, we could easily see that there were four or five of them, though none appeared very large. We saw where the gorillas had run along on all fours, which is their usual mode of progression. We could perceive also where, from time to time, they had seated themselves to chew the canes they had borne off. The chase began to be very exciting.

We had agreed to return to the women and their guards and consult about what was to be done, after we had discovered the probable course of the gorilla; and this was now done. To make sure of not alarming our prey, we moved the whole party forward a little way, to some leafy huts, built by passing traders, and which served us for shelter and concealment. Here we bestowed the women, whose lively fear of the terrible gorilla arises from various stories current among the tribes, of women having been carried off into the woods by the fierce animal. Then we prepared once more to set out on our chase, this time hopeful to get a shot.

Looking once more to our guns, we started off. I confess that I was never more excited in my life. For years I had heard of the terrible roar of the gorilla, of its vast strength, of its fierce courage when only wounded. I knew that we were about to pit ourselves against an animal which even the enormously large leopards of the mountains fear, which the elephants let alone, and which perhaps has driven away the lion out of this territory; for the "king of beasts," so numerous elsewhere in Africa, is not met with in the land of the gorilla.

We descended a hill, crossed a stream on a fallen log, crept under the trees, and presently approached some huge boulders of granite. In the stream we had crossed we could see plainly signs that the animals had just crossed it, for the water was still disturbed. Our eyes wandered everywhere to get a glimpse of our prey. Alongside of the granite blocks lay an immense dead tree, and about this the gorillas were likely to be.

Our approach was very cautious; I wish you could have seen us. We were divided into two parties. Makinda led one, and I the other. We were to surround the granite block, behind which Makinda supposed the gorillas to be hiding. With guns cocked and ready we advanced through the dense wood, which cast a gloom, even in midday, over the whole scene. I looked at my men, and saw that they were even more excited than myself.

Slowly we pressed on through the dense bush, dreading almost to breathe, for fear of alarming the beasts. Makinda was to go to the right of the rock, while I took the left. Unfortunately he and his party circled it at too great a distance. The watchful animals saw him. Suddenly I was startled by a strange, discordant, half human, devilish cry, and beheld four young and half-grown gorillas running towards the deep forest. I was not ready. We fired, but hit nothing. Then we rushed on in pursuit; but they knew the woods better than we. Once I caught a glimpse of one of the animals again; but an intervening tree spoiled my mark, and I did not fire. We pursued them till we were exhausted, but in vain. The alert beasts made good their escape. When we could pursue no more we returned slowly to our camp, where the women were anxiously expecting us.

I protest I felt almost like a murderer when I saw the gorilla this first time. As they ran on their hind legs, with their heads down, their bodies inclined forward, their whole appearance was that of hairy men running for their lives. Add to all this their cry, so awful, yet with something human in its discordance, and you will cease to wonder that the natives have the wildest superstitions about these "wild men of the woods."

In our absence the women had made large fires, and prepared the camp. I changed my clothes, which had become drenched by the frequent torrents and puddles we ran through in our eager pursuit. Then we sat down to our supper, which had been cooked in the meantime. I noticed that all my plantains were gone—eaten up. What was to become of us in the great forest? I had only two or three biscuits, which I kept in case of actual starvation or sickness.

As we lay by the fire in the evening before going to sleep, the adventure of the day was talked over to those who had not gone with us; and, of course, there followed some curious stories of the gorillas. I listened in silence.

One of the men told a story of two Mbondemo women who were walking together through the woods, when suddenly an immense gorilla stepped into the path, and, clutching one of the women, bore her off in spite of the screams and struggles of both. The other woman returned to the village much frightened, and told the story. Of course her companion was given up for lost. Great was the surprise when, a few days afterwards, she returned to her home.

"Yes," said one of the men, "that was a gorilla inhabited by a spirit." This explanation was received by a general grunt of approval.

One of the men told how, some years ago, a party of gorillas were found in a cane-field tying up the sugar-cane in regular bundles, preparatory to carrying it away. The natives attacked them, but were routed, and several killed, while others were carried off prisoners by the gorillas; but in a few days they returned home, not uninjured indeed, for the nails of their fingers and toes had been torn off by their captors.

Then several people spoke up, and mentioned names of dead men whose spirits were known to be dwelling in gorillas.

Finally came the story that is current among all the tribes who are acquainted with the habits of the gorilla, that this animal will hide himself in the lower branches of a tree, and there lie in wait for people who go to and fro. When one passes sufficiently near, the gorilla grasps the luckless fellow with his powerful feet, which he uses like giants' hands, and, drawing the man up in to the tree, he quietly chokes him there.

Hunger and starvation began to tell upon us severely. When we started I did not calculate on meeting with gorillas. I had eaten all my sea bread. There was not a particle of food among us, and no settlement near us. I began to feel anxious for fear that we should die. Berries were scarce; and nuts were hardly to be found. The forest seemed deserted. There was not even a bird to kill. To make matters worse, we had been misled. We were lost—lost in the great forest!—and we failed to reach a certain settlement where we had expected to arrive.

Travelling on an empty stomach is too exhausting to be very long endured. The third day I awoke feeble, but found that one of the men had killed a monkey. This animal, roughly roasted on the coals, tasted delicious. How I wished we had ten monkeys to eat! but how glad and grateful we were for that single one.

Presently, Makinda, looking up, discovered a beehive. He smoked the bees out, and I divided the honey. There might have been a fight over this sweet booty had I not interposed and distributed it in equal shares. Serving myself with a portion not bigger than I gave the rest, I at once sat down, and devoured honey, wax, dead bees, worms, dirt, and all; I was so hungry. I was only sorry we had not more.

I had really a hard time getting through the old elephant tracks, which were the best roads through the jungle. The men seemed to have lost their way. We saw no animals, but found several gorillas' tracks.

At last my men began to talk more cheerfully; they knew where they were: and, soon after, I saw the broad leaves of the plantain, the forerunner of an African town. But, alas! as we approached, we saw no one coming to meet us; and when we reached the place we found only a deserted village. But even for this how thankful I was! Since I left Dayoko I had experienced nothing but hunger and starvation; and these were the first human habitations we had met.

Presently, however, some Mbicho people made their appearance. They were relatives of Mbéné, and their village was close by. They gave us some plantains, but no fowls. I wished very much to get a fowl. I felt *gouamba* (which means hunger) for meat, and knew that a good warm fowl broth would have done me a great deal of good. We spent the evening in the houses, drying and warming ourselves. It was much better than the forest, even if it was only a deserted town.

I asked if we should ever reach the cannibal country, and found that, with the exception of the Mbicho village near at hand, we were already surrounded on three sides by Fan villages.

I was too tired to rest. Besides, I was getting deep into the interior of Africa, and was in the neighbourhood of the Fans, the most warlike tribe that inhabited the country. So I barricaded my hut, got my ammunition ready, saw that my guns were all right, and then lay awake for a long time, before I could go to sleep.

23

MARCH SOUTHWARD

CHARLES CHAILLÉ-LONG

After the conclusion of the Civil War, Union Captain Charles Chaillé-Long accepted an offer to join the army of the Khedive (viceroy) of Egypt. In 1874, 5 years after his arrival in Alexandria, he was summoned to travel south to present-day Uganda with intentions of establishing Egyptian control along the Nile. With only two other soldiers and their servants, Chaillé-Long arrived at the capital of Nyanda in June, just the second white man to visit M'Tsé, the king of Uganda. Chaillé-Long left with a (later disputed) treaty that expanded the Egyptian Empire before continuing his journey down the Nile in search of the river's source. Here he reaches the palace of M'Tsé.

CHAPTER VIII: MARCH SOUTHWARD

ON the morning of the 25th of May, after many attempts that had proved vain, I started southward with the followers heretofore mentioned, with the addition of "Selim." The rains were now almost incessant, and the roads running sluices. My dragoman Ibrahim was becoming drunken, disobedient and surly; more than once he had intimated that I was taking him into the country to die; and his cowardly conduct at "Mögi" left me entirely without the slightest confidence in him. Suleiman, my brave and faithful Saïs, suffering from an old wound, from poisonous grass, that here is very difficult to cure, had become entirely helpless, really in a pitiable state: and I was obliged, much against my will, to leave him at the garrison. Selim was appointed Saïs, and "Uganda" was transferred to his care. As I rode on, in front of my little column that morning, already weakened by fever, and suffering from my now chronic state of wet, I tried to think that I was more hopeful than on the morning I had left Gondokoro, just one month before: but the painful conclusion forced itself upon me, that I was without a reasonable hope of success. I look back to that ride, that morning, as among the darkest hours of my life. More than once I decided to abandon an enterprise that now began to look fool-hardy – for failure meant certain death. In the midst of this gloomy and uncertain mood, we arrived at Kissembois, after four and a half hours' march.

Rionga came to greet me arrayed in his war dress, which consisted of a wonderful robe made of the bark of tree, but wrought in the most beautiful manner; parallel lines of black dots crossed the Roman like costume; whilst with sandals on his feet and spear in hand, "he looked every inch a king." I was quickly surrounded by his men of state, all dressed in cloth similar to that worn by Rionga, but more simple. His numerous wives stood without the circle, and their repeated "Wah! wahs!" proclaimed their astonishment at sight of both white man and horse. Huts were assigned me, and soon his sons came bearing me great pots of milk, bunches of bananas, sweet potatoes, and "merissa" made from compressed bananas. This drink has been highly spoken of by Sir Samuel Baker, and both he and Lady Baker were accustomed to drink it; to me, however, both the odour and flavour were disgusting.

At night, a dance was given in my honour; the novelty of which caused me to forget, for the moment, my sombre thoughts and forebodings. I made them several presents of beads, cloth, tin fifes, &c. I had with me a small magnetic battery with which I gave them a rude exhibition; that is to say, I knocked several of them down. If I were an enthusiast in the idea of the quick regeneration of the African, I would suggest the use of the magnetic battery; it clothes the possessor with every attribute human and divine, and the negro yields a ready submission. This little "Lubari" was an open sesame for me to the African heart and with my horse "Ugunda," my good star had placed in my hands two talismans that were to win success, where others strong in resources, arms, and soldiers had failed.

I scarcely need add that each shock administered them (and they were by no means delicate ones), was received with shouts of laughter and Wah! wahs! of wonder and superstitious awe. I turned from the friendly crowd with a lighter heart; I had a friend in the future I had not counted upon. We then were five, viz. myself, Said and Abd-el, "Ugunda" my horse, and little "Lubari," the magnetic machine.

The mosquitoes here were so thick, and their bites so irritating and poisonous, that sleep was impossible. Kissembois is situated in the bend of the river, that here, in a serpentine way regains its general direction southward or south-eastward. The land is low and boggy, and during the night, Kellerman, Ibrahim, and myself, had a most violent attack of jungle fever: whose first intimation is felt in a benumbed sensation, that crawls like ice along the vertebral column, followed by violent fever and utter prostration.

May 26th—Ba Beker, who now has charge of my porters, delays departure, and claims that he must return to Foueira in order to bring up some porters that have failed to arrive. The excuse is made simply to take advantage of the bounteous hospitality of Bionga; and to drink freely of the large quantity of merissa sent me every day.

I showed them my Reilly Gun, No. 8 Elephant, and established a reputation and sobriquet of "El-Chadide," (the great), by planting an explosive shell in the centre of a tree a hundred yards distant, the ball crashing through, and making a clean ole in its transit. At night, the accustomed dance was given. The ex-king was surrounded by his Mtongoli (ministers) in respectful attitudes on their knees. At the feet of Rionga sat his chief musician, who evoked not unpleasant music from a well-made guitar. The colour of my hair, face, and uniform was a never ending source of remark, and ejaculations of astonishment.

Whilst seated in my hut the door was suddenly darkened by the figure of a boy, who came as porter of an extra jug of "merissa." "Pinto" told me his name, and proclaimed himself at once the favourite and the buffoon of Rionga by his contortions of face and witty sayings (he spoke Arabic from his constant intercourse with the garrison); "Pinto" looked askance at some red beads and red cotton cloth that, as he said, "would make him a Sheik at once." They were given him unfortunately for my peace of mind, for like Oliver Twist he begged for more incessantly.

May 28th—No longer able to restrain my anger, at being compelled by these bacchanalians to remain in this feverish encampment, I called Rionga and begged him to compel my men to march. He did so, and soon packages of food sewed in skins, and my tin cases were distributed among the porters who, as usual, screamed and chattered in angry discussion. When all was ready I bade adieu to Baba Tucka, the Adjutaut-Major who had accompanied me thus far. To him and Rionga I said, "If I come back at all, look for me by the river." Rionga replied to me, "Impossible; you can never return by the river, no one has ever gone or can go to M'tsé by the river: the Keba Regas will prevent you."

Rionga had arrayed himself in the same costume in which he had received me; he came now to bid me adieu, and whispered to me in an undertone as I mounted my horse, "Beware of Ba Beker, he is as false as a fox!" an admonition that proved of service to me; since I watched him closely and checkmated all his endeavours to ruin me, when later he became jealous of the influence I exercised over King M'tsé.

Scarcely had I left camp when Ugunda commenced "to go lame," whether shamming or not, I do not know; but the following day he had quite recovered the use of his leg.

The country is flat with here and there several mountains, which like Pyramids in the distance, rise from its depressed plane, to break the monotony of the scene.

I shall ask the reader to go with me through my itinerary, with its record of perpetual rain, fever, and misery, to the capital at Ugunda.

May 29th—"Mirabile dictu!" no rain last night, the porters make every excuse not to march today, and I am therefore compelled to submit.

The inaction of camp is far more dreaded by me than the fatigue of the march. During the day "Morako," a "Mtongoli," Sheik of an Ugunda province, exasperated with one of his men who had drunk up his "merissa," brutally cut off both his ears. The cries and screams of the victim are terrific, and rendered hideous by the intermingled jeers of laughter from his comrades, who looked unfeelingly on. The punishment by cutting off of the ears is a prerogative of a minister, or "Mtongoli" of Ugunda; whilst to M'tsé alone belongs the power to put to death.

May 30th—We marched seven hours and a half to-day through rain and mist; the water that we are obliged to drink is execrable; the spongy earth quickly absorbs the rain, save that which here and there collects in great holes, the tramping ground of elephant and buffalo. The water is a mixture of their excretions, and of this, with tongue parched with fever, we are obliged to drink. Fetid odours arise from the black marshy ground, and almost asphyxiate us as we pass over it. During the march Ba Beker sends a boy reeking with small pox to march near me; three times I had him sent to the rear, but his return the third time seemed to me so studied, that I was compelled to lecture Ba Beker severely.

May 31st—Fever of last night abated; en route at seven a.m., and pass Mrooli. The Keba Begas (Unyori) come out from their village, and content themselves with savage looks. The river is in sight from here, and has quite a lake-like appearance; at midday we cross the river Kafou, a stream of three feet deep, but which swells later to a much greater depth. It was hence that, following its course for a certain distance. Sir Samuel Baker in his first expedition went westward to the Lake Albert Nyanza; the Kafou being the farthest point that he reached southward.

All my people are ill save Saïd and myself. Abd-el-Rahman has a fearful attack, whilst later in the day a genuine "jungle" seized me, effect of which leaves one almost in a state of collapse. Bananas have become our almost only food, varied now and then with a potage of "dourah," that I make myself, since Adam is perfectly worthless, and Kellerman with strange perversity will not aid me. The natives and my porters envelope the unripe banana in its huge leaf, and putting this in a large earthen pot over the fire, they are thus steamed and rendered palatable to the savage, who scarcely ever eat the ripened fruit. In Ugunda the fruit, in addition to this process, is both roasted and dried; the latter process being preparatory to converting into a flour, from which a very wholesome and palatable bread is made.

June 1st—The storm that prevails prevents us from marching; we cannot see the way, and are thus doomed to inaction. The day is passed in administering from a little store of quinine in my possession to my suffering people. Left alone to my sombre thoughts, with nothing of that exhilarating effect that even the rigours of a campaign sometimes excite in the bosoms of those ever eager to exchange the haunts of civilization for venture in a savage land—hard, stern, self-imposed duty was my only support under these trying circumstances. The country, cold and cheerless, forbade me those sensations of delight and ecstasy that have become stereotyped by almost every traveller in Africa, who, trusting that no other might be so unfortunate as himself, has painted imaginary scenery that might vie with that of a Claude Melnotte. The quaint and uncertain histories of that great Arab traveller, Ibn Batuta, had become a model for his successors, anxious thus to acquire fame and reputation, where the naked truth would perhaps have been coldly received. I have never seen in all Africa any views of landscape that merit notice except the scenery on the Lake Victoria Nyanza.

Whilst encamped here my ten men given me by Rionga presented themselves, asking that I would "shoot three big guns against the country of Unyoro (Keba Rega)," with which their tribe, as already noted, is at constant war. I did not at that moment feel disposed to humour them, and they left me sadly disappointed. On the following morning they again presented themselves, repeating the request of the day before, proffering at the same time a present of Indian corn wrapped in banana leaves. What a treasure, and relief from my now unwholesome diet of "dourah" and bananas! In the enthusiasm of the moment I order three shots to be fired in air "against the country!" which was received with the greatest satisfaction. This was one of the greatest feats of diplomacy I had ever seen in Africa; the stomach had been appealed to instead of the heart, always a vulnerable point with the negro; he had applied the law to me, and had won!

Day after day we march through rain, bog, and slime over the marshy earth. Poor Ugunda groans, and labours to extricate himself from the holes in which he sometimes falls. I am obliged to dismount and very often pull him, aided by my porters, through the black, filthy mud. Rain and misery by day, and misery and rain by night, with the addition of the chilly atmosphere these may be accepted as the leading incidents of the route.

The 9th of June we arrived near Chagamoyo, neutral ground, that separated Unyoro from Uganda, "Morako," the Cheik heretofore mentioned, taking with him my porters from the territorial line into his *own country Ugunda*, for the purpose of making a raid. On inquiry, I found that this was a custom on all roads

passed over by a great Sheik like "Morako," and the people captured were, by right of conquest, his slaves. Here was a feature
of the slavery question I had not yet been brought to consider;
though afterwards I learned by experience, that the greatest
slave-dealer in Central Africa is the Sheik of the tribe himself.

"Morako" returned with three goats, three sheep, three dogs,
and three women; they had rushed, with some old flint-locks,
from the cover of banana-trees into a circular open space, and
with fearful yells had made the above captures. I should have
been inclined to interfere, but the women seemed perfectly con-
tented, and apparently accustomed to this change of life. My
interference however in any positive way would have been as
useless as ill-judged. I was powerless to act, for I was not quite
sure but that a worse fate awaited myself.

The next day the 10th, the country changed for the better,
and the lowlands of Unyoro gave place, as we entered Ugunda,
to roads *well swept*, that, "Morako" tells me, have been widened
and swept by orders of his great master, M'tsé, who had sent him
a messenger, in response to a message sent by Morako, apprising
him of the intended visit of a great White Prince, whose face and
features were unlike those of the Ugunda, and whose strange
"mount" would astonish even M'tsé. The uncertain and difficult
mission which I had imposed upon myself led me (as I became
fully aware of the risk I had undertaken), to study to make up
in diplomacy for my very weak position. I had sent word by the
messenger "that a great Prince would visit him, the great M'tsé,
the greatest King of all Africa" (I meant Central Africa). He was
flattered by the recognition of his greatness, whilst it gave me
a position to treat with him, and secured for me a reception
that was denied Speke, and caused him to leave Ugunda with

his plans almost foiled. (M'tsé never forgave Captain Speke for insisting upon sitting in his presence; whilst to me he accorded a seat near him, and caused his people to prostrate themselves before me.)

A certain exhilaration now replaced the gloom that had pervaded me. My lips were bursting with fever, and bleeding, either the effect of poisonous weeds, that sometimes in a vacant mood I would put in my mouth in passing, or from the fierce rays of the sun that at times broke through the generally overclouded heavens.

M'tsé had ordered these roads to be *swept* and cleared, as they led over steep ascents. The red clay soil marked their direction for miles through a grass-covered country, or climbing the sides of mountains, were lost to view in the misty atmosphere. At the base of these mountains run treacherous muddy streams, almost impassable, through which my horse reared and plunged, and which often obliged me to dismount. I have been forced to flounder waist deep in the disgusting putrid mud, and to wash off the paste from my person and my horse, whilst waiting the tardy passage of the porters. The water that we drank here was execrable, and of the same character as that already referred to. We bivouacked at four o'clock in a banana grove, in the midst of which, as usual, were now to be seen the neat straw huts, divided into compartments, that distinguish in their cleanness the habitations of the Uganda. The inhabitants fled on the approach of their own people—a cause of congratulation in this case, as I was only too glad to exchange the nominal shelter of my tent for the comfortable Uganda hut.

June 11th—The arrival of the Grand Kahotah (Minister of Foreign Affairs), was announced by a rush of his guard, who with drum and horns made a deafening noise. He encamped near me in the banana forest. He has brought me twenty cows (the cows were not given me, but were kept by the Kahotah), bananas, and tobacco; and an invitation to come at once to Uganda, and instructions were given to his messengers not to let the White Prince, "Mbuguru," tread upon grass: that is to say, to make me follow the road that he had caused to be made for my reception.

African diplomacy willed it that I should remain encamped for several days, until the king should prepare a "Zeriba,"— enclosed huts for myself and staff—and also have reported to him whatever he might want to know of me in advance. The "Kahotah" was a man of great importance with M'tsé; besides preparing for M'tsé political dishes, he was also his cook, and alone prepared the food that M'tsé always ate alone. This chief then gave himself all the airs of a man clothed in a little brief authority. His first message to me was, that "he would receive my visit at his hut." Here was a quandary; for to accede was to acknowledge his superiority. I said simply to his messenger (Selim acting as interpreter), that I came to see M'tsé, and not the Kahotah. This seemed to solve the difficulty, since he sent me word that he would come; but the proud fellow never did, and though he escorted me to Ugunda we never met, but sent daily reciprocal salutations. Could anything have been more diplomatic? The faithful minister had doubtless orders that my first interview should be with the king.

My dragoman Ibrahim, however, paid frequent visits to the "Kahotah," whose representations of M'tsé and his court bred in the wily Ibrahim a desire to be a great man also. The stories of great quantities of ivory incited his cupidity, and the natural hypocrisy and deceit of the man induced him to conspire against me. He assumed the role of "fiké," or priest, and so won upon the Kahotah, that he finally believed the most monstrous lies: that "I was going to see M'tsé, and that my intention was to take the country and supplant him as king; and other insinuations tending to prevent my being permitted to enter the capital. The faithful devotion of Saïd and Abd-el-Rahman, however, frustrated the intrigues of Ibrahim. I arrested him on this and other charges, that made his continuance with me impossible, and therefore called upon the Sheik, "Morako," for men to send him to Foueira. By presents I induced him to give me the guard for the moment, leaving him under surveillance at the Zeriba of Morako, near by, until I could ask M'tsé for a guard to send "an unfaithful servant back to Foueira"—this was afterwards granted, and M'tsé made the detail himself—Ibrahim was returned safely in arrest. This was a serious blow to me; for I depended very much upon this fellow as an interpreter and writer, for at that time I spoke but little Arabic; I was, however, favoured by a fortuitous circumstance, for M'tsé had with him a dragoman named "Ide," who served me in his stead. Absolute necessity compelled me to speak Arabic, and I did so finally with great success.

The rigours of the climate may be imagined when Saïid, the last to succumb, has finally fallen a victim to the fever. Born in the malarious districts of the Bahr-el-Abiad, I considered him proof against fever. On the morning of the 18th of June we again resumed the route. M'tsé had finally sent permission, and ordered that I should be pushed on with all haste. Through jungle, mud, and banana grove, we pushed our way followed by the Kahotah, with great tooting of horns and incessant beating of drums; the road, of course, losing itself in these difficult passes. After a long march, however, we came upon a much finer country, where the roads were at least twenty-five feet wide, and well kept. We ascend a steep, hill, and from its height the beautiful panorama of Ugunda unfolds itself to view, spreading itself towards the Lake Victoria, over which hung a misty veil of vapour. The country, cut into hill and dale by its countless, almost continuous banana forests was, by comparison, a scene that well-nigh seduced me into enthusiasm; for I felt I was standing upon the threshold of the mysterious region that enveloped Ugunda and the Lake Victoria.

The 19th of June we left camp; the route lay over a rolling country flanked by the mountains of "Yohomah." We arrived at Gebel Bimbah at nine a.m., whence we continued the route till mid-day, when we bivouacked. In a deserted cabin, my men found and brought me a quantity of pea-nuts of same kind as those which grow so abundantly in California. We found plantains large and delicious here for the first time.

On the morning of the 20th of June the column was in motion, preceded by the "Kahotah" at the head of a mass of men, whose numbers had now swollen to about 4000.

The Uguuda flag consists of a white ground of twelve inches wide from the staff, thirty-six inches red, bordered with three pendant stripes of monkey skin of long hair common to the country. It is a significant fact that this is the only people I had, or have since visited in Africa, who have a flag.

Horns and drums kept up a deafening noise; the latter instrument being accompanied by a vocal imitation of the crow. These people, armed with lances, formed in solid column of forty to fifty front, the roads here permitting this formation; whilst on each side skirmishers dressed in a fantastic uniform, with fez of flannel ornamented with black feathers, performed the most remarkable evolutions, whilst firing the uncertain firelocks with which they were armed, with reckless disregard of aim. These were the body-guards of M'tsé, and had this curious privilege. On each side of the column marched a numerous body of men, wholly dressed in plantain leaves curiously arranged around the body, who with grimace and wild gesticulation kept time in dance and shouts to the accompanying music. A curious throng of young girls peered out with startled gaze from the great banana forests through which the cortege passed; or fled with gazelle fleetness at the sight of man and horse! It was a proud day for Saïd, Abd-el-Rahman, and Selim, as they marched in front of me, dressed in their gay uniform kept for the occasion. "Ugunda," too, seemed proud of the distinction of being the first horse that had ever visited Central Africa; and who, through every season, had defied the reputed, redoubted Tetsé fly. His diet of bananas had in no way depreciated his appearance; though its effect upon me was beginning to tell fearfully upon my health and strength, in the fearful derangement of the stomach from which I was now a constant sufferer. The column halted for a moment on a wide plaza, cleanly swept; a high palisade enclosed numerous well-built huts: whilst at the great portal a mass of women were collected. This was the residence of the Queen-Mother, the widow of the deceased king Suna, the father of M'tsé. A nicely-dressed slave in breathless haste came running from the gate, and throwing himself prostrate at my feet, presented me her royal and gracious salutation and welcome to Ugunda. My soldier Selim interpreted him my thanks and salutations; and the column moved on over hill and ravine, and through sloughs and bogs that, strange to say, characterize every descent of elevated ground, until ascending a high hill, I stood facing an elevation not 500 yards away, the palace of M'tsé, King of Ugunda! I forgot for the moment the physical pain to which I was a victim, in the strange coup-d'oeil that presented itself to my view. A succession of hills, covered with banana groves, rolled away and lost themselves in the vapours, which seemed to hold in mystery the Lake Victoria, and the unknown Nile. On every hillside thousands of people were gathered: whilst directly in front of me, at the outer gate of the palace, stood M'tsé himself, surrounded by a great throng of men and women. For a long distance a mass of men struggling to catch sight of the "Mbuguru;" in the immediate vicinity of my person the natives had prostrated themselves; whilst still mounted I surveyed the novel scene. Soon with lightning-speed several messengers (Marsalah) come running towards me, and throwing themselves at my feet, conveyed to me the welcome of their king. Selim thanked them in my name, and they hasten back. These men merit description here. Chosen for their ferocious appearance, there is the wild glare of brutality in their gleaming eyes, and a long black beard proclaimed them of other origin than the Ugundi, undoubtedly Malay. Their dress consists of a pantaloon of red and black flannel, bordered with black: a tunic of red flannel with black stripes, dolman-like across the breast, from which hangs a fringe of a peculiar monkey skin; a red cloth turban, around which is wound in tasteful coils a finely plaited rope-cord, badge and instrument of their deadly office: for they are the *bourreaux* at the court, executioners of M'tsé's undisputed will! M'tsé sends his messengers to ask that I will approach, that he may see the animal on which I am mounted. Only for a moment I felt a sense of repulsion to all this show; but I was no longer free to risk what had cost me so much suffering, the sympathy and confidence of the king. Gathering the reins in my hand, I drove my spurs into the flanks of Ugunda, and sped down the hill with fearful speed, amid the yells of delight of the assembled throng. An instant the horse slipped and stumbled in a depression of the uneven road; quickly recovering however, I rode towards M'tsé and his hareem, who broke in flight with cries and screams of fright. Returning I regained the hill, welcomed by the excited crowd in loud and hoarse shouts. In the act of dismounting afrightened rush trample of men took place; they had thought me till now a Centaur!

The Mtongoli detailed to my service conducted me to my Zeriba, built expressly for me on the side of the hill, but a few paces from my halting-place. Enclosed by a high palisade with an interior wall, my hut in front of the interior gate was of a form approaching a house with an open front; behind which and joined thereto was my sleeping-chamber, a shed with door that connected with other buildings occupied by my suite. Fifty-eight days passed in travel between Gondokoro and the Lake, delays included, with thirty-one days of actual march: and 165 hours at four kilometres the hour had been accomplished: the five degrees of latitude separating Gondokoro from Ugunda had been made, a distance of 660 kilometres, by reason of the serpentine and difficult way.

Sick and fatigued I sought my hammock at an early hour, and slept soundly despite the myriads of mosquitoes that here rendered life almost insupportable; and the incessant noise of drums and horns that composed the royal band, that had come by orders of the king to honour thus my presence.

CHAPTER IX: RECEIVE A MESSENGER FROM M'TSÉ

The morning of the 21st of June broke with a cloudless sky; at eight o'clock the heat had become excessive. A "marsalah" (messenger) arrived to beg me, in the name of M'tsé, to visit him at once. I immediately donned my uniform, then similar to that worn by the officers of Les Chasseurs d'Afrique, in France. The gold lace and ornaments upon tunic and red pantaloosn, had fortunately escaped injury from the rains and damp. In this, in the language of our English friends, I would be considered by the natives as a "howling Swell," and would astonish the Court circle. At the door stood my horse Ugunda, attended by Selim, now become my interpreter; Saïd and Abd-el-Raliman, in red shirts and white pantaloons, the uniform of the "Forty Thieves." At the entrance of the gate the Ugunda and Egyptian flags had been planted in the ground, whilst thousands struggled for a place to catch a glimpse of the royal (!) guest of their great king. Ba Beker was with me, within the tent, as my aide and interpreter with the court. Followed by them, my appearance as I mounted my horse was greeted by shouts of enthusiasm, that were re-echoed by the distant hills now covered with human beings. At the head of this immense cortege, preceded by banners and music, and the Kongowee (General-in-Chief of the army), I proceeded to the palace situated on the opposite hill, in the centre of an amphitheatre formed by seven high walls or palisades, through which entrance is had by opposing gates to which cow-bells are attached; the interval of twenty yards between the walls being occupied by huts of the ministers and courtiers. Through these I made my way followed only by a favoured few; at each gate an invisible hand rang wildly these bells, and the detached gates slid from view, giving entrance. Passing the seventh gate I found myself in front of a large pyramid-shaped hut supported by a corridor of columns within.

From within a man of majestic mien approached the entrance; this was M'tsé. He appears scarcely thirty-five years of age; certainly more than six feet high; his face is nervous but expressive of intelligence. From his large restless eye, a gleam of fierce brutality beams out that mars an otherwise sympathetic expression; his features are regular, and complexion a light copper tint. He is dressed in a long cloak, common in fashion to that worn by the better class of Arab merchants. The texture is of blue cloth, trimmed with gold; around his head, in graceful folds, is wound a white turban; his waist encircled by a belt in gold, richly wrought, from which is suspended a Turkish scimitar; his feet are encased in sandals of Moorish pattern, procured from Zanzibar. He advanced to meet me, with a graceful salutation, as I dismounted from "Ugunda," to whom alternately his eyes wandered with almost an expression of fear, that gave me the impression that he regarded me as fresh from the Inferno.

The din and noise from horn and drum now became deafening as, leaving Ugunda to Selim, I passed within the open front of the palace, and followed the king, who *retrograded* to his royal seat at the end of the corridor. A chair, over which was thrown a cloth wrought in gold, formed the royal throne. Seated, M'tsé placed his feet upon a pillow, near which was a beautifully polished ivory tusk of milky whiteness, as if to say, *"In hoc signo regno."* When I had taken the seat assigned me by the king, a few moments of awkward silence ensued, of which I profited by turning to take in the particulars of this strangest of all receptions. At each pillar along the corridor leading from the door stood the executioners, of whom I have already spoken.

The fierce gleam of savagery that shone from their eyes, now fastened upon me, caused me just one little moment of uneasiness, as I turned to regard the Mtongoli, that, dressed in white cotton (only members of the court may dress in white), lined each side of this apparent "Hall of Justice," a large room whose sides and ceiling were covered with a cotton cloth, and distinctly marked, as I gazed upwards, "Wachusetts Mills!" bought at Zanzibar from the "Meri-kani." M'tsé has sent from time to time caravans of ivory to Zanzibar in exchange for cottons, copper wire, and shells, which represent now the money of the country. But these expeditions have ceased.

To sit in presence of the king was an honour never before accorded to mortal: it may not seem strange then, that prostrate forms looked up at me with something akin to that awe and fear that hedged around M'tsé. As if to impress me with his importance, (and not in vain), his ministers were called in audience to render reports that concerned their several missions. The "Kon-gowee" (General-in-Chief), throwing himself prone upon his face, cried aloud, with hands clasped and raised alternately, "Yanzig! yanzig! yanzig!" the common salutation of the Ugunda when addressing a superior. It was interpreted to me, that he had successfully escorted me to the palace, to the honour and dignity of the Ugunda army. The second minister called was "Kahotah," who had diplomatically declined the honour of seeing me before M'tsé (court intrigue), and who diplomatically also, had said nothing of his failure to present me the twenty cows, which he was charged to offer me. "Kahotah," however, had not been a courtier long; or he might have known that envy and malice would soon divulge to M'tsé his secret and treachery. Ba Beker had long looked with jealous eye upon this head-cook in cabinet and kitchen of M'tsé; he therefore told M'tsé of the failure of "Kahotah" to visit me, and of his appropriation of the cows. The question became serious, and Kahotah came near losing his head. Appealed to by M'tsé himself, I excused on account of my illness the non-reception of Kahotah, who was therefore saved a humiliating and disagreeable decapitation. Another minister was called, who had accompanied Ba Beker, and had been violently ill en route. I gave him the last dose of medicine I possessed, and succeeded in relieving his pain. He recounted to M'tsé my wonderful art as a medicine man; an unfortunate reputation, since M'tsé never ceased to worry me for medicine (dower) during my stay in his kingdom; in despite of my protestations that I had none, and that I was ill myself.

Ba Beker was now asked as to myself, the object of my mission, and what I thought of M'tsé!

Ba Beker interpreted to him, though he understood me perfectly. I spoke in Arabic, as follows:

"O M'tsé, great king of Africa, I have come in the name of the great Sultan at Cairo to present you his gracious salutations. The world has heard of a great African king, and my August Sovereign in sending me to him, wishes me thus to express his kindly friendship and interest for one, for whom he wishes only continued health and greatness."

This was received with expressions of delight, and by M'tsé smilingly. "Kurungi! kurungi!"

"Good! good!" resounded from all sides: whilst they all rushed forward with wild gesticulation and apparent menace, with neatly carved club-sticks, they screamed and danced in a mimicry of hostile attack against M'tsé, crying "Yanzig! yanzig! yanzig!" which meant that they thanked M'tsé for bringing so powerful a prince to Ugunda!

M'tsé suddenly rose from his seat; a slight but significant contraction of the eye had caused the disappearance of the "marsalah," who quick to do their master's will, snatched from their turbans the plaited cord, and seizing their unresisting victims, to the number of thirty, amid howls and fearful yells, crowned in blood the signal honour of the white man's visit to M'tsé. It required no common effort for me to repress my feelings at this moment, or to assume that careless air that concealed what was going on within: for all eyes were watching me intently, and a sign of feeling would, if nothing more serious, have subjected me to ridicule and loss of prestige. Singular contradictory combination in the negro, that cowardly himself, he most admires coolness in others.

To protest would have been as useless on my part as impolitic. This was a custom common to all African potentates; a prerogative that went with the claim to African greatness. A protest from me would perhaps have consigned me to a like fate: and though impracticable philanthropists would have advised my throwing myself into the "bloody chasm," I confess to a certain selfish congratulation, that neither myself nor my soldiers had been included in the sacrifice. Captain Speke had recorded this propensity, in his voyage through Ugunda. It has fallen to me to vindicate the memory of this gallant voyager from the imputations cast upon him by Dr. Livingstone: who, only a few months before, from Lake Bageolowe had written to Stanley: "I wish some one would visit M'tsé, or Ugunda, without Bombay as interpreter; he is by no means good authority. The King of Daho-mey suffered eclipse after a common sense visitor, and we seldom hear any more of his atrocities. The mightiest African potentate, and the "most dreadful cruelties told of Africa, owe a vast deal to the teller." As if to refute the appreciation of the negro character, here strangely ennobled by the honoured Livingstone, Stanley was at that moment reporting in the Ashantee Expedition the "bloody facts" at Coomassie; the details of which cause the very heart to sicken and recoil.

I cite these facts in the interest of truth alone, yielding to none in the desire to ameliorate the condition of the African. But in heaven's name, let those whose province it is to be the pioneers in the work, speak of him as he is, without regard to those who attribute to him virtues and ideas, that, if possessed, would render him no longer a subject for our commiseration and sympathy.

The interview had now finished, and the drums and horns were silent: the bloody deed had been done, and sickened and oppressed I arose to go. M'tsé followed me to the door, where I was met by the anxious faces of my soldiers Saïd, Abd-el- Rahman, and Selim, who accompanied me at the bidding of M'tsé to a garden on the left in order that he might show me his hareem, more than 100 very pretty women, clothed in the same simple and tasteful garment common to both sexes. They surrounded me, examined carefully the gilt trimmings of my uniform, and laughed in astonishment at my hair, as I lifted my tarbouche from my heated head. When no longer seated upon his throne M'tsé is very gay, and laughs with a freedom that soon convinced me we should be great friends. We strolled through the numerous nicely constructed huts, shaded by the ubiquitous banana trees, followed by the whole of his hareem, by whom he is greatly beloved; as indeed he is by the whole people, who, as time wore on I found to be, as a general rule, a lying, miserable set, who, although certain of being put to death, would sometimes defy his authority. During the walk he had brought to me a pretty boy of about twelve years of age, perfectly white. I did not for the moment, thus taken una-wares, think of the Albinos that have been heretofore recorded as indigenous among some African people; and consequently I looked very much surprised. No less so did the boy, who looked in wonder and seemed pleased to meet with one whose colour approached his own. His hair was rather the crisp wool of the negro but perfectly white; his eyes were blue; his skin of a delicate white tint. M'tsé offered to give him to me, but I refused to take him at the moment, and forgot to do so at the time of my departure from Ugunda.

From this hill the road winds around its base, three hours to Murchison Creek, over a beautiful and picturesque country of banana groves; in the distance a small creek may be seen, like a silver stream winding through the country northward, here called " Bahr Rionga." The sun was now sinking behind the mountains, as, conducted to the gate, having made the detour of his garden, I mounted my horse to ride away. He seemed greatly delighted at the sight, and begged me to show him how fast he could go. Nothing loth to quit his presence, I gave the reins to "Ugunda," and quickly regained the open road, followed by my suite, who arrived soon after at the Zeriba, anxious to exchange impressions at the unexpected character of the reception with which we had been honoured. Ba Beker declared that, next to M'tsé, I was considered the greatest man in Ugunda. Strange to say, my audience were of one accord aft to the greatness of the "Sultan Kam M'tsé," as they called him; whilst the execution was referred to only in its detail.

The conversation was interrupted by the arrival of presents from the king; very timely, for I had absolutely nothing to give my men. There were fifty-six bundles of bananas, twenty earthen jars, three packets of large sugar-cane, two packets of salt, twenty goats, and fifty cows. The latter were a very fine stock, and resembled in appearance the Durham short-horn of England; whilst among them were also very long-horned, large, and beautifully-shaped beasts; and my Zeriba soon resembled a well-stocked farm-yard.

In my *suite* Ba Beker had, unknown to me, brought from the post at Foueira ten Dongolowee, whom he proposed to present as the body-guard of M'tsé. Ba Beker established himself with these men in my Zeriba, until their drunken orgies became so insupportable, that, pistol in hand, I drove the whole of them out, and was no longer annoyed by them.

On each side of my hut was that of Kellerman and Adam; Ugunda and Selim occupied another: whilst Said and Abd-el-Rahman were assigned one very near my door. The front room was very nicely built, and served me for a divan. The nights were very cold and wet, and ill almost incessantly, I was obliged to keep a fire burning at night, kept alive either by Said or Abdel by turns. Wood is very scarce in Ugunda, and my ten men given me by Rionga proved invaluable in searching for it; otherwise we should have suffered severely from cold. My tent served to close the wide portal by hanging it across: whilst my hammock swung across the wide room, in the centre of which a fire was kept constantly burning. How often memory reverts to this scene, when lying ill and helpless, hope of ever returning to Gondokoro seemed like some wild dream.

CHAPTER X: PRESENTS FOR M'TSÉ

The etiquette of Court in Ugunda prescribes that presents should always follow a visit, but much haste in such matters is considered decidedly vulgar. An exception to this rule was made for the vulgar class who daily sent in their offerings of all kinds to M'tsé.

This morning then had been chosen by Ba Beker for presentation of my "salaam-alak" to M'tsé, who had already sent his brother, as well as Ide his dragoman, to find out the nature of my presents. At eight o'clock a "marsalah" arrived to announce that M'tsé was awaiting my visit. Ba Beker, as master of the ceremonies, took charge of the boxes, and we started. Much the same scene took place as on the day before, proceeding in uniform and on horseback, my soldiers preceding me. Certainly not less than five thousand people blocked the road, and blackened the hill-tops. Arrived at the palace, M'tsé arose from his throne, and smilingly beckoned me in. Resuming his seat he motioned me to the chair occupied by me the previous day. A council was now in session here, giving a semblance of order and government; so that the assembly in the hut gave the impression of a Cabinet Council.

M'tsé was dressed to-day in a violet-coloured silk, embroidered with gold and wore a new Egyptian tarbouche (fez) that he had evidently procured from Ba Beker.

Several large cases contained the gifts to be presented. These were brought, and Ba Beker was ordered to lay them one by one at the feet of the "Sultan." Bleached cotton cloths, red Turkey and tarbouches were highly prized; for the white cotton is alone worn by the members of the Court. Calicoes, and an immense lot of beads, necklaces, rings, and bracelets (known as "Suc Suc"), were received with outbursts of admiration. A mass of other articles, that I do not remember, were added. A large mirror, with gilt frame, was an object of great curiosity. A music-box that had served to beguile my weary hours at night, when on the road it played "Tramp, tramp, tramp, the boys are marching," "Dixie," and "Johnny comes marching home" (in a fearfully inebriated state, if one might judge from the stops and uncertain notes), and other airs, was an old friend, from whom I parted with regret. I added a magnificent gun (Reilly, No. 8 Elephant), with cartridges of explosive ball. M'tsé was highly delighted with this, and naively said, "Surely you are a great man to make me a present of a gun like this. Can't you kill Keba Rega for me?" This was his constant theme, owing to a traditional jealousy that existed between the Kings of Unyoro and Uganda; and now on the part of M'tsé a desire to make war upon Keba Rega, which was only checked by the fact that the "Unyori" were a very warlike people, and he was afraid of them. The greatest impression made upon him and his courtiers, over all other of the gifts presented him was the little electric battery—"my little Lubari," that in the early stages of my journey from Kissembois I numbered as one of my five companions. For four hours I tried its effect upon them, amid the most boisterous "wah! wahs!" of astonishment and delight. M'tsé at length deigned to try its electric current, and, when recovered from the shock, gazed at it with an expression of awe mingled with delight. When I rose to go I saw how "Lubari" had aided me; for M'tsé said to me, "You are my brother! anything that you may want to do here you have only to ask me." In subsequent interviews, that were of almost daily occurrence (if I were not too ill), I broached to him my desire to visit the Lake Victoria, and cross to its eastern shore, explore it, and pass thus from the river to Grondokoro. The proposal was received with every mark of disapprobation by the ministers. They said, "The white man is he a fool that he speaks of travelling on the river? 'Speeky' (Captain Speke) tried to do so and could not; and what will he do against the people of Keba Rega?"

I was not disheartened at this, for I expected opposition; besides a strange superstition existed among these people, that the opposite side of the Lake Victoria was inhabited by "Afrites" (devils), beings who exercised a guardianship over these waters, and had frequently caught and killed many of the people of Ugunda. Again and again I referred to the subject; subsequently delivering him a long lecture on the opening of the river for navigation and for the exportation of his ivory. By means of descriptions of houses, palaces, and carriages, finally aided by rude sketches I conveyed to him, what was at first unintelligible; for he could not comprehend a small sketch, but invariably inverted it. At last I made him understand; describing other princes, not so great or powerful as he, who lived in houses, and had carriages, and were surrounded with luxury and comfort: "whilst you, M'tsé, with all your ivory, are little better off than the poorest of your people; for, like them, you have nothing that goes to make up the life of the great King you are." He finally consented that I should visit the Lake, but my return by the river was flatly refused. "No," said he, "you must not go, you will be killed; the river does not go, as you think, to Mrooli: it goes away to the eastward. You will be lost and die of hunger, or be killed, and then your Sultan will come and kill me."

I confess that this reply rather cooled my ardour for the moment. What if the river went eastwards and not to Mrooli? My death might certainly be the consequence, from either of the causes he assigned. But I held fast to my resolve, and in a subsequent interview I said to him, "You refuse then to permit me to return; if so I will stay here and die, and what will be the consequence? Your enemy, Keba Rega, will send word that you have caused my death; and the steamers and boats that would otherwise come to bring you articles of luxury, materials to build your houses, and make you a great king, will all be given to Keba Rega: who, becoming powerful, will some day come and fight you, and perhaps conquer your country." I rested my case upon this, for I saw that I had touched the vital spot (his jealousy and hatred of Keba Rega) whilst his mind, inflamed with a desire to be great in the sense I had represented, I doubted not would cause him to accede to my demand. I did not see him again for several days, for I was quite ill, prostrated completely with fever and a distressing diarrhoea. M'tsé, fearful of my dying on his hands, and dreading the consequences, sent incessantly to know my condition.

On the night of the 23rd, there being no rain, I secretly arranged to send up some rockets and fireworks I had brought with me, reserving several for the river navigation; for I had resolved at all hazards to return that way.

At a given signal the rockets were sent up, and the greatest consternation and alarm prevailed. I had however arranged that M'tsé should be kept but a moment in doubt. The fearful scramble at the palace (the fright was reported to me as really terrible), was succeeded however by a corresponding expression of delight.

My visits were now less frequent at the palace, for I was seriously ill; and besides, almost every visit was attended by a human sacrifice: and my soul sickened at this kind of honour!

The 24th and 25th I was seriously ill, and confined to the hut. I was so weak as to be scarcely able to walk: whilst my flesh was nearly transparent: and my once muscular legs and arms were mere skin and bone. Unfortunately I was without proper medicine, and chewed leaves in the vain hope to find them astringent or tonic. Kellerman and Adam were now likewise on their backs, and absolutely cried like children. Kellerman said to me, "I am utterly without hope of ever returning," and gave up to despair. I never could induce him to go to the palace: though M'tsé frequently asked for him. I was half inclined to believe that Kellerman never doubted but that one day I too would be sacrificed: as he was always very anxious about my return, whenever absent at the palace.

During all this time I had received a great many visits, and reserved some presents (secretly given) for those visitors. I endeavoured to trace, by patient questioning, some tradition, that might give a show of reason to the origin ascribed to them. Here, as elsewhere, I failed to discover it. The customs of one king, as of one Sheik, are lost in the egotism and vanity of his successor. Personal rule, especially among savages, ever has this disadvantage, the successor obliterating all traces of his predecessor—hence even tradition ceases. In my navigation and exploration of the river Juba, on the eastern coast of Africa, half a degree below the Equator, I found numerous tribes speaking languages in which, on comparing a small vocabulary of words, there was an evident correspondence with the language of the Ugundi. Thus "Mezi" (water), in this language is the identical word in the language of "M'yooah," who, like the Ugunda, prefix M'—M'Ugunda, to designate the "country of;" " Bosi" (a goat), is "Unbosi" in Ugunda; "Koko" (chicken), the same, and many other words are synonymous.

Central Africa, subsequent to the flow of the Moslem invasions on its eastern coast, had been invaded doubtless by the Arab nomad, kindred spirit to that noted Arab traveller, Ibn Batutah, imbued with a desire to discover its mysteries, or actuated by the greed of gain to collect its gold, its ivory, and its slaves. Whilst bearing with him the banner of Mahomet, he implanted in his march among the negroes the first idea of a divinity, scarcely definable to-day; and by amalgamation, operating a change in the colour, and the typical characteristics of the negro of Central Africa. For although the woolly hair is still there, the nose and mouth have in these regions lost—the former its flatness, and the latter its thickness—whilst the tint of the Ugunda is of dark copper colour. Among these people however, I have noticed that there are many of the real negro type in colour, hair, &c., showing thus perhaps the original type of the natives of the country prior to amalgamation.

Later, in an expedition to the Makraka Niam, on the confines of the Monbutto country, I remarked that the tribes on the river Yeh—the Mundo, Muro, Abaker, Kiyéh, and others—though speaking different languages, bore a striking resemblance in colour, hair, habits, dress, and music with the people of Ugunda, showing thus an original unity of race in the negro. The traditions so often accredited to the negro, so far as my experience goes, have no other foundation than in his vanity or his caprice. M'tsé, when asked as to his origin, replied by pointing proudly to the Albino boy: to be considered as of the white race being a great point in his ambition, remarked among other negroes as well. In probable connexion with the theory here advanced I have to cite that, during an interview, when I had given him a gilt and Turkey-red bound volume of Burton's "Travels," he produced a voluminous Arab manuscript, worn and discoloured by age, "that I might bind it, and make it like the book I had given him." Fearing a loss of prestige if I attempted it, I endeavoured to make him understand that I was not a bookbinder: that work of that nature required special labour, &c.: all to no effect however. I took the book, and with the aid of Kellerman succeeded in making a plain cover of paper; using as paste a mucilage made of the flour of the banana. This book was highly reverenced, and had been given him by the late King Suna, his father. How it had readied Ugunda he could not say; but Ide, his dragoman and instructor in Arabic, told me that it was of such ancient date, and the writing so different from his Arabic, that he could decipher but a few words here and there. This served to strengthen my conviction, that the Arabs referred to above, coming from the east coast, without doubt had brought this manuscript with them: the preservation of which, however, was as unique as strange in the history of a race which ever strives to forget and obliterate the past, rather than retain records of it.

June 26th—Though ill and suffering, and supported by my two soldiers, I responded to the pressing invitation of M'tsé to go to the palace. He said to me, "Mbguru, come and see my women; they are 'kurungi' (good)." He dragged me after him, and seemed delighted to present me to his wives, that thronged around me, no longer abashed as on the first visit; and this familiarity encouraged by me at length went so far as to be checked abruptly by M'tsé, who said, "Let us leave them now, as they will annoy you." This was said whilst I fancied that a shadow of jealousy flitted across his face, and with a flash of the eye, that told me he would in no way consent to play the role of a "mari sage," like Offenbach's good king Menelaus.

Whilst walking among the banana groves I again touched upon the subject of his permitting me to explore the opposite shore of the lake, and to return by the river. In imagination I drew for him houses of wood and brick that would replace the grass-huts of his people: and how his army, now consisting of twenty or thirty men, armed with old firelocks, would all have beautiful guns and uniforms like those of my soldiers, Said and Abd-el: and he himself a carriage and a horse, to carry him in state as a king. I would have desisted had I known the price of the impression I had made upon his exalted imagination: for he now resolved, despite the opposition of his ministers, to accede to my demand. These men hated me intensely, as Selim reported me their conversation, and had instructed him to tell me the most horrible stories of cruelties practised by the people on the river. Selim exaggerated, without doubt, these stories, for both he and Kellerman regarded me as mad, in persisting in what they thought must lead to certain death. Saïd and Abd-el-Hahman shared in these feelings I could easily see, but they did not say so in the conversations I had with them: for they were my constant companions, and almost my every thought found expression to them in the long nights, when the rain and storm howled without, and when we were obliged to huddle close around the fire in my hut. The wood burned badly, for it was wet and soggy, and gave out little heat. Kellerman and Adam were always in their lints, wrapped in their blankets; while Selim and his numerous wives had the same hut with "Ugunda," who was again becoming sleek and fat upon Ugunda grass, and his now almost habitual regime of large golden bananas or plantains. Selim told me that he occasionally gave him "merissa" to drink: and that the Ugunda, who daily came in great crowds to look at him, regarded him with awe and fear, encouraged by the wily Selim, who told them fabulous stories of what "Ugunda" said about them, naively remarking that his chief complaint was that the natives did not give him enough merissa—an intoxicating drink of which Selim was himself over-fond.

On the 29th the constant fever and dysentery of the past few days had now merged into delirium. Attended alone by Saïd, for Abd-el- Rahman, in common with all, save Saïd and Selim, was suffering fearfully from fever, I cried incessantly for ice and snow. "Tortoni's" at Paris became the one sole cry, the North Pole of my fever-racked brain. When its fury was spent I was so weak and emaciated, that I heard my men more than once discussing what they should do in the event of my death: and consternation was written on their features, as they were brought to consider the impossibility of their return; the more so since Ba Beker had rendered himself an object of hatred and suspicion to all, and who would doubtless, should anything happen to me, revenge himself upon them.

Adam, my cook, as if roused to action by the consciousness of what threatened him, in common with the rest, came to me and told me that Ba Beker, to whom he had applied to kill an ox to make me soup, had absolutely refused to do so; stating that the cattle sent me, now numbering sixty heads of splendid beasts, were all his. I sent for him, and in my anger I denounced him as an ingrate scoundrel; to which he only bent his head in submission, astonished that there was still enough vitality in me to make a scene. From this moment Ba Beker became my bitter enemy; secretly he conspired against me, and caused me all the subsequent trouble on the road to Urondogani detailed hereafter. Though he used every art to convince M'tsé that I was in Ugunda for the purpose of dispossessing him, M'tsé remained faithful to his pledged friendship to me; otherwise I could never have left Ugunda alive.

From this day till the 6th of July I was unable to move from my hammock, guarded by my faithful and devoted soldiers. In the interval, as in mockery, M'tsé sent frequently to me, asking for "dower" (medicine), for which all Africans have a strange infatuation, declaring that he had stomach-ache, and buzzing in his ears, and sore eyes: all of which Ide, who knows that I have no medicine, tells me is false. Instead of Sir Samuel Baker's idea of the regeneration of the negro, by "a man in full highland dress and bagpipes, who would set all psalms to lively tunes, and the negroes would learn to sing them immediately;" it would work better to send an apothecary well stocked with drugs. Sir Samuel, however, in giving this idea as to success of bag-pipes, may have been actuated by a desire to transfer those doubtfully melodious instruments to a field of more usefulness and appreciation!

I had been here now sufficiently long to form an idea of the country, its people, and its products.

The country is rolling and picturesque; its groves of banana trees, that everywhere abound, adorn the verdant landscape on hill and dale. But nothing—absolutely nothing—of that grand and magnificent spectacle depicted by the pens of more enthusiastic travellers, who would make, to willing readers, a Paradise of Africa, which in reality is, and must ever be a grave-yard to Europeans. The soil is richly impregnated with iron, rock crystal, and granite. The principal tree in Ugunda is the wild fig, from whose bark a cloth is manufactured by incessant pounding.

Exposed to the air it assumes a light-brown colour, when the different pieces are sewn together. The products are Indian corn, sweet potatoes, sugar-cane of a superior quality. Tobacco, resembling the famous "perique" of Louisiana, is grown in large quantities; and could be made a valuable article of export on account of its delicious flavour.

There are no fruits except the banana and plantain, which grow wild and in greatest luxuriance. The tree is very large, and the watery matter contained in the stock serves the Ugunda for water, when he cannot procure it elsewhere. The banana is scarcely ever eaten in a ripe state, save by the females, who extract from it an unfermented and delicious liquor. Gourds of bottle-shape are strung around their necks, from which, from time to time, they drink The banana, the principal article of food, is prepared either by roasting or by a sweating process already described. "Merissa" (fermented liquor, whether of banana or dourah) is the drink of the male, and a source of much intemperance. The cattle of the country equal the choice breeds of England: they do not however form a part of the diet of the people. Sheep and goat's flesh is almost the only animal food that is eaten.

The industry of the country consists in the tanning of skins of animals, in which a favourable comparison may be made with that of Europe. The cultivation of the soil is by the women, and only sufficient to support life. The men occupy themselves with the elephant chase, for ivory, which they do in the manner hereafter described as practised by the people west of the Bahr-el-Abiad.

The animal kingdom comprises almost all the beasts common to Africa: elephant, lion, giraffe, leopard, wild cat, hippopotamus, and crocodile; the zebra is said to be found here, but in vain I essayed to procure one. It is in the tanning of skins that they are especially skilled, vying in finish with specimens of European work.

Sugar-cane is considered a great luxury, and very often one sees the IJgunda passiug, chewing the end of a long cane that trails behind him.

European goods, copper, and shells, constitute the money of the country, in exchange for ivory or cattle.

They are very skilful workers in iron, and their lances are very nicely finished.

The cloth, referred to above, from the bark of tree, is not so thick as that manufactured by the Makraka Niam-Niam, but the same in every other respect. Their music horns are composed of elephant tusks. Their drums are very large, and their hoarse sounds, accompanied by cawing in imitation of the crow, are anything but agreeable.

M'tsé has a form of government unique, perhaps, among all African potentates. There is division of labour, and a distribution of the service of state among chiefs, whose appellation of Mtongoli, with their attributes, entitle them to rank as Ministers of State and Members of Cabinet. These officials come next in rank to the "Kahotah," who takes precedence with "Kongowee," Generalissimo of the army. This important personage is at the head of all the natives, who are at all times armed with the lance; a few only being armed with muskets (flint-locks), and these are generally detailed for service in the immediate vicinity of the king. Many of these men had lost their flints, and came to me as a great favour to beg them. I had none, of course: but to their utter bewilderment I picked them up from their own earth; a precious discovery to them, since the very few they possessed had been procured with the guns at Zanzibar.

The population of Ugunda proper, I esteemed at 500,000, whilst a number of Sheiks of adjacent tribes, whose numbers are unknown, are tributary. Their huts are built of jungle-grass, the walls of which are of sugar-cane. The interior is divided into compartments, and kept very clean.

The salutation of the Ugunda is very peculiar. As two persons meet the word "Ouangah!" is responded to by "Oh hi!" which continues from an elevated voice to a lower tone until it becomes scarcely audible; then, and not till then, does the conversation commence. The word "Agambe!" is frequently used in conversation, and corresponds to "Do you listen?" To superiors the salutation is different; the prostrate form is then elevated to squatting on the haunches with legs under the body, the hands extended flat upon the ground, as an expression of humility or of thanks, the hands clasped are raised in quick succession, whilst the word "Yanzig! yanzig! yanzig!" is constantly repeated.

On the 6th of July I had sufficiently recovered to respond to the pressing invitation of the king to go to the palace. M'tsé had never yet condescended to visit me; it would have been a want of dignity that even the Ugunda, passionately devoted to him, would doubtless have resented. M'tsé was for them the sole King of Africa, and was the constant theme of their conversations. He could and did send them to be decapitated, but this was his privilege alone, and they were content, nay happy, that the Mtongoli had no other authority over them than the cutting off of their ears; the Mtongoli himself often sharing the same fate as the mass. What secret of government M'Tsé possessed to govern these people so rudely, and yet be beloved by them, was an enigma to me. To return to the palace then where I saw assembled on that morning a great mass of men:—in front of the palace door sat seven men in the posture above described.

Drums and horns were making the usual din, whilst the throng without was dense. Within sat along the wall the Mtongoli: and at their accustomed posts, along the corridors, the fiery-eyed and fiendish looking executioners; their fantastic uniform in brilliant contrast to the neat white shirt of the Mtongoli. M'tsé sat on his royal chair, a questioner of and listener to the men crouched at the door.

Motioned to my accustomed seat by M'Tsé, I leaned feebly against the post, weak and faint. Unable to comprehend the conversation, my eyes wandered over this strange assembly, and gradually losing myself in reflection I thought of the world beyond, shut out from me by thousands of miles of weary, deadly travel. Distant from Gondokoro even more than 600 miles, I felt myself succumbing to disease that now had me completely in its grasp, I no longer dared hope of return; and a feeling stole over me that my persistence with M'Tsé to permit me to return by the river was useless. Despair was taking the place of the energy and hope that till now had kept me alive. I had reached that point, where the pain of freezing limbs gives place to the fatal happy slumber, half waking half conscious, the precursor of death!

A crash of horns and sound of drums broke upon my ears and awakened me, startled from my reveries—the seven men had disappeared, and the cries without too truly told me that the executioners, no longer in their place, were plying their deadly office. My last conversation had resulted in determining M'Tsé to grant my request; this was this bloody price paid that the world might know something of this mysterious region. I have said here before that they believed demons, "Afrites," guarded with jealous care the opposite side of the lake, and the river Victoria Nile running there from north. M'Tsé in consenting to my going there, had caught several of these evil guardians; with what result the executions made apparent. I felt for a moment as if fixed to the spot, and my anxious look of inquiry caused M'tsé to speak thus:—"O Mbuguru, thou hast asked to go and visit regions inaccessible to men; that thou mightest do so I have killed these men, otherwise they would have killed you. It hurts my heart ("batn," belly, is always used by Africans instead of heart), to kill these Afrites, but they have already done my people great injury."

M'Tsé had doubtless heard that I condemned the practice: and I had told him myself that a Great King in the outer world never committed such acts to prove His greatness: hence his apology.

Though I felt elated at the permission of visiting the Lake, there came a shadow of regret as I thought of the now mangled bodies without, and my indirect complicity in their death.

Immediately after a number of warriors rushed in, headed by the "Kongowee," who made a sham attack, vociferating, gesticulating, and brandishing their clubs, and throwing themselves at the feet of M'Tsé; a ceremony which meant to testify their approbation of the act: saying at the same time, "You are the Great M'Tsé, and we are your servants." Said and Abd-el stood at the door and witnessed the executions; M'Tsé beckoned them to approach, which they did with somewhat doubtful step. I saw that for the moment a suspicion, that a like "fantasiah" might be in store for us all, was quickly flashing through the minds of the two soldiers, who advanced directly towards me. I felt greatly relieved when this strange capricious king begged me to cause them "to play soldier;" as he wanted me to organize and drill his army; telling me that he would give me any quantity of ivory; and make me a king. The first proposition I accepted, the other I refused, telling him that I wished him to send his ivory over the road I should open to commerce by the river. Said and Abd-el went through the manual of arms, the facings and firings, to his great delight, and amid cries of the Mtongoli of "Kurungi! Kurungi!" (good). Soon after I begged his permission to retire. He arose and accompanied me to the door, looking in wonder at my horse. As I mounted and rode away he said, "Mbuguru, you will not forget to give me a carriage and a horse." I said, "Yes, M'Tsé, anything you may ask." Like all Africans he was a great beggar, and was never appeased.

On the 9th I went to the palace to make my adieu. I was received with great ceremony, and M'Tsé was arrayed in a white robe for the first time. I thanked him in a few words for his great kindness to me, and assured him that the world should hear more of him, as indeed I found him to be a great African King. I hoped that he would soon profit by my visit, and that ere long a steamer would be on the river; when he might go without fatigue, and see himself the scenes which I had heretofore detailed to him of a world unseen. He begged me to stay and build him a house and carriage, and in fact made every effort to cause me to remain. He had already sent me an escort and porters for my luggage, and I had arranged that Kellerman and Adam should go direct to Urondogani with baggage and porters, and await me there: until my passage across the Lake to the eastern shore;

then to turn northward, to reach Urondogani by the river; a design which was frustrated, as will hereafter appear.

I left M'Tsé, and the court, where I had been nearly a month. They all crowded around me, and M'tsé warmly pressed my hand, telling me, "I love you, Mbuguru, you are my brother: you will find boats for you at Urondogani; let me know if you have any trouble." I turned my back on the capital, accompanied by my two soldiers and Saïs, and a numerous escort of honour. As the column wound round the hill on which was

Through the enclosure, to wave me adieu. I had only commenced the march when a furious storm broke over our heads, sending the guard for shelter in every direction. I was finally obliged to return. For several days the storm continued with unabated fury; and during this time I was again seized with a most violent fever, as the temperature became cold, and the dampness obliged us all to hover around our at all times miserable fire.

The interval of my delay was unmarked by any incident: except that M'Tsé, who was immediately informed of my return, sent one night to ask that Selim might be allowed to remain, as he wished to send him to bring a white man then at Ujiji. The Ugunda go frequently to that place, making the journey in ten days. I supposed the white man to be Lieutenant Cameron, as it afterwards proved to be. Of course I could not accede to this request, under the circumstances.

On the 12th I went to pay another visit to the king, to repeat my thanks and kindly appreciation of the services he had and would render me. On returning to my "Zeriba," I found a quantity of cow, leopard, and rat skins most beautifully tanned and sewed together, making large sheets. There were ten large ivory tusks, and many other articles of jewelry, necklaces and bracelets made of ivory, and ten large bolts of native cloth.

The transportation through Unyoro of the ivory and cloth and many other articles that I was obliged to leave (and which I received several months afterwards by the route of Unyoro), cost him in slain forty of his men. This is cited here to show the good faith of M'tsé, in his promise to me to throw his ivory in the market, by sending it to Gondokoro: or at least to Foueira, near by, if the river, heretofore unknown, proved to be the same as at Foueira, and navigable, the point on which I insisted and was about to test.

SOURCES

"Chapter VII: Two Beautiful Black Eyes" and "Chapter VIII: Aden to Colombo," from *Around the World in Seventy-Two Days*, by Nellie Bly, 1890, http://digital.library.upenn.edu/women/bly/world/world.html.

"Into the Madhouse with Nellie Bly: Girl Stunt Reporting in the Late Nineteenth Century America," from *American Quarterly*, by Jean Marie Lutes, June 2002.

"Chapter XVIII: A Day in the African Alps – the Col de Tirourda," from *Algerian Memories: A Bicycle Tour over the Atlas to the Sahara*, by Fanny Bullock Workman, 1895, http://digital.library.upenn.edu/women/workman/algerian/algerian.html#XVIII.

Game Faces: Five Early American Champions and the Sports They Changed, by Thomas H. Pauly, University of Nebraska Press, 2012.

"Chapter VIII: The Convict Trail," from *Jungle Peace*, by William Beebe, 1920, http://www.gutenberg.org/files/37614/37614-h/37614-h.htm#chap1.

The Remarkable Life of William Beebe: Explorer and Naturalist, by Carol Grant Gould, Washington: Island Press, 2012.

"Chapter XVII: Machu Picchu," from *Inca Land: Explorations in the Highlands of Peru*, by Hiram Bingham III, 1922, http://www.gutenberg.org/files/10772/10772-h/10772-h.htm#d0e3571.

"Chapter VI: Sacred City of the Living Buddha," from *Across Mongolian Plains: A Naturalist's Account of China's "Great Northwest,"* by Roy Chapman Adams, 1921,

https://archive.org/stream/acrossmongolianp00andr/acrossmongolianp00andr_djvu.txt.

"Roy Chapman Andrews," from *Journey: An Illustrated History of Travel*, by Smithsonian, 2017.

"Chapter XI: From the Little Colorado to the Foot of the Grand Canyon"
To the Foot of the Grand Canyon," from *Canyons of the Colorado*, by John Wesley Powell, 1895, http://www.gutenberg.org/files/8082/8082-h/8082-h.htm.

"Thursday 13," from *History of the Expedition under the Command of Captains Lewis and Clark, Volume I*, prepared by Paul Allen, 1814, http://www.gutenberg.org/files/16565/16565-h/16565-h.htm.

"Chapter XII: Seventy-Two Days without a Port," from *Sailing Alone around the World*, , by Joshua Slocum, 1900, https://www.gutenberg.org/files/6317/6317-h/6317-h.htm.

"Joshua Slocum and His Travels." Joshua Slocum Society International. http://www.joshuaslocumsocietyintl.org/jshistory.htm

"Chapter XIX: How to Travel in Tropical Africa," from *A Yankee in Pigmy Land: Being the Narrative of a Journey across Africa from Mombasa through the Great Pigmy Forest to Banana*, by William Edgar Geil, 1905, https://archive.org/details/ayankeeinpigmyl02geilgoog.

"William Edgar Geil papers" PACSCL Finding Aids. http://dla.library.upenn.edu/dla/pacscl/detail.html?id=PACSCL_HSP_DOY03

"Chapter XV: The Pole!" and "Chapter XVI: The Fast Trek Back to Land," from *A Negro Explorer at the North Pole*, by Matthew Henson, 1912, http://www.gutenberg.org/files/20923/20923-h/20923-h.htm.

Brendle, Anna. "National Geographic News." news.nationalgeographic.com. https://news.nationalgeographic.com/news/2003/01/0110_030113_henson.html

"Did You Know... A Customs Employee was the 'First Man to Sit on Top of the World?'" U.S. Customs and Border Protection. https://www.cbp.gov/about/history/did-you-know/first-man

"Mystic Nedief: The Shia Mecca," from *National Geographic Magazine*, Vol. XXVI, by Frederick Simpich, July–December, 1914, https://archive.org/stream/nationalgeograph261914nati/nationalgeograph261914nati_djvu.txt.

"Necrologies Frederick Simpich," from *The Chronicles of Oklahoma*, Vol. XXVIII, Oklahoma Historical Society, by Grant Foreman, Spring 1950.

"Chapter XVI: A Second Attempt on Huascarán," from *The Search for the Apex of America: High Mountain Climbing in Peru and Bolivia, Including the Conquest of Huascaran, with Some Observations on the Country and*

People Below, by Annie S Peck, 1911, https://archive.org/stream/asearchforapexa00peckgoog/asearchforapexa00peckgoog_djvu.txt.

A Woman's Place Is at the Top: A Biography of Annie Smith Peck, Queen of the Climbers, by Hannah Kimberley, St. Martin's Press, 2017.

"Chapter XXII: The Trap Is Sprung," from *Marooned in Moscow: The Story of an American Woman Imprisoned in Russia*, by Marguerite E. Harrison, 1921, https://archive.org/stream/maroonedinmoscow00harr/maroonedinmoscow00harr_djvu.txt.

Women of the Four Winds: The Adventures of Four of America's First Women Explorers, by Elizabeth Fagg Olds, Houghton Mifflin, 1985.

"Adventures with a Camera in Many Lands," from *National Geographic Magazine*, Vol. XXXIX, by Maynard Owen Williams, January–June 1921, https://archive.org/stream/nationalgeograp401921nati/nationalgeograp401921nati_djvu.txt.

Maynard Owen Williams, Class of 1910, Kalamazoo College, by Lawrence H. Conrad Sr., 1968.

Presenting America's World: Strategies of Innocence in National Geographic Magazine, 1888–1945, by Tamar Y. Rothenberg, Ashgate, 2007.

"Chapter XII: Discovery of Some New Islands," from *Voyages & Discoveries in the South Seas*, by Edmund Fanning, 1833, https://archive.org/stream/voyagesroundwor00fanngoog/voyagesroundwor00fanngoog_djvu.txt.

"Some Wonderful Sights in the Andean Highlands," from *National Geographic Magazine*, Vol. XIX, by Harriet Chalmers Adams, 1908, http://www.archive.org/stream/nationalgeograph19natiuoft/nationalgeograph19natiuoft_djvu.txt.

"Woman Explorer's Hazardous Trip in South America," *New York Times*, August 18, 1912.

"CHAPTER XXII. Dog-Driving," from *Tent Life in Siberia*, by George Kennan, 1870, http://www.gutenberg.org/cache/epub/12328/pg12328-images.html.

"This day in Geographic History: February 16, 1845: Happy Birthday, George Kennan" National Geographic. https://www.nationalgeographic.org/thisday/feb16/happy-birthday-george-kennan/

"VIII. The River of Doubt," from *Through the Brazilian Wilderness*, by Theodore Roosevelt, 1910, http://www.gutenberg.org/cache/epub/11746/pg11746-images.html.

The River of Doubt: Theodore Roosevelt's Darkest Journey, by Candice Millard, New York: Anchor Books, 2006.

"Theodore Roosevelt" WhiteHouse.gov. https://www.whitehouse.gov/about-the-white-house/presidents/theodore-roosevelt/

"Chapter XIII: The Joys of Polar Sledging," from *The Aerial Age*, by Walter Wellman, 1911, https://archive.org/stream/aerialage00wellgoog/aerialage00wellgoog_djvu.txt.

To the Pole: The Diary and Notebook of Richard E. Byrd, 1925–1927, edited by Raimund E. Goerler, 1998.

"Chapter XVII: Preparations for visiting the Ruins," from *Incidents of Travel in Central America, by Chiapas and Yucatan*, by John Lloyd Stephens, 1841, https://archive.org/stream/incidentsoftrave02stepuoft/incidentsoftrave02stepuoft_djvu.txt.

"By Motor through the East Coast and Batak Highlands of Sumatra," from *National Geographic Magazine*, Vol. XXXVII, by Melvin Hall, January–June, 1920, https://archive.org/stream/nationalgeograp371920nati/nationalgeograp371920nati_djvu.txt.

Princeton Alumni Weekly, Good Reading, February 1950, Volume 1, Number 1

Worlds to Explore: Classic Tales of Travel & Adventure from National Geographic, edited by Mark Jenkins, National Geographic, 2006.

"Chapter VII: Our Journey through the Wilderness Continued," from *Stories of the Gorilla Country*, by Paul Du Chaillu, 1867, http://www.gutenberg.org/files/52444/52444-h/52444-h.htm.

"Chapter VIII: March Southward," "Chapter IX: Receive a Messenger from M'tsé," and "Chapter X: Presents for M'tsé," from *Central Africa: Naked Truths of Naked People*, by Charles Chaillé-Long, 1877, https://archive.org/details/centralafricanak00chai_1.

Icenogle, David. "The Expeditions of Chaille-Long." Aramco World. http://archive.aramcoworld.com/issue/197806/the.expeditions.of.chaille-long.htm